First World War
and Army of Occupation
War Diary
France, Belgium and Germany

2 CAVALRY DIVISION
Divisional Troops
Royal Army Service Corps
Headquarters Divisional Army Service Corps (424
Company A.S.C.)
13 March 1915 - 31 March 1919

WO95/1128/1

The Naval & Military Press Ltd
www.nmarchive.com
Published in association with The National Archives

Published by

The Naval & Military Press Ltd

Unit 10 Ridgewood Industrial Park,

Uckfield, East Sussex,

TN22 5QE England

Tel: +44 (0) 1825 749494

www.naval-military-press.com

www.nmarchive.com

This diary has been reprinted in facsimile from the original. Any imperfections are inevitably reproduced and the quality may fall short of modern type and cartographic standards.

© **Crown Copyright**
Images reproduced by permission of The National Archives, London, England, 2015.

Contents

Document type	Place/Title	Date From	Date To
Heading	WO95/1128/1		
Heading	1915-1919 2nd Cavalry Division. H.Q. Divl. A.S.C. Mar 1915-Mar 1919 (424 Coy ASC)		
Heading	War Diary of Headquarters 2nd Cavalry Divisional A.S.C. April 13/3/15 to 31/3/15 Volume VII		
War Diary		13/03/1915	31/03/1915
War Diary		24/03/1915	29/03/1915
Miscellaneous	Composition of Detachment from N. Midland Division.		
Miscellaneous	Appendix "B"	15/03/1915	15/03/1915
Miscellaneous	Appendix "C"	16/03/1915	16/03/1915
Miscellaneous	Appendix "D"	18/03/1915	18/03/1915
Miscellaneous	Appendix "E"	18/03/1915	18/03/1915
Miscellaneous	2nd Cavalry Division. Appendix "F"	31/03/1915	31/03/1915
Miscellaneous	O.C. Supply Column.	31/03/1915	31/03/1915
Heading	###		
Heading	###		
Heading	War Diary of 2nd Cavalry Division A.S.C From 1/4/15 To 30/4/15 Volume VIII		
War Diary		01/04/1915	22/04/1915
War Diary	Vieux-Berquin	23/04/1915	24/04/1915
War Diary		25/04/1915	30/04/1915
Miscellaneous	A.A. & Q.M.G. 2nd. Cav. Division. Appendix G.	09/04/1915	09/04/1915
Heading	War Diary of 2nd Cavalry Divisional A.S.C From 1/5/15 to 31/5/15 Volume IX		
War Diary		01/05/1915	31/05/1915
Heading	War Diary of 2nd Cavalry Division A.S.C. From 1/6/15 to 30/6/15 Volume X		
War Diary		01/06/1915	04/06/1915
War Diary	La Nieppe	05/06/1915	15/06/1915
Heading	War Diary of 2nd Cavalry Divisional A.S.C. From 1/8/15 to 31/8/15 Volume XII		
War Diary	La Nieppe	01/08/1915	05/08/1915
War Diary	Roquetoire West	06/08/1915	31/08/1915
Heading	War Diary of 2nd Cavalry Divisional A.S.C. From 1/9/15 To 30/9/15 Volume XIII		
War Diary	Roquetoire West	01/09/1915	20/09/1915
War Diary	Quiestede	21/09/1915	24/09/1915
War Diary	Roquetoire	25/09/1915	30/09/1915
Heading	War Diary of 2nd Cavalry Divisional A.S.C. From 1/10/15 To 31/10/15 Volume XIV		
War Diary	Roquetoire	01/10/1915	19/10/1915
War Diary	St Martin. D'Hardinghem	20/10/1915	31/10/1915
Heading	War Diary of 2nd Cavalry Divisional A.S.C From 1/11/18 To 30/11/15 Volume XV		
War Diary	St Martin D'Hardinghem	01/11/1915	30/11/1915
Heading	War Diary of 2nd Cavalry Divisional A.S.C. From 1/12/15 To 31/12/15 Volume XVI		
War Diary	St Martin D'Hardinghem	01/12/1915	31/12/1915
Heading	War Diary of 2nd Cavalry Divisional A.S.C From 1/1/16 To 31/1/16. Vol XVII		

War Diary	St Martin D'Hardinghem	01/01/1916	31/01/1916
Heading	War Diary of 2nd Cavalry Divisional A.S.C. From 1/2/16 To 29/2/16 Volume XVIII		
War Diary	St Martin D'Hardinghem	01/02/1916	29/02/1916
Heading	War Diary of 2nd Cavalry Divisional A.S.C. From 1/3/16 To 30/3/16 Volume XIX		
War Diary	St Martin D'Hardinghem	01/03/1916	31/03/1916
Heading	War Diary of 2nd Cavalry Divisional A.S.C. From 1/4/16 To 30/11/16 Volume XX		
War Diary	St Martin. D'Hardinghem	01/04/1916	30/04/1916
Heading	War Diary of 2nd Cavalry Divisional A.S.C. From 1/5/16 To 31/5/16 Volume XXI		
War Diary	St Martin D'Hardinghem	01/05/1916	05/05/1916
War Diary	Lumbres	06/05/1916	31/05/1916
Heading	War Diary of 2nd Cavalry Divisional A.S.C. From 1/6/16 To 30/6/16 Volume XXII		
War Diary	Lumbres	01/06/1916	21/06/1916
War Diary	Hazebrouck	22/06/1916	30/06/1916
Heading	War Diary of 2nd Cavalry Divisional A.S.C. From: 1st July To 31st July. 1916. Vol 1		
War Diary	Hazebrouck	01/07/1916	31/07/1916
Heading	War Diary of H.Q., A.S.C., 2nd Cav. Div for August, 1916. Vol XXIV		
War Diary	Hazebrouck	01/08/1916	31/08/1916
Heading	War Diary of O.C., 2nd Cavalry Divisional A.S.C. For September, 1916 Vol 3		
War Diary	Hazebrouck	01/09/1916	05/09/1916
War Diary	Hamet Billet	06/09/1916	06/09/1916
War Diary	Monchy Cayeur	07/09/1916	07/09/1916
War Diary	Vacqueriette	08/09/1916	09/09/1916
War Diary	Villers L'Hopital	10/09/1916	10/09/1916
War Diary	Vignacourt	11/09/1916	11/09/1916
War Diary	Lahoussoye	12/09/1916	14/09/1916
War Diary	Position 50 Yds N of C in Ville Sous Corbie Map Reference Map 17 scale 1/100,000	15/09/1916	30/09/1916
Heading	War Diary of H.Q. 2nd Cavalry Divl. A.S. Corps. October, 1916 Vol 4		
War Diary	Position 50 Yds N of C in Ville Sous Corbie Map Map 17 seale 1/100,000	01/10/1916	31/10/1916
Heading	War Diary of Headquarters, 2nd Cavalry Divisional A.S.C. November, 1916 Vol 5		
War Diary	Position 50 Yds N of C in Ville Sous Corbie Map Map 17 seale 1/100,000	01/11/1916	07/11/1916
War Diary	Bussy-Les-Daours	08/11/1916	08/11/1916
War Diary	Belloy-Sur-Somme	09/11/1916	09/11/1916
War Diary	Bonneval	10/11/1916	10/11/1916
War Diary	Dompierre	11/11/1916	30/11/1916
Heading	War Diary of Headquarters, 2nd Cavalry Divisional A.S.C. December, 1916 Vol. 6		
War Diary	Dompierre	01/12/1916	31/12/1916
Heading	War Diary of H.Q., 2nd Cavalry Divisional A.S.C. January, 1917 Vol. XXIX		
War Diary	Dompierre	01/01/1917	31/01/1917
Heading	War Diary of O.C. A.S.C., 2nd Cavalry Division. February, 1917 Vol. XXX.		
War Diary	Dompierre	01/02/1917	28/02/1917

Heading	War Diary of Headquarters, 2nd Cavalry Divisional A.S.C. March, 1917 Vol. XXXI.		
War Diary	Dompierre	01/03/1917	31/03/1917
Heading	War Diary of Headquarters, 2nd Cavalry Divisional A.S.C. April, 1917 Vol. XXXII		
War Diary	Dompierre	01/04/1917	07/04/1917
War Diary	Dompierre & Wavan	07/04/1917	08/04/1917
War Diary	Henu	09/04/1917	27/04/1917
War Diary	Frohen-Le-Grand	28/04/1917	30/04/1917
Heading	War Diary of Headquarters, 2nd Cavalry Divl. A.S.C. May, 1917-Col. XXXIII		
War Diary	Frohen-Le-Grand	01/05/1917	11/05/1917
War Diary	St Ouen	12/05/1917	12/05/1917
War Diary	Bussy-Les-Daours	13/05/1917	13/05/1917
War Diary	Lamotte-En-Santerre	14/05/1917	14/05/1917
War Diary	Roisel	15/05/1917	31/05/1917
Heading	War Diary of Headquarters, 2nd Cavalry Divisional A.S.C. From 1st June, To 30th June, 1917 (Volume XXXIV)		
War Diary	Roisel	01/06/1917	25/06/1917
War Diary	Roisel K.10.C.3-5.	26/06/1917	30/06/1917
Heading	War Diary of Headquarters 2nd Cavalry Divisional A.S.C. From 1st July 1917 To 31st July 1917. (Volume XXXV)		
War Diary	Roisel K.10.C.3.5	01/07/1917	08/07/1917
War Diary	Buire	09/07/1917	12/07/1917
War Diary	Suzanne	13/07/1917	13/07/1917
War Diary	Treux	14/07/1917	14/07/1917
War Diary	Thievres	15/07/1917	15/07/1917
War Diary	Houvigneul	16/07/1917	31/07/1917
Heading	War Diary of Head Quarters, A.S.C., 2nd Cavalry Division For August 1917 (Volume XXXVI)		
War Diary	Houvigneul	01/08/1917	31/08/1917
Heading	War Diary of Headquarters 2nd Cavalry Divisional A.S.C. From 1st September1917 To 30th September 1917. Volume XXXVII		
War Diary	Houvigneul	01/09/1917	30/09/1917
Heading	War Diary of H.Q., 2nd Cavalry Divisional Army Service Corps. From 1st October 1917, To 31st October 1917 (Volume. XXXVIII)		
War Diary	Houvigneul	01/10/1917	07/10/1917
War Diary	Heuchin	08/10/1917	18/10/1917
War Diary	Houvigneul	19/10/1917	19/10/1917
War Diary	Domart-En-Ponthieu	20/10/1917	20/10/1917
War Diary	St Sauflieu	21/10/1917	31/10/1917
Heading	War Diary of Headquarters 2nd Cavalry Division Army Service Corps. From:- 1st November 1917 To 30th November 1917 Volume XXXIX		
War Diary	St Sauflieu	01/11/1917	15/11/1917
War Diary	Mericourt	16/11/1917	16/11/1917
War Diary	Monchy Lagache	17/11/1917	19/11/1917
War Diary	Villers Faucon E.16.C.3.7	20/11/1917	30/11/1917
Heading	War Diary of Headquarters, 2nd Cavalry Divisional A.S.C. From:- 1st December 1917. To:- 31st December 1917. (Volume 40.)		
War Diary	Camp N of Fins on Metz road	01/12/1917	05/12/1917

War Diary	Cartigny	06/12/1917	06/12/1917
War Diary	Bussy-Les-Daours	07/12/1917	07/12/1917
War Diary	Quevauvillers	08/12/1917	31/12/1917
Heading	War Diary of Headquarters, 2nd Cavalry Divisional A.S.C. January, 1918-Volume XLI.		
War Diary	Quevauvillers	01/01/1918	31/01/1918
Heading	War Diary of Headquarters 2nd Cavalry Divisional A.S.C. From 1st February 1918 To 28th February 1918. (Volume XLII)		
War Diary	Quevauvillers	01/02/1918	04/02/1918
War Diary	Marcelcave	05/02/1918	05/02/1918
War Diary	Athies	06/02/1918	28/02/1918
Heading	War Diary of Headquarters, 2nd Cavalry Divisional Army Service Corps. From 1st. March To 31st March 1918. Volume XLIII.		
War Diary	Athies	01/03/1918	12/03/1918
War Diary	Quesmy	13/03/1918	22/03/1918
War Diary	Pontoise	23/03/1918	23/03/1918
War Diary	Bailly	24/03/1918	25/03/1918
War Diary	Rovallieu	26/03/1918	26/03/1918
War Diary	Joncquieres	27/03/1918	27/03/1918
War Diary	Moyvillers	28/03/1918	28/03/1918
War Diary	Erquinvillers also Noyons St Martin	29/03/1918	29/03/1918
War Diary	Plachy-Buyon	30/03/1918	31/03/1918
Heading	War Diary of Headquarters, 2nd Cavalry Divisional Army Service Corps. From 1st April To 30th April 1918. Volume XLIV.		
War Diary	Plachy-Buyon	01/04/1918	01/04/1918
War Diary	Salouel	01/04/1918	02/04/1918
War Diary	Rivery.	03/04/1918	05/04/1918
War Diary	Ailly Le Haut Clocher	06/04/1918	10/04/1918
War Diary	Auxi Le Chateau	10/04/1918	12/04/1918
War Diary	Bomy	12/03/1918	13/04/1918
War Diary	Blaringhem	13/04/1918	28/04/1918
War Diary	Coyecque	29/04/1918	30/04/1918
Heading	War Diary Headquarters of 2nd Cavalry Divisional, Army Service Corps. From: 1st May, 1918 To: 31st May, 1918. Volume XLV.		
War Diary	Coyecque	01/05/1918	05/05/1918
War Diary	Alette	06/05/1918	31/05/1918
Heading	War Diary of Headquarters, 2nd Cavalry Divisional A.S.C. From. 1st June, 1918. To 30th June, 1918. Volume XLVI.		
War Diary	Alette	01/06/1918	30/06/1918
Heading	War Diary Vol XLVII of H.Q. 2nd Cavalry Divisional A.S.C. From 1st To 31 July 18		
War Diary	Alette	01/07/1918	13/07/1918
War Diary	Wail	14/07/1918	14/07/1918
War Diary	Lacauroy	15/07/1918	21/07/1918
War Diary	Wail	22/07/1918	22/07/1918
War Diary	Alette	23/07/1918	31/07/1918
Heading	War Diary of Headquarters, 2nd Cavalry Divisional. A.S.C. From. 1st August, 1918 To 31st August. 1918. Vol 26		
War Diary	Alette	01/08/1918	03/08/1918
War Diary	Moulmel	04/08/1918	04/08/1918

War Diary	Coaurs	05/08/1918	05/08/1918
War Diary	Breilly	06/08/1918	07/08/1918
War Diary	Longueau	08/08/1918	11/08/1918
War Diary	Mop. Ref. Sheet 66 E 1/40,000 E. 13.6.6.3	12/08/1918	14/08/1918
War Diary	Belloy-Sur Somme	15/08/1917	15/08/1917
War Diary	Canaples	16/08/1918	16/08/1918
War Diary	Fontaine L Etalon	17/08/1918	20/08/1918
War Diary	Grenas	21/08/1918	23/08/1918
War Diary	Camp Barincourt Bailleumont road	24/08/1918	25/08/1918
War Diary	Grenas	26/08/1918	31/08/1918
Heading	War Diary of Headquarters. 2nd Cavalry Divisional A.S.C. From 1st September To 30th September. 1918.Volume XlIX		
War Diary	Grenas	01/09/1918	10/09/1918
War Diary	Mondicourt	11/09/1918	30/09/1918
Heading	War Diary of Headquarters 2nd Cavalry Divnl. A.S.C. From 1st To 31st October, 1918. Volume L.		
War Diary	Mondicourt	01/10/1918	31/10/1918
Heading	War Diary of H.Q. 2nd Cavalry Divl. A.S.C. November. 1918 Volume LI.		
War Diary	Mondicourt	01/11/1918	05/11/1918
War Diary	Bihucourt	06/11/1918	06/11/1918
War Diary	Cambrai	07/11/1918	12/11/1918
War Diary	Boussies	13/11/1918	13/11/1918
War Diary	Taisnieres	14/11/1918	14/11/1918
War Diary	South site of road between Douxies Maubeuge main Road	15/11/1918	16/11/1918
War Diary	Thuin	17/11/1918	17/11/1918
War Diary	Morialme	18/11/1918	20/11/1918
War Diary	Bouvignes	21/11/1918	21/11/1918
War Diary	Leignon	22/11/1918	22/11/1918
War Diary	Marche	23/11/1918	30/11/1918
Heading	War Diary of Headquarters, Royal Service Corps, 2nd Cavalry Division. From:- 1st December, 1918 To:- 31 December, 1918. Volume LII		
War Diary	Marche	01/12/1918	15/12/1918
War Diary	Theux	16/12/1918	31/12/1918
Miscellaneous	Appendix 1 to Dec 1918 War Diary.		
Miscellaneous	Appendix 2 to Dec 1918 War Diary.		
Heading	War Diary of Headquarters, 2nd Cavalry Divisional R.A.S.C. From 1st to January 1919. Volume. 53		
War Diary	Theux	01/01/1919	31/01/1919
Heading	War Diary of Headquarters: 2nd Cavalry Divisional R.A.S.C. From:- 1st February, 1919 To:- 28th February, 1919. Volume LIV		
War Diary	Theux	01/02/1919	28/02/1919
Heading	War Diary of H.Q. 2nd Cav Div 1/3/19-31/3/19 (Volume LV)		
War Diary	Theux	01/03/1919	09/03/1919
War Diary	Heusy	10/03/1919	31/03/1919

WD 95/1128/1

1915-1919
2ND CAVALRY DIVISION

H.Q. DIVL. A.S.C.

MAR 1915-MAR 1919

(424 COY ASC)

Confidential
War Diary of

Headquarters 2nd Cavalry

Divisional A.S.C.

From 13/3/15 to 31/3/15

Volume VII.

Mar 1919

WAR DIARY
INTELLIGENCE SUMMARY

Volume VII

Army Form C. 2118.

Instructions regarding War Diaries and Intelligence Summaries are contained in F.S. Regs., Part II. and the Staff Manual respectively. Title pages will be prepared in manuscript.

(Erase heading not required.)

Hour, Date, Place	Summary of Events and Information	Remarks and references to Appendices
13/3/15.	Still in same billets at VIEUX BERQUIN. The Detachment from N. MIDLAND DIVISION, joined the 2nd Cav. Division on 13/3/15, and is called the NOTTS and DERBY Brigade. Lieut. Spinney, Requisitioning Officer, Divisional Troops went to the mines at BRUAY & obtained 3 tons of coal - 2 tons for the NOTTS & DERBY Brigade - 1 ton Divisional Troops. D.C, A.S.C, 2nd Cav. Division, inspected the lorries of the Am[munitio]n Park - the vehicles were in good order & the recovery & repairs well kept. Report rendered to D.A.D.A.M.S on same. There is no information to report on the British front. The weather is warm & sunny & the roads have dried up considerably.	Strength of NOTTS & DERBY Brigade - See Appendix A. OAH
Sunday 14/3/15.	Still in same billets at VIEUX BERQUIN. The Summary of Information states that the British had gained 4000 yds of Trenches including the village of NEUVE CHAPELLE. 2000 dead Germans have been counted in the lines & another 3,000 are estimated to have been killed. A very lively cannonade was kept up from 5 p.m - 10 p.m in the direction of NIEPPES, rifle firing could be heard. The weather was very fine, sunny & quite mild. The roads have dried up.	OAH
Monday 15/3/15.	Still in same billets at VIEUX BERQUIN. The Summary of Information states that the village of ST ELOI has been taken by the Germans & that we have lost several trenches but are in the progress of retaking them. The weather is very mild but dull & inclined to be misty. Pte Cunningham, clerk in this office & surplus to establishment was sent to the Base, H.T. Depot, HAVRE.	OAH

Army Form C. 2118.

WAR DIARY
INTELLIGENCE SUMMARY.
(Erase heading not required.)

Instructions regarding War Diaries and Intelligence Summaries are contained in F.S. Regs., Part II. and the Staff Manual respectively. Title pages will be prepared in manuscript.

Hour, Date, Place	Summary of Events and Information	Remarks and references to Appendices
Tuesday 16.3.15.	Instructions received from A.A. & Q.M.G. 2nd Cav. Div. that as the weather is milder, the Cloak or coat British & warm will be discarded, & that the transport for these will be returned to Advanced Horse Transport Depot. The vehicles & horses, 2 & 198 respectively, were ordered to entrain at HAZEBROUCK at 6 P.M. & be sent to Advanced H.T. Depot, ABBEVILLE. The following transport was entrained at 6 P.M. — { 5th Brigade and Wagon } { 1st Battery } 9 wagons, 24 horses, 2 horses, 1 man, 2 men. The weather was very mild but dull. The roads are dry & reported to be during at HAZEBROUCK Station. Still in farm billets at VIEUX BERQUIN.	See Appendix B. See Appendix C. Ditto
Wednesday 17.3.15.	The A.D. of S. & T. Cavalry Corps inspected the horses of the Supply Column & ordered himself satisfied in every way. Went to the 16th Farriers to arrange about getting riders and to take them one to-morrow. The weather remains fine & mild. We are still in the same billets at VIEUX BERQUIN. There is nothing to report.	Ditto

WAR DIARY
or
INTELLIGENCE SUMMARY.
(Erase heading not required.)

Army Form C. 2118.

Hour, Date, Place	Summary of Events and Information	Remarks and references to Appendices
Thursday 18/3/15	Inspected No. 2 Cavalry Field Ambulance. To Report See Appendix D. Handed over 7 wagons to 4th Brigade of which the 3rd Hussars took 5 wagons & the 6th Dragoons took 2 wagons. The unserviceable wagons brought in by these units were left at the station to be railed away. Return of Supply details sent in. The weather is mild but on absence of sunshine & towards evening became very dark & rained slightly. Still in same billets at VIEUX BERQUIN.	Appendix D. See Appendix E. D/H
Friday 19/3/15	Sent in Field Return & Motor Car Return. Still in same billets at VIEUX BERQUIN. The weather has turned cold & snow is on the ground & a bitter cold wind is blowing.	D/H
Saturday 20/3/15	Supply officers diaries inspected. Vauxhall Cars of 1st Cav. Div. inspected with a view to exchanging the Sunbeams in our Division. Closed Daimler belonging to A.A. & Q.M.G. inspected with a view to exchanging for an open car. Went into St OMER to try & get Vauxhalls in exchange for two Bollee & Daimler. No Vauxhalls obtainable. Weather mild & warm.	D/H

Army Form C. 2118.

WAR DIARY
or
INTELLIGENCE SUMMARY.
(*Erase heading not required.*)

Instructions regarding War Diaries and Intelligence Summaries are contained in F. S. Regs., Part II. and the Staff Manual respectively. Title pages will be prepared in manuscript.

Hour, Date, Place	Summary of Events and Information	Remarks and references to Appendices
Sunday 21-3-15.	Still in same billets at VIEUX BERQUIN. Weather very fine & mild.	OK HH
Monday 22-3-15.	Returned from Boller - M.662, to G.H.Q. & got receipts for Same. Took Drencher, M.9408 in change. Authority A D R of T 43/3/15. Still in same billets. Weather mild & warm.	OK HH
Tuesday 23-3-15.	Received 5 Chargers from the 16th Lancers, 3 of the Chargers are bad & not fit for Officers' Chargers. Changed billets into Farm as a case of measles has broken out in our former billets. Nothing to report. The weather is mild & dull.	OK HH

WAR DIARY
or
INTELLIGENCE SUMMARY.

(Erase heading not required.)

Army Form C. 2118.

Instructions regarding War Diaries and Intelligence Summaries are contained in F. S. Regs., Part II. and the Staff Manual respectively. Title pages will be prepared in manuscript.

Hour, Date, Place	Summary of Events and Information	Remarks and references to Appendices
Tuesday 30-3-15.	Still in same Billets. I.G.S. Wagon + 1 Maltese Cart arrived, with 5 horses. Met + obtained above at HAZEBROOK + have taken them on our strength. Team of horses very good. Horse for Maltese Cart unused to job. Inspected the Transport of the 5th Bn. Lieut. E.L.B. Ravenhill joined + was posted to 6th Cav. Bde. as Transport Officer.	PAH. See Appendices F for Report.
Wednesday 31-3-15.	Still in same Billets. Weather fine + dry. Return of Officers rendered.	PAH.

Army Form C. 2118.

WAR DIARY
or
INTELLIGENCE SUMMARY.
(Erase heading not required.)

Instructions regarding War Diaries and Intelligence Summaries are contained in F.S. Regs., Part II and the Staff Manual respectively. Title pages will be prepared in manuscript.

Hour, Date, Place	Summary of Events and Information	Remarks and references to Appendices
Wednesday 24/3/15.	In Same Billetts. Weather very changeable, rain prevalent. Daimler M.1247 returned to G.H.Q.	OAH
Thursday 25/3/15.	In Same Billetts. Weather fine. Vauxhall M.9595 arrived from G.H.Q. for A.A. & Q.M.G. in place of Daimler M.1247. Exchanged Chestnut horse received from 16th Lancers for a black Cob from the Notts & Derby Bde. State of Supply Details rendered. Returned 2 horses received from 16th Lancers to the 16th Lancers, as they are useless for our purpose.	OAH
Friday 26/3/15.	In Same Billetts. Weather fine. Wolseley M.550 arrived from G.H.Q. for Head Quarter General Staff. Field Plate & summary of Motor Vehicles rendered.	OAH

Army Form C. 2118.

WAR DIARY
or
INTELLIGENCE SUMMARY.
(Erase heading not required.)

Instructions regarding War Diaries and Intelligence Summaries are contained in F.S. Regs., Part II. and the Staff Manual respectively. Title pages will be prepared in manuscript.

Hour, Date, Place	Summary of Events and Information	Remarks and references to Appendices
Saturday. 27-3-15.	Still in Same Billets. Weather fine & warm. Received a mail. Cab from D.A.A & Q.M.G. + took it on our strength. Lieut. Vale joined as Reg. Officer 4th Cav. Bde. + hut Dudley ordered to report at BOULOGNE. D² Crissel admitted to Hospital.	PH
Sunday. 28-3-15.	Still in Same Billets. Weather fine.	PH
Monday 29-3-15.	Still in Same Billets. weather fine but cold wind. Snow at one time + unable to walk freely.	PH

A

A.A.&Q.M.G.2nd.Cav.Div.Q.L.2439.

HQ.2/Cav.Div.A.S.C.125.

Composition of Detachment from N.Midland Division.

Notts and Derby Brigade.

5th Battalion Notts and Derby Regt.

6th   " "   " "   " " .

7th   " "   " "   " " .

8th   " "   " "   " " .

Detachments from a Brigade Amnt Column and N.Midland Div.Amnt Col.

1st Field Ambulance complete.

Supply Section of the Train.

3 Amnt. Park Lorries.

Supply Column Section.
----

4 Lorries.   ))
1 First Aid.   )   Under an Officer.
2 Spare.   )

****

APPENDIX 'B'
****

Telegram

TO.---   3rd, 4th, and 5th, Cavalry. Brigades.

To reduce transport and as weather is milder it has been decided to discard either the cloak or Coat Warm British also third Blanket per man. These should be handed into the Railhead Ordnance Representative being sent in by the Rug cart which will be no longer required and will also be returned to Railhead for dispatch to Advanced Horse Transport Depot. Please report when this has been done and whether Cloaks or Coats warm have been returned. Torn or unserviceable Coats Cloaks or Blankets should not be returned but destroyed

15/3/15.   (sgnd). J.G. Griffiths. Major. D.A.
                                   for. A.A. & Q.M.G.
                                        2nd. Cav. Division.

APPENDIX "C"

Telegram.

O.C.A.S.C.
      2nd.Cav.Divn.

Following wire received from Traffic G.H.Q.begins.
Your 27.Vehicles and 108 pnt. horses should entrain HAZEBROOK
18.00.to-day. The vehicles and horses should be sent to
Advanced Horse Transport Depot ABBEVILLE.

16/3/15.   (sgnd).J.G.Griffiths.Major.D.A.
                          for.A.A.&.Q.M.G.
                                2nd.Cav.Divn.

APPENDIX. "D".

D.A.A. & Q.M.G.

    2nd Cav Divn.

I inspected this day 6 Mark 1 Light Ambulances of the 2nd. Cavalry Field Ambulance.and found them serviceable.

I would reccommend that one complete spare set of springs be carried and authority obtained for issue of the necessary articles.

The following stores for the upkeep and maintenance of the vehicles are on demand from the A.O.D. could they be hastened please as they are urgently required viz..

    12.Brake shoes.

    4.covers Ambulance.

18/3/15.   (sgnd) A.F.Perry.Knox.Gore.Major

                            O.C.Head.Qrs.2nd.Cav.Div.A.S.C.

APPENDIX "E".

The following wagons taken in exchange by the 3rd.Brigade.
at Steenbecque.Railway.Station.

3rd.HUSSARS'

H.Q.Mark.8. ------------------------------E.16568.

Asq.Mark.9. ------------------------------E.19178.

H.Q.Mark.8. ------------------------------E.~~00000~~.11776.

Bsq.Mark.10. -----------------------------E.19878.

Csq.Mark.10. -----------------------------E.17243.

OXFORDSHIRE.HUSSARS'
!!!!!!!!!!!!!!!!!!

Mark.10. --------------------------------935.

Mark.10. --------------------------------E'44283.

                              (sgnd)P.A.Arden.Capt.for Major.

18/3/15.   O.C.A.S.C.2nd.Cav.Div.

Appendix "E"

No. 225.

D.A.A. & Q.M.G.

2nd Cavalry Division.

I beg to report that yesterday March 30th I inspected the Transport of 5th Cavalry Brigade & found it serviceable with the undermentioned exceptions.

Head Quarters, 5th Cav. Bde.

1 G.S. Wagon. Mark Vlll. requires new rear wheel.

12th Lancers.

Harness Pole draught should be obtained for Water Cart recently received, as at present shaft draught harness is being used - the latter is not satisfactory.

x   One tail board requires repairs.

x   Maltese Cart requires repairs.

x   Tank Water Cart - one pump out of action owing to lead from pump being damaged.

I am arranging to have items marked (x) adjusted by the Supply Column.

On all G.S. Mark Vlll. wagons the rear wheels require attention being in my opinion too slack on the axle arm. The wear is due to the length of time the vehicles have been in use and not to any lack of lubricant. The end play of wheels on axle arms could be taken up by the aid of mild steel or phosphor bronze washers which should be of varying thickness, viz:- $\frac{1}{8}$", 3/16" & $\frac{1}{4}$".

I would suggest that the A.O.D. be asked to arrange for the Inspector of Ordnance Machinery to report on this matter, as I understand there is an I.O.M. at Cavalry Corps Railhead with workshops & staff of Artificers.

31/3/15.   sd.   A.F. Pery Knox Gore.

No. 225.

O.C.
   Supply Column.

Vehicles on charge of 12th Lancers require minor repairs as under. Can you effect the necessary repairs & name a convenient date.

(a)   One tail board iron support requires removal, welding & replacing.
(b)   Repairs to side standard of Maltese Cart.
(c)   Pump lead on Water Cart broken.

It ould perhaps be as well to send out a Foreman to see what work is required. He should report to the Qr. Mr. 12th Lancers.

31/3/15.   sd.   A.F. Pery Knox Gore.

B.E.F. FRANCE & FLANDERS.

2 CAV DIVISION. TROOPS.

H.Q. 2 CAVALRY DIVISION
ARMY SERVICE CORPS.
(424 COY A.S.C.)
1915 MAR TO 1919 MAR.

2 CAV DIV AUXILARY
HORSE TRANSPORT
(575 COY A.S.C.)
1915 SEPT TO 1919 JUNE.

2 CAV DIV AMMUNITION PARK
(56 COY A.S.C.)
1914 AUG TO 1917 SEPT.

B.E.F. FRANCE & FLANDERS.

2 CAV DIVISION. TROOPS.

H.Q. 2 CAVALRY DIVISION
ARMY SERVICE CORPS.
(424 COY A.S.C.)
1915 MAR TO 1919 MAR.

2 CAV DIV AUXILARY
HORSE TRANSPORT
(575 COY A.S.C.)
1915 SEPT TO 1919 JUNE.

2 CAV DIV AMMUNITIION PARK
(56 COY A.S.C.)
1914 AUG TO 1917 SEPT.

1128

Confidential
War Diary
of 2nd Cavalry Divisional A.S.C

From 1/4/15 to 30/4/15.

Volume VIII

Volume VIII

Army Form C. 2118.

WAR DIARY
INTELLIGENCE SUMMARY.
(Erase heading not required.)

Instructions regarding War Diaries and Intelligence Summaries are contained in F. S. Regs., Part II. and the Staff Manual respectively. Title pages will be prepared in manuscript.

Hour, Date, Place	Summary of Events and Information	Remarks and references to Appendices
Thursday 1-4-15.	Still in same Billets. T. Lieut A.F.H. Bonvalôt. T. Lieut. J. M. Grenade. T. 2/Lt J. Logan-Bell. Joined our Head Quarters. Weather fine & dry.	
Friday 2-4-15.	Still in same Billets. T.2/Lt J. Logan-Bell attached to the 2nd Cav. Div. Supply Column. Weather fine & dry.	
Saturday 3-4-15.	Still in same Billets. Weather wet & misty.	

Army Form C. 2118.

WAR DIARY
or
INTELLIGENCE SUMMARY.
(Erase heading not required.)

Hour, Date, Place	Summary of Events and Information	Remarks and references to Appendices
Sunday. 4-4-15.	Still in same Billets. Weather wet + misty.	
Monday. 5-4-15.	Still in same Billets. Weather very wet.	
Tuesday. 6-4-15.	Still in same Billets. Weather fine in morning — wet afternoon	

Instructions regarding War Diaries and Intelligence Summaries are contained in F.S. Regs., Part II and the Staff Manual respectively. Title pages will be prepared in manuscript.

Army Form C. 2118.

WAR DIARY
INTELLIGENCE SUMMARY.
(Erase heading not required.)

Instructions regarding War Diaries and Intelligence
Summaries are contained in F.S. Regs., Part II
and the Staff Manual respectively. Title pages
will be prepared in manuscript.

Hour, Date, Place	Summary of Events and Information	Remarks and references to Appendices
Wednesday. 7-4-15.	Still in same Billets. Dr Jones reported at ARSENAL & sent to HAVRE to report. Weather fine.	
Thursday. 8-4-15.	Still in same Billets. Staff & supply details rendered. Weather wet. Cleared up towards evening.	
Friday 9-4-15	Still in same Billets. Total state & return of Motor Cars rendered. Weather changeable. Experiments made with finding S.S. wagon as to its return. Carrying Capacity at STEENBECQUE STATION.	See Appendix "G"

Army Form C. 2118.

WAR DIARY
or
INTELLIGENCE SUMMARY.

(Erase heading not required.)

Instructions regarding War Diaries and Intelligence Summaries are contained in F.S. Regs., Part II and the Staff Manual respectively. Title pages will be prepared in manuscript.

Hour, Date, Place	Summary of Events and Information	Remarks and references to Appendices
Saturday. 10-4-15	Still in same Billets. Weather wet.	
Sunday. 11-4-15	Still in same Billets. Sent small lot that was obtained from D.A.D.M.G. to Mob. Mobile Veterinary Section as it was too light for its work. Weather fine.	
Monday. 12-4-15	3-ton lorry left Head Qrs. for 1st Cav. Div. Supply Column. Weather fine. Still in same Billets	

Army Form C. 2118.

WAR DIARY
or
INTELLIGENCE SUMMARY.
(Erase heading not required.)

Instructions regarding War Diaries and Intelligence Summaries are contained in F.S. Regs., Part II. and the Staff Manual respectively. Title pages will be prepared in manuscript.

Hour, Date, Place	Summary of Events and Information	Remarks and references to Appendices
Tuesday. 13-4-15.	Still in same Billets. 2 lorries from + 3 lorries from the Ammⁿ Park left this Division to from the 9th Cavalry Bde. Weather wet + windy.	
Wednesday. 14-4-15.	Still in same Billets — weather fine.	
Thursday. 15-4-15.	Sent Chestnut horse that we received from the 16th Lancers to No. 4. Reserve Park to be exchanged. Weather fine — Still in same Billets. Sent in return of Motor Cars + Supply Details	

(73989) W4141—463. 400,000. 9/14. H.&J.Ltd. Forms/C. 2118/10.

WAR DIARY
or
INTELLIGENCE SUMMARY.
(Erase heading not required.)

Army Form C. 2118.

Hour, Date, Place	Summary of Events and Information	Remarks and references to Appendices
Friday 16-4-15	Received a van man from No. 6. Reserve Park. Took over the cor of 6. Head Quarters draught horses. No rugs were sent with their horses two motorcycles. Received from Abbeville H.T. Depot on forage Cart with two light draught horses. Remained Field Return & Inventory of Motor vehicles. Still in farm Pollets - weather fine.	
Saturday 17-4-15	Weather fine - Still in farm Pollets. Took over 2 G.S. Wagons + 4 horses from Head Quarters 2nd Cav. Division. Work after.	

Army Form C. 2118.

WAR DIARY
INTELLIGENCE SUMMARY.
(Erase heading not required.)

Instructions regarding War Diaries and Intelligence Summaries are contained in F.S. Regs., Part II. and the Staff Manual respectively. Title pages will be prepared in manuscript.

Hour, Date, Place	Summary of Events and Information	Remarks and references to Appendices
Sunday 18-4-15	Still in Same Billets. Weather fine. Dr. Kelly, R. No. T2/14215 joined from Advanced B.A.T. Depot	
Monday 19-4-15	Still in Same Billets. Weather fine.	
Tuesday 20-4-15	Still in Same Billets. Weather very fine.	
Wednesday 21-4-15	Still in Same Billets. Weather fine. Received orders that E.J. & D. Batt. R.H.A. were being sent to 7th Inf. Div. and would leave for duty as follows: on 23rd E.J.+J also ration of Ammn Col. on 24th the feeding of Batts & Ammn Col. Still to be performed by 2nd Cav: Divn. Dr Lloyd & Dr Feather joined from No 2. Cav. Field. Amb.	
Thursday 22-4-15	Still in same Billets. Weather fine. Issued necessary orders to Supply Off: regarding supply of any proceeding for duty with 7th Inf. Div:.	

Army Form C. 2118.

WAR DIARY
INTELLIGENCE SUMMARY.
(Erase heading not required.)

Hour, Date, Place	Summary of Events and Information	Remarks and references to Appendices
9.a.m. 23-4-15. VIEUX-BERQUIN	Received orders that fighting portion of Brigades & "A" Echelon Transport would concentrate at 12 noon ready to march N. head of Column STRAZEELE Str:- Division to march via METEREN and BERTHEN apex FLETRE to BOESCHEPE- fighting portion of Army Corps remaining at cross roads ½ mile N.E. of FLETRE. "B" Echelon Transport to remain in present billets ready to move at short notice. Still in same billets. Dr. Jones. A.S. T/4255. admitted into Hospital	Supply arrangements S.O.S to have the lorries carrying food in convenient road so as not to hinder movement of troops, split loads so as to feed "B" Echelon later up food for "A" Echelon & fighting troops when latter have halted for night. Previous instructions re R.H.A. cancelled.
Sunday 24-4-15. VIEUX-BERQUIN	"B" Echelon Transport Concentrated & ready to move at short notice. Still in Same Billets. Weather fine. Received two men from Advanced Horse Transport Depôt to complete our establishment.	

Army Form C. 2118.

WAR DIARY
or
INTELLIGENCE SUMMARY.

(Erase heading not required.)

Instructions regarding War Diaries and Intelligence
Summaries are contained in F. S. Regs., Part II.
and the Staff Manual respectively. Title pages
will be prepared in manuscript.

Hour, Date, Place	Summary of Events and Information	Remarks and references to Appendices
Sunday 25-4-15.	Still in same billets - Weather very hot. Dr Jones M.O. T/4253 rejoined from hospital	
Monday 26-4-15.	Still in same Billets, weather very hot	
Tuesday 27-4-15.	Still in same Billets - weather not so hot today.	

(73989) W4141—463. 400,000. 9/14. H.&J.,Ltd. Forms/C. 2118/10.

Army Form C. 2118.

WAR DIARY
or
INTELLIGENCE SUMMARY.

(Erase heading not required.)

Instructions regarding War Diaries and Intelligence Summaries are contained in F. S. Regs., Part II and the Staff Manual respectively. Title pages will be prepared in manuscript.

Hour, Date, Place	Summary of Events and Information	Remarks and references to Appendices
Wednesday 28-4-15.	Still in Same Billets - Weather hot + dry.	
Thursday 29-4-15-	Still in Same Billets - Weather hot + dry. State of Supply details rendered.	
Friday 30-4-15-	Still in Same Billets - Weather hot + dry. B.213 A rendered, also summary of Motor Vehicles & Return of Officers.	

Appendix G

A.A.& Q.M.G.
    2nd.Cav.Division.

The front portion of a G.S. Wagon will carry the undermentioned supplies.

(1).   400 rations Biscuit.

             or

(2).   816 rations Preserved Meat.

             or

(3).   576 rations Preserved Meat.
        560 rations Bacon.
        600 rations Jam.
        850 rations Sugar.

             or

(4).   450 rations Biscuits.
        650 rations Cheese.
        760 rations Tea.

             or

(5).   200 rations Preserved Meat.
        200   " "   Biscuit.
        200   " "   Cheeses
        200   " "   Sugar.
        200   " "   Bacon.
        200   " "   Jam.

             or,

(6).   300 rations Preserved Meat.
        300 rations Biscuit.
        300 Iron Grocery Rations.

             or,

(7).   13 sacks of oats @ 30 lbs per Sack = Rations for 86 horses @ 12 lbs per horse--(3½.L.G.S. Wagons to carry oats for a Cavalry Regt.).

(3) & (4). Are a good combination as with the front and rear portion of a limbered G.S. wagon Mens rations for a Cavalry Regt..could, allowing for some casualties and "B" echelon not being with fighting portion of the Regt.. be carried.

<u>NOTES.</u>   The packing has to be carefully done and lashings would be necessary to prevent the load falling off when travelling over rough ground.

                                   (sgnd) A.F.Pery.Knox.Gore.
                                                  Major.
9/4/15.   O.C.Head.Qrs.2nd.Cav.Divn.A.S.C.

Confidential.

War Diary

of 2nd Cavalry Divisional A.S.C.

from 1/5/15 to 31/5/15

Volume IX.

Army Form C. 2118.

Volume IX

WAR DIARY
or
INTELLIGENCE SUMMARY.

(Erase heading not required.)

Instructions regarding War Diaries and Intelligence Summaries are contained in F.S. Regs., Part II and the Staff Manual respectively. Title pages will be prepared in manuscript.

Hour, Date, Place	Summary of Events and Information	Remarks and references to Appendices
Saturday 1st May 1915.	Still in same Billets – weather very hot.	
Sunday 2nd May 1915.	Still in same Billets – weather very hot. Received orders to get ready to move following morning at 9 a.m. Starting Point of "B" Echelon. 200 yds to VIEUX BERQUIN side of the Railway Crossing at STRAZEELE. Everything packed up & ready to move.	
11.30 p.m.	Orders received cancelling move.	

(73989) W4141—463. 400,000. 9/14. H.&J.Ltd. Forms/C. 2118/10.

WAR DIARY
INTELLIGENCE SUMMARY.
(Erase heading not required.)

Army Form C. 2118.

Hour, Date, Place	Summary of Events and Information	Remarks and references to Appendices
Monday 3rd May.		
8.15 a.m.	Received orders to be at previous starting point at 11 a.m. & to move via CAESTRE, STEENVOORDE, ECQUES to HERZEELE.	
11.45 a.m.	Moved off from starting point & marched to STEENVOORDE where fresh orders were received to move to ESQUELBEC & take up billets there.	
7.p.m.	Arrived ESQUELBEC & found billets. Weather very hot & dry. Weather next halting.	

Army Form C. 2118.

WAR DIARY
or
INTELLIGENCE SUMMARY.
(Erase heading not required.)

Instructions regarding War Diaries and Intelligence Summaries are contained in F. S. Regs., Part II. and the Staff Manual respectively. Title pages will be prepared in manuscript.

Hour, Date, Place	Summary of Events and Information	Remarks and references to Appendices
Tuesday, 4th May.	In Billets at ESQUELBEC. Thunderstorm in afternoon. Horses picketted in the open.	
Wednesday, 5th May.	In same billets. Weather most sultry. Exchanged buckboard Car of senior supply officer for a Vauxhall from G.H.Q. Supply Col. Thunderstorm in afternoon + a lot of rain. Received two mules in lieu of one H.D. Horse.	
Thursday, 6th May.	In same billets. Weather still sultry. Rain very prevalent all day but away light from Rhine to "B" echelon 2nd Cav. Div. Field Ambulance as a Ruler.	See references Q

(73989) W4141—463. 400,000. 9/14. H.&J.Ltd. Forms/C. 2118/10.

Army Form C. 2118.

WAR DIARY
or
INTELLIGENCE SUMMARY.
(Erase heading not required.)

Instructions regarding War Diaries and Intelligence Summaries are contained in F.S. Regs., Part II and the Staff Manual respectively. Title pages will be prepared in manuscript.

Hour, Date, Place	Summary of Events and Information	Remarks and references to Appendices
Friday 7th May	Received orders to to proceed to move back to our old billets at VIEUX BERQUIN.	
1.15 p.m.	Received orders to proceed to starting point at VIEUX BERQUIN. Received starting point 2.15 p.m. & followed in behind the "B" Echelon of 5th Bde. Waited in CASSELS horse while the Cavalry went through. Proceeded to VIEUX BERQUIN & took up our old billets at 10.0 p.m.	
Saturday 8th May	In same billets. Weather very hot & dry.	
11.0 p.m.	Received orders to entrain to at 5 a.m. following morning.	

Army Form C. 2118.

WAR DIARY.
INTELLIGENCE SUMMARY.
(Erase heading not required.)

Instructions regarding War Diaries and Intelligence Summaries are contained in F.S. Regs., Part II. and the Staff Manual respectively. Title pages will be prepared in manuscript.

Hour, Date, Place	Summary of Events and Information	Remarks and references to Appendices
Sunday, 9th May 1915.	Stood to all day. Weather fine & very hot.	
Monday, 10th May 1915.	Still in same Billets. Weather very hot today.	
Tuesday, 11th May.	Still in same Billets. Weather very hot & dry. Received orders to carry on as usual. D: Smith joined 146th Fd. & 6th Gurkha came in his place.	
Wednesday 12th May.	Still in same Billets. Weather hot & dry. Received orders at 11 p.m. that the Regiment must move by bus to HAZEBROUCK at 11 A.M.	

(73989) W4141—463. 400,000. 9/14. H.&J.,Ltd. Forms/C. 2118/10.

WAR DIARY
INTELLIGENCE SUMMARY.

(Erase heading not required.)

Army Form C. 2118.

Hour, Date, Place	Summary of Events and Information	Remarks and references to Appendices
Thursday 13th May	Still in Same Billets. Weather hot & dry.	
11 p.m.	Received orders that the fighting portion of the Brigade would move by Bus into the vicinity of VLAMERTINGE. "B" Echelon to remain in the same Billets until further orders.	
Friday 14th May	Still in Same Billets. Weather wet & cold.	
Saturday 15th May	Still in Same Billets. Weather wet & cold.	

Army Form C. 2118.

WAR DIARY
or
INTELLIGENCE SUMMARY.
(Erase heading not required.)

Instructions regarding War Diaries and Intelligence Summaries are contained in F. S. Regs., Part II and the Staff Manual respectively. Title pages will be prepared in manuscript.

Hour, Date, Place	Summary of Events and Information	Remarks and references to Appendices
Sunday 16th May	Still in same Billets. Weather cold & wet.	
Monday 17th May	Still in same Billets. Weather wet & rubby.	
Tuesday 18th May	Lt. Caine joined 5th Cav: Bde. & Cpl. Bryants joined to take his place. Dr. Knowles joined Supply Col. & Cpl Tuke joined to take his place.	
Wednesday 19th May	Still in same Billets. Weather wet & rubby. Dr Horton sick & admitted to Hospital. Still in Same Billets. Weather wet.	

(73989) W4141—463. 400,000. 9/14. H.&J.Ltd. Forms/C. 2118/10.

Army Form C. 2118.

WAR DIARY
INTELLIGENCE SUMMARY.
(Erase heading not required.)

Hour, Date, Place	Summary of Events and Information	Remarks and references to Appendices
Thursday 20th May	Still in Same Billets — Weather fine & warm.	
Friday 21st May	Still in Same Billets — Weather fine & warm.	
Saturday 22nd May	Still in Same Billets — Weather fine & warm. 9= Tuke returned to Supply Col. & relieved by Dr Finney.	

Army Form C. 2118.

WAR DIARY
or
INTELLIGENCE SUMMARY.
(Erase heading not required.)

Instructions regarding War Diaries and Intelligence Summaries are contained in F. S. Regs., Part II. and the Staff Manual respectively. Title pages will be prepared in manuscript.

Hour, Date, Place	Summary of Events and Information	Remarks and references to Appendices
Sunday 23rd May.	Still in Same Billets – weather fine & warm. Yeo/M. Hall, sent to Advanced M.T. Depot, to return French horse harness complete. This turnout was evacuated by No. 7 Mobile Vet. Sect. & handed to this lorratum.	
Monday 24th May.	Still in Same Billets – weather fine & warm. Two H.D. horses, surplus to Establishment were sent to RENESCURE to meet representative of Reserve Parks.	
Tuesday 25th May.	Still in Same Billets – weather fine & warm.	

Army Form C. 2118.

WAR DIARY
or
INTELLIGENCE SUMMARY.
(Erase heading not required.)

Instructions regarding War Diaries and Intelligence Summaries are contained in F.S. Regs. Part II. and the Staff Manual respectively. Title pages will be prepared in manuscript.

Hour, Date, Place	Summary of Events and Information	Remarks and references to Appendices
Wednesday 26th May.	Still in same Billets. Weather fine & warm.	
Thursday 27th May.	Still in same Billets. Weather fine but cold. S/Sgt. Hall returned from H.T. Depot on completion of duty.	
Friday 28th May	Still in same Billets. Weather fine.	

(73989) W4141—463. 400,000. 9/14. H.&J.Ltd. Forms/C. 2118/10.

WAR DIARY
or
INTELLIGENCE SUMMARY.
(Erase heading not required.)

Army Form C. 2118.

Hour, Date, Place	Summary of Events and Information	Remarks and references to Appendices
Saturday 29th May.	Still in same Billets. Weather fine & warm. Arranged for the Supply Column horses into HAZEBROUCK. Found good billets for workshop tete.	
Sunday 30th May.	Still in Same Billets. Weather fine & warm. Received unofficial orders that the Division would move to LE NIEPPE to-morrow. Went to LE NIEPPE + arranged billets in case of move.	
Monday 31st May.	Received orders that the Division Head Quarters would move to LE NIEPPE. The O.C. A.S.C. to take charge of B. Echelon Head Qrs., Am't Col, Field Ambulances. Spare horses + Police, on the march. Starting Point 7 Roads South of STRAZEELE.	

Army Form C. 2118.

WAR DIARY
INTELLIGENCE SUMMARY.
(Erase heading not required.)

Instructions regarding War Diaries and Intelligence Summaries are contained in F.S. Regs., Part II. and the Staff Manual respectively. Title pages will be prepared in manuscript.

Hour, Date, Place	Summary of Events and Information	Remarks and references to Appendices
Monday 31st May	Moved off from Starting Point at 9 a.m. Shave lorries & police jointed from the Column. Arrived LE NIEPPE at 2 p.m. & got settled down in new Billets.	

Confidential
War Diary
of 2nd Cavalry Divisional A.S.C.
From 1/6/15 to 30/6/15

Volume X.

Volume X

Army Form C. 2118.

WAR DIARY
INTELLIGENCE SUMMARY.
(Erase heading not required.)

Instructions regarding War Diaries and Intelligence Summaries are contained in F. S. Regs., Part II. and the Staff Manual respectively. Title pages will be prepared in manuscript.

Hour, Date, Place	Summary of Events and Information	Remarks and references to Appendices
Monday 31st May	Moved off from starting point at 9 a.m. Stone horses & police joined before the Column arrived LEMETTE. 2 p.m. & got settled down in new billets.	
Tuesday 1st June.	In Same Billets - Weather fine & warm. Leave commences.	
Wednesday 2nd June.	Major Fay. Knox. Gore left the Divinon before No. 14. Div Amm. Park. Major Prott. Eliott. took over as O.C. A.S.C. In Same billets - weather fine & warm. Interviewed Col Swaby.	

Army Form C. 2118.

WAR DIARY
INTELLIGENCE SUMMARY.
(Erase heading not required.)

Hour, Date, Place	Summary of Events and Information	Remarks and references to Appendices
Thursday 3rd June.	Inspected the Supply Column & found all correct. Col. Swales called & interviewed Col' Murray & H.Q. Secretary. In Franc Billets, weather fine & warm.	
Friday 4th June.	Inspected H.Q. Ammunition Park & 2nd Cav. Div. Ambulance Workshop unit. Lieut Kahane joined unit as Reynolds Officer. Interviewed Col. Crosby with regard to above Officer as to is helpless. Lieut Kahane to remain & await further orders. Vauxhall Car 7563 exchanged for December 1214 — Vauxhall Car 7563 the front to G.H.Q. Supply est ... for refreshment overhaul.	

WAR DIARY
INTELLIGENCE SUMMARY.
(Erase heading not required.)

Army Form C. 2118.

Hour, Date, Place	Summary of Events and Information	Remarks and references to Appendices
LA NIEPPE		
Saturday 5th June 1915	Capt. P.A. Brown, Adjutant, of this unit, to proceed to England & report to Officer i/c of D.G.S.T., War Office for duty. Vauxhall Car T363, sent to Supply Col. for necessary report of deficiencies & overhaul, before the departure for G.H.Q. Supply Col.	
6th June 1915.	Visited 4th Cav Bde.	
7th June 1915.	Visited A.D.S.&T. Cav Corps afternoon	
8th June 1915.	Visited Field and Workshop unit.	
11th June 1915.	Visited Supply Col in the morning	
12th June 1915.		
13th June 1915.	Visited 4th Bde H.Q. and inspected Transport	
14th June 1915.		
15th June 1915.	Visited Field and Workshop unit in the morning and Supply Col in afternoon	

Confidential
War Diary
of 2nd Cavalry Divisional A.S.C.
From 1/8/15 to 31/8/15

Volume XII

Volume XII

WAR DIARY
INTELLIGENCE SUMMARY.
(Erase heading not required.)

Army Form C. 2118.

Instructions regarding War Diaries and Intelligence Summaries are contained in F.S. Regs., Part II. and the Staff Manual respectively. Title pages will be prepared in manuscript.

Hour, Date, Place	Summary of Events and Information	Remarks and references to Appendices
1915 1st August Le Nieppe	Still in same billet. Very hot & thundery today.	
2nd August Le Nieppe	Still in same billet. Showery today.	
3 August Le Nieppe	Still in same billet. Rained nearly all day	
4th August Le Nieppe	Still in same billet. Cloudy. Went over draw near billets at Roquetoire.	
5th August Le Nieppe	Still in same billets. Fine today. Preparing to move.	

Army Form C. 2118.

WAR DIARY
or
INTELLIGENCE SUMMARY.
(Erase heading not required.)

Instructions regarding War Diaries and Intelligence Summaries are contained in F.S. Regs., Part II. and the Staff Manual respectively. Title pages will be prepared in manuscript.

Hour, Date, Place	Summary of Events and Information	Remarks and references to Appendices
Friday 6th August Roquetoire. West.	Moved away from La Thieuloye old billet at 10.30 a.m. arriving at starting point. T road La Bouf & La La Barone on the St Omer to Laval road at 10.50 a.m. Left there at approx. 11.00 a.m. in the following order. H.Q. & Car Park, H.Q, A.S.C. H.Q, R.H.A. D. Eshlor field Ambulance & H.A. Route taken through Renescure thence Wavringhem crossed main road began to come about a mile on the road after crossing main road the column often split up here H.Q. and H.A ars a War fox. went to Roquetoire Eastwest. West e the R H A to Reginues the Field Ambulance to Couchie d'Equier. It started to rain just before morning off & kept it up As we were all near our new billets the roads were all in a very good condition and the column moved with ease arriving at new billets 1-30 p.m. H.Q, A.S.C. Having arrived wagons were put into fields & a temporary horse line put up at 3.00 p.m. Men & horses were all fed & officers men cooking under new homes not altogether.	
7th August Roquetoire. West.	Still in same billet. The whole day was spent in fixing up horse lines & bivouacs for men. Fine day but not bright.	

Army Form C. 2118.

WAR DIARY
or
INTELLIGENCE SUMMARY.

(Erase heading not required.)

Instructions regarding War Diaries and Intelligence Summaries are contained in F.S. Regs., Part II. and the Staff Manual respectively. Title pages will be prepared in manuscript.

Hour, Date, Place	Summary of Events and Information	Remarks and references to Appendices
8th August. Roquetoire West.	Still in same billet. Cleaned up the field & place for horses. Made 1 remount arrived same day.	
9th August. Roquetoire West.	Still in same billet. Same day. The French aircraft was seen as report over Aire. One wagon & team of horses went over to Fort de Blairmont and got a load of wood, two sick horses were cleared out - no one to put horses in. Meeting of Supply officers in the afternoon.	
10 August. Roquetoire West.	Still in same billet - horses went on exercise at 8 o'clock for two hours. Weather fine, heavy shower in afternoon lasting about ½ of an hour.	

(73989) W4141—463. 400,000. 9/14. H.&J.Ltd. Forms/C. 2118/10.

Army Form C. 2118.

WAR DIARY
or
INTELLIGENCE SUMMARY.
(Erase heading not required.)

Instructions regarding War Diaries and Intelligence
Summaries are contained in F. S. Regs., Part II.
and the Staff Manual respectively. Title pages
will be prepared in manuscript.

Hour, Date, Place	Summary of Events and Information	Remarks and references to Appendices
11th August. Roquetoire. West.	Still in same billet. Reveille Parade at 8 a.m. 1 wagon out for rations. Gone for green forage. Weather very fine. Rations hot.	
12th August. Roquetoire. West.	Still in same billet. Reveille Parade at 6 a.m. very good. Ra rations. Weather very fine.	
13th August. Roquetoire. West.	Still in same billet. Reveille Parade at 6 a.m. 1 wag gone for rations. Weather very fine. 2. Linkwell G.S. wagon arrived from. 8 Div: R.A.A. Am. Column for 39 Mobile. Vet. Section. Stopped men & equipment.	
14th August. Roquetoire. West.	Still in same billet. Reveille Parade at 8 a.m. 1 wagon out rations. Weather very fine. R.H.A. man been 1 wagon for rations. 1 wagon still here.	

(73989) W4141—463. 400,000. 9/14. H.&J.Ltd. Forms/C. 2118/10.

WAR DIARY
INTELLIGENCE SUMMARY

(Erase heading not required.)

Army Form C. 2118.

Instructions regarding War Diaries and Intelligence Summaries are contained in F.S. Regs., Part II. and the Staff Manual respectively. Title pages will be prepared in manuscript.

Hour, Date, Place	Summary of Events and Information	Remarks and references to Appendices
15th August. Roquetoire West.	Still in same billet. Received horses 8 a.m. 1 waggon for rations. 1 for green forage. No firing from enemy.	
16th August. Roquetoire West.	Still in same billet. Received horses 8 a.m. 1 waggon for rations. 1 waggon to draw green in for trench former. Strong feet round waggon horses cleaned weather fine.	
17th August. Roquetoire West.	Still in same billet. Left after a route march, went to Béthune - arriving at the starting point. 7 a.m. its appointed time. Place Béthune. Cauchie d'Esquas route taken from starting point to report thereover when within two kilometres of village turned to the right & got on to the Thérouanne - St Omer road as am turning to the right a getting into ditch & kilometres of Thérouanne from turned to the right passing through Esquio to Cauchie d'Esquas where the Column spent at all. Going to have refreshments billets. H.Q. d.d.g. arriving Baril 10 a.m. march carried out in very good order & at 11 a.m. I'd marched half & lapsed at rest all day. 2nd Lt. A. Gray reported for duty on R.O. Per Lists.	

Army Form C. 2118.

WAR DIARY
INTELLIGENCE SUMMARY.
(Erase heading not required.)

Instructions regarding War Diaries and Intelligence Summaries are contained in F. S. Regs., Part II. and the Staff Manual respectively. Title pages will be prepared in manuscript.

Hour, Date, Place	Summary of Events and Information	Remarks and references to Appendices
18th August. Roquetoire. Wet.	Still in same billet. 1 waggon for rations & 1 for wood. O.C. A.S.C. & Lieut. Orr went to inspect the route march of the 3rd Brigade. Heavy showers in the morning, rest of the day fine.	
19th August. Roquetoire. Wet.	Still in same billet. 3 waggons out 1 for rations 1 for green forage, one for drawing in green for present — 2 men prisoners. Horse went out to exercise at 6. a.m. - boy made report the same, gate put up to entrance of field.	
20th August. Roquetoire. Wet.	Still in same billet - 2 waggons & 1 cart out. cart for forage & rations, a waggon to draw green for the french people & Lieut. G. Simpson + 6 men to men left for the Fat Cow Ret at Enquetberg Fine day. I.O. inspected same made pick out road out bad.	

(73989) W4141-463. 400,000. 9/14. H.&J.Ltd. Forms/C. 2118/10.

Army Form C. 2118.

WAR DIARY
INTELLIGENCE SUMMARY.
(Erase heading not required.)

Instructions regarding War Diaries and Intelligence Summaries are contained in F.S. Regs., Part II. and the Staff Manual respectively. Title pages will be prepared in manuscript.

Hour, Date, Place	Summary of Events and Information	Remarks and references to Appendices
21st August Roquetoire West	Still in same billet. 2 waggons out drawing straw in for French farmers. 1 cart for rations & green forage. V.O. inspected all the horse. & found them all in good condition. Any mule to be worked on Tuesday. Fine day.	
22 August Roquetoire West	Still in same billet. 1 cart for rations horse exercise from 9 a.m. till 10.30. a.m. a very fine day.	
23 August Roquetoire West	Still in same billet. Horses watered at 8. a.m. 1 officer went into Hazpier. 1 cart for rations. 1 waggon for French farmer. Duffy Officers Meeting.	
24th August Roquetoire West	Still in same billet. Horses watered at 8 a.m. 1 cart for rations. 1 waggon for wood for H.Q. Div. 1 waggon for French farmer. 1 for green forage weather fine. men rest in for ?	

Army Form C. 2118.

WAR DIARY
INTELLIGENCE SUMMARY.
(Erase heading not required.)

Instructions regarding War Diaries and Intelligence Summaries are contained in F. S. Regs., Part II. and the Staff Manual respectively. Title pages will be prepared in manuscript.

Hour, Date, Place	Summary of Events and Information	Remarks and references to Appendices
25th August Roquetoire West	Still in same billet. Horses went out to exercise at 8. a.m. 1 cart for ration 1 wagon for hay. went to Wardrecques for supplying of old hay which, weather very good.	
26th August Roquetoire West	Still in same billet. Horses went out to exercise at 8. a.m. 1 cart for ration & 1 for straw very hot day.	
27th August Roquetoire West	Still in same billet. Horses went out to exercise at 8. a.m. 1 wagon for ration. 1 for St Omer for trench guinea and 1 for wash for the R.Q.M.S.C. very hot day.	
28th August Roquetoire West	Still in same billet. Exercise horses at 8 a.m - 1 cart for ration. a very hot day. few drops of rain fell at 5 p.m. from a thunderstorm passing over some distance off.	

(73989) W4141—463. 400,000. 9/14. H.&J.Ltd. Forms/C. 2118/10.

Army Form C. 2118.

WAR DIARY
or
INTELLIGENCE SUMMARY.
(Erase heading not required.)

Instructions regarding War Diaries and Intelligence Summaries are contained in F.S. Regs., Part II. and the Staff Manual respectively. Title pages will be prepared in manuscript.

Hour, Date, Place	Summary of Events and Information	Remarks and references to Appendices
29th August. Roquetoire West.	Still in same billet. 1 cart for rations. Horses exercised at 9 a.m. - started to rain at 3 o'clock & kept it up till 10 o'clock. Driver returned from hospital	
30th August Roquetoire West	Still in same billet. 1 cart for rations. 1 wagon for green forage. Horses exercised at 9 a.m. Supply Officers meeting in the afternoon. V.O. Inspected horses. One with bad back doing very well. Weather fine but a little cold. O.C. C.A.S.C. inspected Route March of the B. Echelon of the 5th Brigade	
31st August. Roquetoire West.	Still in same billet. Horses exercised at 9 a.m. 1 cart for rations. 1 wagon for hay. Inspection at Wardrecques. Weather fine but cold.	

Confidential
War Diary
of 2nd Cavalry Divisional ASC.

From 1/9/15 to 30/9/15

Volume XIII.

Volume XII

Army Form C. 2118.

WAR DIARY
or
INTELLIGENCE SUMMARY.
(Erase heading not required.)

Instructions regarding War Diaries and Intelligence Summaries are contained in F.S. Regs., Part II. and the Staff Manual respectively. Title pages will be prepared in manuscript.

Hour, Date, Place	Summary of Events and Information	Remarks and references to Appendices
1st September 1915 Roquetoire West	Still in same billets. Horses went out Exercise at 8 a.m. 1 Cart for rations. Fine morning but rain in the afternoon. Fine evening.	
2nd September Roquetoire West	Still in same billets: 17 men & 2 officers left billets at 7.30 a.m. & proceeded to the 3rd Cav Brigade for the demonstration of musketry defence, every body there put on three schemes & went through a French field of fire, carried out very satisfactorily. arriving home at 11 a.m. started to rain at 1 p.m. & was showery the rest of the day.	
3rd September Roquetoire West	Still in same billets. rained hard all day. Men & horses moved smaller shelter for the night. field in a very bad state.	

Army Form C. 2118.

WAR DIARY
INTELLIGENCE SUMMARY.
(Erase heading not required.)

Instructions regarding War Diaries and Intelligence Summaries are contained in F. S. Regs., Part II. and the Staff Manual respectively. Title pages will be prepared in manuscript.

Hour, Date, Place	Summary of Events and Information	Remarks and references to Appendices
4th September. Roquetoire West.	Still in same billets. Horses went out to Exercise at 8 a.m. 1 cart for ration 1 wagon for green forage. Showery all day.	
5th September. Roquetoire West.	Still in same billets. Horses went out to Exercise at 8 a.m. 1 cart for ration. Fine day.	
6th September. Roquetoire West.	Still in same billets. Horses went out to Exercise at 8 a.m. 1 cart for ration, 1 wagon for green forage & 1 for manure. Batty officers meeting. Very fine day.	
7th September. Roquetoire West.	Still in same billets. Horses went out to Exercise at 8 a.m. 1 cart for ration, 1 for cinders, 1 for straw. Very fine day.	

(73989) W4141—463. 400,000. 9/14. H.&J.Ltd. Forms/C. 2118/10.

Army Form C. 2118

WAR DIARY
or
INTELLIGENCE SUMMARY

(Erase heading not required.)

Instructions regarding War Diaries and Intelligence Summaries are contained in F. S. Regs., Part II. and the Staff Manual respectively. Title Pages will be prepared in manuscript.

Place	Date	Hour	Summary of Events and Information	Remarks and references to Appendices
Roquetoire West	8th September		Still in same billets. Horses went out to exercise at 8 a.m. 1 cart for rations. 1 wagon for A.D.S.O. Very fine day.	
Roquetoire West	9th September		Still in same billets. Horses went out to exercise at 8 a.m. 1 cart for rations. 1 wagon for hay sweeping. Very fine day.	
Roquetoire West	10th September		Still in same billets. 1 wagon went out to exercise. 1 wagon brought back grain for sick farmer. 2 carts for green forage & straw. 1 for hay sweeping. O.C. went and inspected Route March of 15 Echelon of 7th Cav. Brigade. Very fine day.	
Roquetoire West	11th September		Still in same billets. Horses went out to exercise at 8 a.m. 1 cart for rations. Very fine day.	

WAR DIARY
INTELLIGENCE SUMMARY
(Erase heading not required.)

Army Form C. 2118

Instructions regarding War Diaries and Intelligence Summaries are contained in F. S. Regs., Part II. and the Staff Manual respectively. Title Pages will be prepared in manuscript.

Place	Date	Hour	Summary of Events and Information	Remarks and references to Appendices
Roquetoire West.	12th September.		Still in same billets. Horses went out to exercise at 8 a.m. Parade at 11 a.m. 1 cart for rations. Very fine day.	Church
Roquetoire West.	13th September.		Still in same billets. Horses went out to exercise at 8 a.m. 2 wagons out. 1 cart for rations. V.O. inspected Horses. 1 went into football with very bad luck with Duffy. Officers meeting. Very fine day.	
Roquetoire West.	14th September.		Still in same billets. Horses went out to exercise at 8 a.m. 1 wagon for stores. 1 cart for rations. Dull morning with a little rain. Fine afternoon.	
Roquetoire West.	15th September.		Still in same billets. 2 wagons for coal from Aire. 1 wagon to column for farrier. 1 cart for rations. Very fine day.	French newspaper

Army Form C. 2118

WAR DIARY
INTELLIGENCE SUMMARY

(Erase heading not required.)

Instructions regarding War Diaries and Intelligence Summaries are contained in F.S. Regs., Part II. and the Staff Manual respectively. Title Pages will be prepared in manuscript.

Place	Date	Hour	Summary of Events and Information	Remarks and references to Appendices
Roquetoire West.	16th September		Still in same billets. Horses went out to exercise at 8 a.m. 1 cart for rations. 1 wagon for hay sweepings. 2 Lt J.R. Jones & 2 Lt E.W. Hutchinson reported for duty & billeted today. Fine day.	
Roquetoire West.	17th September		Still in same billets. 2 wagons for hay sweeping. 1 wagon for Green forage & straw. Very fine day. 1 cart.	
Roquetoire West.	18th September		Still in same billets. Horses went out to exercise at 8 a.m. 1 cart for rations. 2 Lt E.W. Hutchinson left for the 8th Sqn Brigade to take over Transport Officers. Very fine day.	
Roquetoire West.	19th September		Still in same billets. Horses went out to exercise at 8 a.m. very fine day. Afternoon for rations. Church parade at 11 a.m.	

1875 Wt. W593/826 1,000,000 4/15 J.B.C. & A. A.D.S.S./Forms/C. 2118.

WAR DIARY

INTELLIGENCE SUMMARY

(Erase heading not required.)

Army Form C. 2118

Place	Date	Hour	Summary of Events and Information	Remarks and references to Appendices
Rognatier Wad.	20th September		Still in same billet. Horses went out to exercise at 9 a.m. I was sent for hay-carrying. I cant for rations received orders to be ready to move to-morrow at 1.30. every fine day.	
Quevatite	21st September		Moved to Quevatite. Leaving Oct. billet at 6 o'clock all settled in by 6 o'clock. O.C. address saw all B. Echelon of Div in a settled down everything day. 2nd Lt J.R. Jowett went to Abbeville to take over the Blanchet Horse Transport from B. nd Car. Div.	
Quevatite	22nd September		Still in same billets. O.C. went a visited B. Echelon horse went out exercise at 9 a.m. Very fine day.	
Quevatite	23 September		Still in same billets. Horses went out to exercise at 9 a.m. O.C. visited B. Echelon. Started to rain at 6.30 & continued all night.	

Army Form C. 2118

WAR DIARY
INTELLIGENCE SUMMARY
(Erase heading not required.)

Instructions regarding War Diaries and Intelligence Summaries are contained in F. S. Regs., Part II. and the Staff Manual respectively. Title Pages will be prepared in manuscript.

Place	Date	Hour	Summary of Events and Information	Remarks and references to Appendices
Quiedede	24th September		H.Q. A.S.C. moved into the Chateau at Roguetoire leaving old billet at 8 a.m. 12.6 reserved a 3 horses & motor cars went forward with the Division. O.C. A.S.C. went & saw B. Echlon move to new billets weather showery.	
Roguetoire	25 September		Still in same billets. Horses went out to exercise at 8 a.m. Capt. Murphy came over reported everything alright in supply column. O.C. went to B. Echlon. Issued most of the day	
Roguetoire	26th September		Still in same billets. Horses went out to exercise at 8 a.m. 3 horses & 2 men went down to the base. O.C. went to B. Echlon. Lt. Grenall arrived to take command of escorting force. Remount Company went out with O.C. to found Reliefs got billets at Ropetoire Same	
Roguetoire	27th September		Still in same billets. The Auxillery Pans transport arrived very early this morning arriving at billets about 10 o'clock today O.C. went to see the Adjutant of the Company weather showery.	

Army Form C. 2118

WAR DIARY
~~INTELLIGENCE SUMMARY~~

(Erase heading not required.)

Instructions regarding War Diaries and Intelligence Summaries are contained in F. S. Regs., Part II. and the Staff Manual respectively. Title Pages will be prepared in manuscript.

Place	Date	Hour	Summary of Events and Information	Remarks and references to Appendices
Roquetoire	28th September		Still in same billet. Nurses went out to auxerre at 8 a.m. 1 sect went to clive. O.C. went over & inspected "O" Eshelon every thing went the Ambulance horse transport were all prov at an new billets weather showery.	
Roquetoire	29th September		Still in same billet. O.C. went over to "O" Echelon & Ambulance Horse Transport every thing all correct issued lead all day	
Roquetoire	30th September		Still in same billet. O.C. went to "O" Echelon & Shrewsbury Horse transport; the later draws rations from same station to-day weather showery & very cold. nights	

Confidential

War Diary

of 2nd Cavalry Divisional H.S.C.

From 1/10/15 to 31/10/15

Volume XIV.

Confidential

Volume XIV

Army Form C. 2118

WAR DIARY
or
INTELLIGENCE SUMMARY

(Erase heading not required.)

Instructions regarding War Diaries and Intelligence
Summaries are contained in F. S. Regs., Part II.
and the Staff Manual respectively. Title Pages
will be prepared in manuscript.

Place	Date	Hour	Summary of Events and Information	Remarks and references to Appendices
Roquetoire	1st October 1915		Still in same billet. O.C. went over to "B" Echelon. Everything correct. Fine day. Cold nights.	
Roquetoire	2nd October		Still in same billet. O.C. went over to "B" Echelon. 3rd Brigade had route march. Fine day. Cold nights	
Roquetoire	3rd October		Still in same billet. O.C. went over to "B" Echelon. Everything correct. Fine day. Cold nights.	
Annezin	4th October		Still in same billet. O.C. went over to "B" Echelon. 3rd Brigade route march. Showery, cold nights.	
Roquetoire	5th October		Still in same billet. O.C. went over to "B" Echelon. 4th Brigade route march. Fine day. Cold nights. Visit inspected by Col. Daracko.	

Army Form C. 2118

WAR DIARY
or
INTELLIGENCE SUMMARY
(Erase heading not required.)

Instructions regarding War Diaries and Intelligence Summaries are contained in F. S. Regs., Part II. and the Staff Manual respectively. Title Pages will be prepared in manuscript.

Place	Date	Hour	Summary of Events and Information	Remarks and references to Appendices
Roquetoire	6th October		Still in same billet. 5th Brigade. "B" Echelon inspected by O.C. all this morning. weather fine. cold. nights.	
Roquetoire	7th October		Still in same billet. O.C. went to "B" Echelon. weather fine nights still cold.	
Roquetoire	8th October		Still in same billet. The whole of "B" Echelon were inspected by Brig. General Lyzart at 3.30 on the main road going from Wardrecques to Thérouanne. the head of column halted opposite a Reinforced garde of "Cadré d'Esquerres". The General was very satisfied with the turn out in general. dull cold day.	
Roquetoire	9th October		Still in same billet. O.C. went to "B" Echelon every thing correct at 7.30 p.m. orders came that the Brigade # surgeon of "B" Echelon to be at Clarety au: Bois 10. a.m. to morrow. weather fine but still cold.	

Army Form C. 2118

WAR DIARY or INTELLIGENCE SUMMARY

(Erase heading not required.)

Instructions regarding War Diaries and Intelligence Summaries are contained in F.S. Regs., Part II. and the Staff Manual respectively. Title Pages will be prepared in manuscript.

Place	Date	Hour	Summary of Events and Information	Remarks and references to Appendices
Roquetoire	10th October		Still in same billet. The 10th Batln wagons moved off this morning under Lt-Col Beath-Eliot. Head of Column at Renery 8.30. marched off at 8.45. Route taken farmery through Racki. on reaching the main road, came to Thérouanne turned to the right leaving the main road again & taking the road to the left & passing through Mentin. There Lieut Rault was sent at Marts for 10 minutes after he Rault was sent to the main road. Johntourame to Estree Blanche. we turned to our left having passed through Estree Blanche to Mells there were many halts indeed. & Rolls and Tabin bofs & after the village arriving at Auchy - au - Bois at 10.0.8. & the line stated was 14.0'clock. The transp went very swiftly at this last point. The Column ratio'd out & moved to their own billets. O.C. Co. S.C. returning back to old Bu.Hd.".	
Roquetoire	11th October		Still in same billets. The dismounted men of 1st & 2nd Cav Div went out to their respective units. L.D.O. Coms Comm. to bid goodbye to them men written from.	

Army Form C. 2118

WAR DIARY
or
INTELLIGENCE SUMMARY
(Erase heading not required.)

Instructions regarding War Diaries and Intelligence Summaries are contained in F.S. Regs., Part II. and the Staff Manual respectively. Title Pages will be prepared in manuscript.

Place	Date	Hour	Summary of Events and Information	Remarks and references to Appendices
ROQUETOIRE	12th October 1915.		Still in same billet. O.C. went down to "B" Echelon. everything correct- weather fine.	
ROQUETOIRE	13th October 1915.		Still in same billet. O.C. went down. to "B" Echelon. everything correct. Major Craig. S.S.O. came down about clash for 5th Batt. weather fine.	
ROQUETOIRE	14th October 1915		Still in same billet. O.C. went down to "B" Echelon. everything correct. Lt. Moore went to the Advance 3rd Batt. weather fine.	
ROQUETOIRE	15th October 1915.		Still in same billet. O.C. went down to "B" Echelon. everything correct. weather fine.	

1875 Wt. W593/826 1,000,000 4/15 J:B.C. & A. A.D.S.S./Forms/C. 2118.

Army Form C. 2118

WAR DIARY
or
INTELLIGENCE SUMMARY

(Erase heading not required.)

Place	Date	Hour	Summary of Events and Information	Remarks and references to Appendices
ROQUETOIRE	16th October		Still in same billet, got orders to move back to old billets to-morrow. Orders came at 10-30 p.m. Fine day.	
ROQUETOIRE	17th October		Moved back to our old billets as the Divisional Horse Transport had taken over old billets. Horses all under cover & men in empty barns. Left the Chateau at ROQUETOIRE at 9.0 o'clock, all settled in by 12.0 o'clock at 1'Eclus. The Cavalry about to move have to similar billets. Returned to "D" Echelon.	
ROQUETOIRE	18th October		Still in same billet. 3rd & 4th Bdes at "D" Echelon moved back to order. Orders came to move to-morrow. H.Q. A.S.C. H.Q. to AE MARTIN, Divisional Horse Transport to BOMY. DE LA VILLE 5" Bde "B" Echelon to & with Ammunition Horse Transport. Weather fine.	
ROQUETOIRE	19th October		Moved this morning leaving billets at 9 o'clock. The H.Q. wagons were to follow late the order of march H.Q. 4 A.S.C. H.Q. Divisional Horse Transport Cart. Route taken through CAUCHIE D'ECQUES leaving the village of CLARQUES on our left also THÉRDUANNE on reaching the THÉROUANNE, HERBELLE road turned sharp right arriving at your road cross off to the left then turn to first turning to the left	

Army Form C. 2118

WAR DIARY
or
INTELLIGENCE SUMMARY

(Erase heading not required.)

Instructions regarding War Diaries and Intelligence Summaries are contained in F. S. Regs., Part II. and the Staff Manual respectively. Title Pages will be prepared in manuscript.

Place	Date	Hour	Summary of Events and Information	Remarks and references to Appendices
ROQUETOIRE	19th October		Left, following the road till we came onto the main road - ST OMER, FAUQUEMBERGUES where we turned sharp left again passing through AVROULT arriving at BOUT DE LA VILLE at 1-15pm the new billet of the Bdre. HQ Conv, after entering the village of FAUQUEMBERGUES taking the road to the right & arriving at the new billet of HQ A.S.C. at 1-45 at ST MARTIN D'HARDINGHEM. The HQ Div Amn. proceeded to HQ THIEMBRONNE O.C. A.S.C. returned to his billet after seeing everybody in their new billets. Weather fine & roads in very good order.	
ST MARTIN D'HARDINGHEM	20th October		Billets very hard to find for men & horses. Received the messages & horses from HQ. O.C. went to see Col. Chanes the commanding there transport & he sent to Brigadier Capt Greenall came over to get orders. Weather fine & cold.	
ST MATIN D'HARDINGHEM	21st October		Still in same billets the blankets wagons of the 8th Brigade were handed over to the Transport Officer of the Brigade this morning. 1 Ambulance from the Army Reserve supplied us on way to base. 10 G S wagons from the Army HT Conv. Sent to WARDRECQUES for coal returned at 6.0 pm. Weather fine. a little shower in the evening	

WAR DIARY
of
INTELLIGENCE SUMMARY

(Erase heading not required.)

Army Form C. 2118

Instructions regarding War Diaries and Intelligence Summaries are contained in F. S. Regs., Part II. and the Staff Manual respectively. Title Pages will be prepared in manuscript.

Place	Date	Hour	Summary of Events and Information	Remarks and references to Appendices
	22nd October		Still in same billet got four more horses meander cover got shelter for the men	
ST. MATIN D'HARDINGHEM			O.C. & S.O. went to Supply Column - weather fine	
	23rd October		Still in same billet all horses under cover O.C. went to see A.A. & Q.M.G. in the morning weather fine	
ST. MATIN D'HARDINGHEM				
	24th October		Still in same billet started to rain very cold - O.C. went to see A.A. & Q.M.G.	
ST. MATIN D'HARDINGHEM				
	25th October		Still in same billet rained most of the day. O.C. went to see A.A. & Q.M.G.	
ST. MATIN D'HARDINGHEM				
	26th October		Still in same billet. O.C. & D.S.O. went out to 5th Bde. Hors of tis	
ST. MATIN D'HARDINGHEM			started to rain late in the afternoon.	
	27th October		Still in same billet OC went to see A.A. & Q.M.G. rained all day - another transport	
ST. MATIN D'HARDINGHEM			went into AIRE for chipord.	

Army Form C. 2118

WAR DIARY
or
INTELLIGENCE SUMMARY

(Erase heading not required.)

Instructions regarding War Diaries and Intelligence Summaries are contained in F.S. Regs., Part II. and the Staff Manual respectively. Title Pages will be prepared in manuscript.

Place	Date	Hour	Summary of Events and Information	Remarks and references to Appendices
ST. MARTIN, D'HARDINGHEM	28th October		Still in same billet. O.C. went to see C.R.E. & Q.M.O. rained hard all day. both cars from H.Q. A.S.C. in workshops.	
ST. MARTIN, D'HARDINGHEM	29th October		Still in same billet. O.C. & A.O. went to see A.A & Q.M.G. fined day. but cold.	
ST. MARTIN, D'HARDINGHEM	30th October		Still in same billet. O.C. & A.O. went to see C.R.E. & Q.M.G. fine day. still cold.	
ST. MARTIN D'HARDINGHEM	31st October		Still in same billet. O.C. went to see C.R.E. & Q.M.G. rained most of the day. digging party from the Brigade left to dig for the trenches	

Confidential
War Diary
of 2nd Cavalry Divisional ASC
From 1/11/15 to 30/11/15

Volume XV

Volume XV

Army Form C. 2118

WAR DIARY
or
INTELLIGENCE SUMMARY

(Erase heading not required.)

Instructions regarding War Diaries and Intelligence Summaries are contained in F. S. Regs., Part II. and the Staff Manual respectively. Title Pages will be prepared in manuscript.

Place	Date	Hour	Summary of Events and Information	Remarks and references to Appendices
	1st November 1915			
ST MARTIN D'HARDINGHEM			Still in same billet. O.C. stayed up to see CSos, QM & reveal Pash all day.	
ST MARTIN D'HARDINGHEM	2nd November		Still in same billet. O.C. went up to see CSos, & QM & reveal Pash all day.	
ST MARTIN D'HARDINGHEM	3rd November		Still in same billet. O.C. went to see CSos, QM.C. S.S.O. had a smash up with his car - another car came into him for the extra body, damage rained hard all day.	
ST MARTIN D'HARDINGHEM	4th November		Still in same billet. O.C. went to see 19.W. & QM.C. started to cover gravel for the Château & H.Q. 19.S.C. weather very cold but fine to-day. O.C. proceeded on leave. Major Ores g acting in his stead.	
ST MARTIN D'HARDINGHEM	5th November		Still in same billet. Last order that none of the personnel in billets were to join the R.E. weather fine in the morning rained a little in the afternoon.	

Army Form C. 2118

WAR DIARY
or
INTELLIGENCE SUMMARY

(Erase heading not required.)

Instructions regarding War Diaries and Intelligence Summaries are contained in F.S. Regs., Part II. and the Staff Manual respectively. Title Pages will be prepared in manuscript.

Place	Date	Hour	Summary of Events and Information	Remarks and references to Appendices
	6 November		Still in same billet. OC Chance called this afternoon to see about hay. 9 more G.S. wagons Whaley out. returned to Etaps. Love turn now but cold	
ST.MARTIN.D.HARDINGHEM	7 November		Still in same billet. 1 wagon for stones. One for rations. weather fine & cold	
ST.MARTIN.D.HARDINGHEM	8 November		Still in same billet. 1 wagon for gravel. One for hay. & one for rations. weather fine & cold	
ST.MARTIN.D.HARDINGHEM	9 November		Still in same billet. 3 wagons out for gravel. 1 cart for rations. weather rained nearly all day	
ST.MARTIN.D.HARDINGHEM	10 November		Still in same billet. 3 wagons out for gravel. 1 wagon for rations. weather fine	
ST.MARTIN.D.HARDINGHEM				

WAR DIARY or INTELLIGENCE SUMMARY

Army Form C. 2118

(Erase heading not required.)

Place	Date	Hour	Summary of Events and Information	Remarks and references to Appendices
ST.MARTIN.D.HARDINGHEM.	11th November.		Still in same billet. 3 wagons for grand. 1 wagon for rations weather fine in the morning rained hard of the day.	
ST.MARTIN.D.HARDINGHEM.	12th November.		Still in same billet. rained hard all day. 1 wagon for rations O.C. A.S.C. returned last night from leave.	
ST.MARTIN.D.HARDINGHEM.	13th November.		Still in same billet. wagon turned out to draw gravel, unable to work at gravel pit. very strong wind blowing rained in the morning fine afternoon.	
ST.MARTIN.D.HARDINGHEM.	14th November.		Still in same billet. one wagon for ration. O.C. & S.S.O. went to MIELLES-LEZ-BLEQUIN. to see about a piquet for a coal dump. found 1 B.L. & S. Bolls 1 B.L. & S. Bolls. weather fine & cold.	
ST.MARTIN.D.HARDINGHEM.	15th November.		Still in same billet. 3 wagons out. two to forage. one for ration. O.C. & A.S.O. went to see A.D.S.T. weather fine & cold.	

Army Form C. 2118

WAR DIARY
or
INTELLIGENCE SUMMARY
(Erase heading not required.)

Instructions regarding War Diaries and Intelligence Summaries are contained in F. S. Regs., Part II. and the Staff Manual respectively. Title Pages will be prepared in manuscript.

Place	Date	Hour	Summary of Events and Information	Remarks and references to Appendices
	16th November		Still in same billet. Horses sent out to exercise 1 cart for rations	
ST MARTIN. O HARDINGHEM			In afternoon O.C. went to see C.A. & A.D. of D.A.D. - arrived hard frost night & roads worn in a very bad state. the following morning, & they froze & cold	
	17th November		Still in same billet. 2 wagons & 1 cart for gravel. roads in bad state snow	
ST MARTIN. O HARDINGHEM			roads, all gone by evening O.C. went to see D.A.D. & D.A.D. fine and cold.	
	18th November		Still in same billet. 1 car from H.Q. 2 Can. Div transferred to G.H.Q. Reserve Supply Column.	
ST MARTIN. O HARDINGHEM			Weather fine & cold.	
	19th November		Still in same billet. 2 wagons for gravel, 1 for rations & two cars arrived 1 for P.S. the other for Field Cashier & Paymaster.	
ST MARTIN. O HARDINGHEM			Weather fine & hard frost.	
	20th November		Still in same billet. 2 wagons went to Lumbres for coal. 2 cart to AVROULT	
ST MARTIN. O HARDINGHEM			The old car of Field Cashier returned to Supply Column. Weather fair still cold.	

Army Form C. 2118

WAR DIARY
or
INTELLIGENCE SUMMARY

(Erase heading not required.)

Place	Date	Hour	Summary of Events and Information	Remarks and references to Appendices
ST MARTIN, D HARDINGHEM	21st November		Still on same billet. 1 wagon for rations. Stormy weather superior. Fine. Still road about	
ST MARTIN D HARDINGHEM	22nd November		Still on same billet. 2 wagons to AVROULT, 1 for rations & 1 wagon to OUVE WIRQUIN for wood for wheeler. Weather fine	
ST MARTIN, D HARDINGHEM	23rd November		Still in same billet. 2 wagons to AVROULT for rations & 1 for wood. 2 motor Bicycles surplus from H & S signal Coys returned to Supply Column & Cavalry Division. Weather fine all day. Rain in the evening	
ST MARTIN, D HARDINGHEM	24th November		Still in same billet. 2 wagons to AVROULT, 1 for rations & 1 for straw. Hay. 3 mule wagons from 3 & 5 returned to their own H.Q. weather rain all day	
ST MARTIN, D HARDINGHEM	25th November		Still in same billet. 2 wagons to AVROULT, 1 for rations. 15 mule wagons left their billets & reported to local detachment at ETTLINGHEM for work with digging parties. 3 of those returned. Ic. 8 & 5 wagons of the 4th Bde. weather	

Army Form C. 2118

WAR DIARY
or
INTELLIGENCE SUMMARY
(Erase heading not required.)

Instructions regarding War Diaries and Intelligence Summaries are contained in F. S. Regs., Part II. and the Staff Manual respectively. Title Pages will be prepared in manuscript.

Place	Date	Hour	Summary of Events and Information	Remarks and references to Appendices
ST MARTIN D. HARDINGHEM	26th November		Still in same billet 1 wagon and 1 cart went to Elnes for rations & wagon for rations weather fine & hard frost.	
ST MARTIN D. HARDINGHEM	27th November		Still in same billet 2 wagons for rations, 1 wagon for rations weather fine & hard frost.	
ST MARTIN D. HARDINGHEM	28th November		Still in same billet 1 wagon for rations weather fine very cold.	
ST MARTIN D. HARDINGHEM	29th November		Still in same billet 2 wagons went to ESTREE BLANCHE for coal 1 wagon & cart to Lloyd D'Haut. O.C. & C. Infantil and Cavalry fell Ambulance report everything in very good order. Stables harness & horses weather round all along.	
ST MARTIN D. HARDINGHEM	30th November		Still in same billet 2 wagons for rations drawn from NIELLES-LEZ-BLEQUIN 1 wagon for rations weather fine showing to wards evening. A. & a.a. Clementharter at 1 & 5th Brigade for Divisional troops & 5th Brigade.	

1875 Wt. W593/826 1,000,000 4/15 J.B.C. & A. A.D.S.S./Forms/C.2'18.

Confidential

War Diary

of 2nd Cavalry Divisional A.S.C.

From 1/10/15 to 31/10/15

Volume XVI

Volume XVI • December

Army Form C. 2118

WAR DIARY
or
INTELLIGENCE SUMMARY
(Erase heading not required.)

Instructions regarding War Diaries and Intelligence Summaries are contained in F. S. Regs., Part II. and the Staff Manual respectively. Title Pages will be prepared in manuscript.

Place	Date	Hour	Summary of Events and Information	Remarks and references to Appendices
ST MARTIN, D, HARDINGHEM	1st December	1915	Still in same billet. 3 wagons for Canteen at Elnes. 1 wagon for rations. Weather fine, much milder.	
ST MARTIN, D, HARDINGHEM	2nd December		Still in same billet. 4 wagons for escort at NIELLES-LEZ-BLEQUIN from the Ame M.T. Coy. O.C. of S.C. went to see commandant Park. Weather fine. Recruit in the evening.	
ST MARTIN, D, HARDINGHEM	3rd December		Still in same billet. 3 wagons east for wood at NIELLES-LEZ-BLEQUIN. 1 cart for rations. O.C. of S.C. went + inspected Shoek H.T. Coy. this afternoon. Weather poured all day. Duty Officers meeting at H.Q. of S.C. his afternoon.	
ST MARTIN, D, HARDINGHEM	4th December		Still in same billet. 1 cart for rations. 2 TSA. Cox reported for duty as A.O. Sir dorto O.C. ASC. went down to Lumbres Owen. to see the Inspection by the A.D.S.T. man all day. a strong cross wind.	

1875 Wt. W593/826 1,000,000 4/15 J.B.C. & A. A.D.S.S./Forms/C. 2118.

Army Form C. 2118

WAR DIARY
or
INTELLIGENCE SUMMARY
(Erase heading not required.)

Instructions regarding War Diaries and Intelligence Summaries are contained in F. S. Regs., Part II. and the Staff Manual respectively. Title Pages will be prepared in manuscript.

Place	Date	Hour	Summary of Events and Information	Remarks and references to Appendices
ST MARTIN, D. HARDINGHEM	5th November		Still in same billet. O.C. & 2 O.C. went to Hes-W.M.V.T. & sent for rations. weather showery. 2nd Lt. Gray left for Abbeville for duty.	
ST MARTIN D. HARDINGHEM	6 November		Still in same billet. 2 wagons for cinders at ELNES car. 68 to be down one of the front wheels. Came off. saved Bert all day.	
ST MARTIN, D. HARDINGHEM	7th November		Still in same billet. Hoar. horse. went to 8 "Hotel Wilhelmen" car. 68 went into workshop returned in the evening. 2 wagons for Hay & rations saved the rest of the day. Can't for rations good morning.	
ST MARTIN, D. HARDINGHEM	8th November		Still in same billet. 2 wagons for cinders from ELNES. coal arrived. weather fine.	
ST MARTIN D. HARDINGHEM	9 November		Still in same billet. horses went out to exercise 1 wagon for rations. O.C. & S.S.M. Inspected No. 2 Sec. Field cart horses good condition absence and to last. Saddles and every except Harness in good condition	

Army Form C. 2118

WAR DIARY
or
INTELLIGENCE SUMMARY
(Erase heading not required.)

Instructions regarding War Diaries and Intelligence Summaries are contained in F.S. Regs., Part II. and the Staff Manual respectively. Title Pages will be prepared in manuscript.

Place	Date	Hour	Summary of Events and Information	Remarks and references to Appendices
ST.MARTIN.D.HARDINGHEM.	10th December 1915		Still in same billet. Horse went out to exercise. Sent a confidential to Lieut. H.T. Coop. at OUDRY Farm at RENESCURE giving instr. as to his sub. condition stables needing a little repair. Most progs to them. Harness in good condition except Saddles not in a little more cleaning weather wet morning fine afternoon strong wind	
ST.MARTIN.D.HARDINGHEM.	11th December		Still in same billet. One wing on to LUMBRES from and 4 section. O.C. and 2C. inspected the F.A.W.U. & Cor. his not very satisfactory weather rained hard all day 4 sect.	
ST.MARTIN.D.HARDINGHEM.	12th December		Still in same billet. One cart for salvage at tephra time & Harness inspected today. found in very good order. weather very dull dry a little snow turned much colder.	
ST.MARTIN.N.HARDINGHEM.	13th December		Still in same billet. Started to cart manure from stables & wagon to CAMPAGNE. with straw & veg. weather fine much colder.	

Army Form C. 2118

WAR DIARY
or
INTELLIGENCE SUMMARY
(Erase heading not required.)

Instructions regarding War Diaries and Intelligence Summaries are contained in F. S. Regs., Part II. and the Staff Manual respectively. Title Pages will be prepared in manuscript.

Place	Date	Hour	Summary of Events and Information	Remarks and references to Appendices
ST.MARTIN, D.HARDINGHEM.	14th December		Still in same billet. 1 wagon to ESTRÉE BLANCHE for coal. 1 wagon for Hay & 1 cart for rations & stores also drew out Monane weather fine but quite cold.	
ST.MARTIN, D.HARDINGHEM.	15th December		Still in same billet. 1 wagon for coal. 1 cart for rations. Men went & had a bath at MERCK. O.C. & 2 i/c went to see CARPENTT. Weather showery & very cold.	
ST.MARTIN, D.HARDINGHEM.	16th December		Still in same billet. Horses went out to exercise 1 man on pass to Calais. O.C. & 2 i/c went to visit A.D.V.S. & T all base machine this afternoon. Drafields went into hospital weather fine but cold.	
ST.MARTIN, D.HARDINGHEM.	17th December		Still in same billet. Horse went out to exercise 1 wagon for rations. Men inspected by the A.D.V.S. everything a/ up. O.C. attended a meeting at the G.O.C. Chateau. Deputy officers meeting held at H.Q. of L.o.C. Weather fine morning snow in the afternoon.	

1875 Wt. W593/826 1,000,000 4/15 J.B.C. & A. A.D.S.S./Forms/C. 2118.

Army Form C. 2118

WAR DIARY
or
INTELLIGENCE SUMMARY
(Erase heading not required.)

Instructions regarding War Diaries and Intelligence Summaries are contained in F. S. Regs., Part II. and the Staff Manual respectively. Title Pages will be prepared in manuscript.

Place	Date	Hour	Summary of Events and Information	Remarks and references to Appendices
ST MARTIN, Q HARDINGHEM	18th December		Still in same billet. 1 wagon out for wood & rations & coal. I horse arrived from 8th Mobile V.S. All horses evacuated are gone today. Every one always weather F & S in the morning	
ST MARTIN, Q HARDINGHEM	19th December		Still in same billet. 2 wagons for rations. O.C. & A.D.S. attended meeting at A.D. of S & T at 12.15 also attended another meeting at 3 P.M. G.O.C. Chatieu HERVARRE. weather fine still cold.	
ST MARTIN, Q HARDINGHEM	20th December		Still in same billet. 2 wagons for rations 1 wagon out to COMPAGNE with coal for heat station. weather fine	
ST MARTIN, Q HARDINGHEM	21st December		Still in same billet 2 wagons for rations 1 wagon for hay & straw weather remained fine all day	
ST MARTIN, Q HARDINGHEM	22nd December		Still in same billet 2 wagons for rations 1 wagon for wood at OUVE WIRQUIN O.C. went to meeting at A.D. of T. also went to supply Column in afternoon. weather misty & rain	

1875 Wt. W593/826 1,000,000 4/15 J.B.C. & A. A.D.S.S./Forms/C. 2118.

Army Form C. 2118

WAR DIARY
or
INTELLIGENCE SUMMARY

(Erase heading not required.)

Instructions regarding War Diaries and Intelligence Summaries are contained in F. S. Regs., Part II. and the Staff Manual respectively. Title Pages will be prepared in manuscript.

Place	Date	Hour	Summary of Events and Information	Remarks and references to Appendices
ST MARTIN, O. HARDINGHEM.	23rd December		Still in same billet. 2 wagons for rations. Weather rained all day.	
ST MARTIN, O. HARDINGHEM.	24th December		Still in same billet. 3 wagons for rations. death serene to-day. O.C. went to Mielles-lez-Bleguin. Duffy Officers meeting. O.C. A.M.S.C. urgent call to see 5 O.C. 2nd Car. Rio weather showery	
ST MARTIN, O. HARDINGHEM.	25th December		Still in same billet. weather showery.	
ST MARTIN, O. HARDINGHEM.	26th December		Still in same billet. 2 wagons for rations. O.C. went to Ammunition Park. weather showery.	
ST MARTIN, O. HARDINGHEM.	27th December		Still in same billet. 2 wagons for rations. O.C. went to BOULOGNE to 4 Oct C.O. & Duffy Column weather fine.	

WAR DIARY or INTELLIGENCE SUMMARY

Army Form C. 2118

(Erase heading not required.)

Instructions regarding War Diaries and Intelligence Summaries are contained in F. S. Regs., Part II. and the Staff Manual respectively. Title Pages will be prepared in manuscript.

Place	Date	Hour	Summary of Events and Information	Remarks and references to Appendices
	28th December		Still in same billet. 6 carts drew rations. O.C. went to A.A. & Q.S. & Supply column	
ST MARTIN D'HARDINGHEM			Weather fine. Comdt. H.T. Coy moved from REMESCURE to ESQUERDES. All dispy parties moved into billets.	
	29th December		Still in same billet. 1 wagon drew rations. O.C. went OSC meeting at A.D.S.T. (O&M) H.T. Comt all located with details for horses for humans & ydrs. Reports & head of one of Div Weather fine	
ST MARTIN D'HARDINGHEM				
	30th December		Still in same billet. 1 wagon to rations. H.Q. details left today for CHOCQUES. O.C. & 13 O.C. went to 6 other Major Duffy came AD Staff in the morning. Div trpt. went down to BESVRES to see all return but no travis weather fine	
ST MARTIN D'HARDINGHEM				
	31st December		Still in same billet. 1 wagon for rations. O.C. went to NEILLES LES BLEQUIN in morning. Dv trpts went to WISSERN to see R.E. & Composite Field Amb. off weather fine	
ST MARTIN D'HARDINGHEM				

Confidential

War Diary

of 2nd Cavalry Division A.I.C.

From 1/1/16 to 31/1/16.

Volume XVII

Volume XVII

WAR DIARY
or
INTELLIGENCE SUMMARY

Army Form C. 2118

January.

Place	Date	Hour	Summary of Events and Information	Remarks and references to Appendices
ST.MARTIN.D.HARDING-HEM.	1st January	AM	Still in same billet. 1 wagon for rations. O.C went out.	
			To MIELLES-LEZ-BLEQUIN also. O.A.D.H. & H.T.Y. Supply. Stores. Weather fine.	
ST.MARTIN.D.HARDING-HEM.	2nd January		Still in same billet. 1 wagon for rations. Weather turned hard all day.	
ST.MARTIN.D.HARDING-HEM.	3 January		Still in same billet. 1 wagon for rations. O.C. went yesterday. Field Cash & Workshop Unit. Weather fine.	
ST MARTIN D HARDING HEM	4th January		Still in same billet. 1 wagon for coal at MIELLES-LEZ-BLEQUIN. Can't for ration. Weather turned misty all day.	
ST MARTIN D HARDING HEM	5th January		Still in same billet. 1 cart for ration + one for hay + straw. O.C. A.S.C. attended meeting at A.D of L.S.T. Weather fine.	

Volume XVII

Army Form C. 2118

WAR DIARY
or
INTELLIGENCE SUMMARY

(Erase heading not required.)

Instructions regarding War Diaries and Intelligence Summaries are contained in F.S. Regs., Part II. and the Staff Manual respectively. Title Pages will be prepared in manuscript.

Place	Date	Hour	Summary of Events and Information	Remarks and references to Appendices
ST MARTIN D. HARDINGHEM	6th January 1916		Still in same billet 2 wagons returned from 3rd Reserve Pk for carg? to return tomorrow for remainder of unit	
ST MARTIN D. HARDINGHEM	7th January		Still in same billet 2 wagons returned from 3rd Reserve Park all correct. Weather fine	
			1 cart for rations. O in C.Offrs meeting	
ST MARTIN D. HARDINGHEM	8th January		Still in same billet 1 wagon to MELLES-LEZ-BLEQUIN for coal. 1 for rations. Weather fine	
ST MARTIN D. HARDINGHEM	9th January		Still in same billet 1 wagon for rations. O.C. cart went to meeting at A.O.d.S+T. Weather fine	
ST MARTIN D. HARDINGHEM	10th January		Still in same billet 1 wagon for rations. Duty offrs meeting this afternoon. Weather fine	

Army Form C. 2118

WAR DIARY
or
INTELLIGENCE SUMMARY

(Erase heading not required.)

Instructions regarding War Diaries and Intelligence Summaries are contained in F. S. Regs., Part II. and the Staff Manual respectively. Title Pages will be prepared in manuscript.

Place	Date	Hour	Summary of Events and Information	Remarks and references to Appendices
ST MARTIN, D. HARDINGHEM	11 January		Still in same billet. 2 wagons for hay & straw & 1 for rations & 1 cart to CAMPAGNE to return with hay. Weather fine.	
ST MARTIN, D. HARDINGHEM	12 January		Still in same billet. 2 wagons for rations 1 cart for rations & C still owing to today cancelled. Weather fine.	
ST MARTIN, D. HARDINGHEM	13 January		Still in same billet 1 wagon to ESTREE BLANCHE for coal. One cart for rations. Weather fine.	
ST MARTIN, D. HARDINGHEM	14 January		Still in same billet. 1 wagon for coal from FAUQUEMBERGUES 2 wagons for road from Surrounded Rd. A.D.M.S. officers meeting. Weather fine. Gen Peterson & Staff returned to day.	
ST MARTIN, D. HARDINGHEM	15 January		Still in same billet 2 wagons & 1 cart of Div. H.Q. returned to day from Command Div 2 wagons & 1 cart for rations. Two detachments 2 N.C.O. & 2 C each of the Cyclist section again weather fine R.C. R.C. evening. Capt Colman in the of town.	

Army Form C. 2118

WAR DIARY
or
INTELLIGENCE SUMMARY
(Erase heading not required.)

Instructions regarding War Diaries and Intelligence Summaries are contained in F. S. Regs., Part II. and the Staff Manual respectively. Title Pages will be prepared in manuscript.

Place	Date	Hour	Summary of Events and Information	Remarks and references to Appendices
ST MARTIN,D.HARDINGHEM	16th January		Still in same billet. 2 wagons 1 cart for rations. 1st 2/10/47 single section again in wagon line	
ST MARTIN,D.HARDINGHEM	17th January		Still in same billet. 1 wagon for rations rest of horses exercised in the morning heavy rain hearing day	
ST MARTIN,D.HARDINGHEM	18th January		Still in same billet. 1 wagon to NIELLES-LEZ-BLEQUIN for coal 2 wagons to AVROULT for carrots. O.C. cdxx went to CATS q ms. weather served all day	
ST MARTIN,D.HARDINGHEM	19th January		Still in same billet. O.C. A.D.S.C. & S.S.O went to APO 64T 2 wagons for rations 2 Out with carts. weather fine	
ST MARTIN,D.HARDINGHEM	20th January		Still in same billet. 3 wagons for coal at NIELLES-LEZ-BLEQUIN 2 carts for rations O.C. ADS went off to office. weather fine	
ST MARTIN,D.HARDINGHEM	21st January		Still in same billet. 1 wagon for wood. 1 for rations O.C. went to see A.s. G.O.S. Duffy. Officers meeting. weather fine morning afternoon misty rain	

1875 Wt. W593/826 1,000,000 4/15 J.B.C. & A. A.D.S.S./Forms/C. 2118.

WAR DIARY or INTELLIGENCE SUMMARY

Army Form C. 2118

(Erase heading not required.)

Instructions regarding War Diaries and Intelligence Summaries are contained in F.S. Regs., Part II. and the Staff Manual respectively. Title Pages will be prepared in manuscript.

Place	Date	Hour	Summary of Events and Information	Remarks and references to Appendices
ST.MARTIN,D'HARDINGHEM	22nd January		Still in same billet. 2 wagons to MUELLES-LEZ-BLEQUIN for coal. 1 wagon for rations. O.C. W.S.C. went to Q. Office. weather fine.	
ST.MARTIN,D'HARDINGHEM	23rd January		Still in same billet. 1 wagon for rations. 1 wagon & cart for drawing rations. weather fine.	
ST.MARTIN,D'HARDINGHEM	24th January		Still in same billet. 1 wagon for rations. 1 wagon & cart for drawing fire. O.C. W.S.C. went to visit Q. Office & H.Q. last week fine.	
ST.MARTIN,D'HARDINGHEM	25th January		Still in same billet. 2 wagons for stores at AVROULT. 1 wagon for rations. O.C. W.S.C. went to Q. Office. Weather fine.	
ST.MARTIN,D'HARDINGHEM	26th January		Still in same billet. 1 wagon for cinders at ELNES. 2 carts for manure. Receipt of Lt. Nghans, who's input account was found short of 29/1/1/1/5. + 80 cartridges. Inquiry held today at H.Q. W.S.C. on handing over when Lt. is going to the Infantry.	
ST.MARTIN,D'HARDINGHEM	27th January		Still in same billet. 1 wagon + contribution to form the dump being moved to Q. Office. weather fine. 1 man C. H. Roy. Court. 8 O.R.s for hospital in return to T. D.	
			BOOT-DE-LA-VILLE B.Q. cart went to H.Q. for W. Q. mess 3 Co. left as T.D.	
			R.A.e	

Army Form C. 2118

WAR DIARY
or
INTELLIGENCE SUMMARY
(Erase heading not required.)

Instructions regarding War Diaries and Intelligence Summaries are contained in F. S. Regs., Part II. and the Staff Manual respectively. Title Pages will be prepared in manuscript.

Place	Date	Hour	Summary of Events and Information	Remarks and references to Appendices
ST. MARTIN D. HARDINGHEM	28th January		Still in same billet. 1 wagon & cart for rations. Two carts drawing manure. Duffy, Officer's mess tins. O.C. will went to G. Officers meeting fine.	
ST. MARTIN D. HARDINGHEM	29th January		Still in same billet. 1 wagon & cart for rations. 1 man to hospital cast rem our rein. & cart for manure. weather fine	
ST. MARTIN D. HARDINGHEM	30th January		Still in same billet. 1 wagon & cart for rations. A & G mgs. called at H.Q. with officer weather fine. Lt. J. Davy joined unit today as R.O. arrived from Y. Base Res. 3rd Cav. Res. was is been using the Pub N.T.O.	
ST. MARTIN D. HARDINGHEM	31st January		Still in same billet. 1 wagon & cart for rations. 1 wagon & cart for wood & water. O.C. & S.B. officer here morning. weather fine.	

Confidential
War Diary
of 2nd Cavalry Divisional A.S.C.
From 1/2/16 to 29/2/16

Volume XVIII

Army Form C. 2118

Volume XVIII

WAR DIARY
or
INTELLIGENCE SUMMARY

(Erase heading not required.)

Instructions regarding War Diaries and Intelligence Summaries are contained in F. S. Regs., Part II. and the Staff Manual respectively. Title Pages will be prepared in manuscript.

Place	Date	Hour	Summary of Events and Information	Remarks and references to Appendices
ST MARTIN D.HARDINGHEM	1st February 1916		Still in same billet. 1 wagon & cart for rations, 1 wagon & cart for holding 1 wagon & cart for rations & coal. O.C. & A.C.O. went to A.D. office about leave.	
ST MARTIN D.HARDINGHEM	2nd February		Still in same billet. 1 wagon & cart for rations. O.C. A.C.O. & S.O. went to office. Left for the D.C.S. meeting at A.D.V.S. office. Weather fine but cold.	
ST MARTIN D.HARDINGHEM	3rd February		Still in same billet. 1 wagon & cart for rations. O.C. were out A.D.S. & office.	
ST MARTIN D. HARDINGHEM	4th February		Still in same billet. 1 wagon & cart for rations on ex. horse of Merck one to Harault. 1 wagon L.O.C. clerk & S.O. went to railhead & D. office. Supply appearing weather showery.	
ST MARTIN D. HARDINGHEM	5th February		Still in same billet. 1 wagon & cart for rations & wagon for coal at Merckeghem-Blarum. O.C. went to A.D office weather fine.	
ST MARTIN D.HARDINGHEM	6th February		Still in same billet. 1 wagon & cart for rations, also one wagon & cart for coal. Rain in the afternoon	

Army Form C. 2118

WAR DIARY
or
INTELLIGENCE SUMMARY

(Erase heading not required.)

Instructions regarding War Diaries and Intelligence Summaries are contained in F. S. Regs., Part II. and the Staff Manual respectively. Title Pages will be prepared in manuscript.

Place	Date	Hour	Summary of Events and Information	Remarks and references to Appendices
ST MARTIN D. HARDINGHEM	7th February		Still in same billet. 1 wagon & cart for rations. 1 wagon to ETAPLES. 3 arch for sand batteries at Quesqueen returned to Etaples. O.C. ACC went up to Offrey new station seen in the morning full of snow.	
ST MARTIN D. HARDINGHEM	8th February		Still in same billet. 1 wagon & cart for rations. Supply officers return called on. Bapis went buying hay. Straw potatoes all to be bought. Outright. Weather fine cold.	
ST MARTIN D. HARDINGHEM	9th February		Still in same billet. 2 wagon & 2 cart for hay. 1 wagon & cart for rations. O.C. ACC A.D.S.D. went to meeting at A.D.S.S.T. weather fine.	
ST MARTIN D. HARDINGHEM	10th February		Still in same billet. 1 wagon & cart for rations. 2 wagon & cart for hay & straw O.C. ACC went to 9 offices & then on 2 lorries of A divisions colliery in trace. weather fine.	
ST MARTIN D. HARDINGHEM	11th February		Still in same billet. 1 wagon & cart for rations. 2 wagon to NIELLES LEZ BLEQUIN to coal. 2 carts for straw & roots. Court of inquiry held at the Supply Column 2nd Cav. Div. on Pte Warmington for damaging his car. weather rained all day.	
ST MARTIN D. HARDINGHEM	12th February		Still in same billet. 1 wagon & cart for rations court of inquiry held at H.Q. A.S.C. Cav. Div. to inquiry into the cause of a mule grazing loose & knocking an old French woman down. O.C. ASC went to G. office in the afternoon interviewed Major Murphy & Capt Hawkey. weather wet & snowing this afternoon.	

1875 Wt. W 593/826 1,000,000 4/15 J.B.C. & A. A.D.S.S./Forms/C. 2118.

Army Form C. 2118

WAR DIARY
or
INTELLIGENCE SUMMARY

(Erase heading not required.)

Instructions regarding War Diaries and Intelligence Summaries are contained in F.S. Regs., Part II. and the Staff Manual respectively. Title Pages will be prepared in manuscript.

Place	Date	Hour	Summary of Events and Information	Remarks and references to Appendices
	13th February		Still in same billet. 1 wagon & cart for rations. O.C. CASC went to see A.D.M.S. & T. Weather fine	
ST MARTIN D. HARDINGHEM				
	14th February		Still in same billet. 1 wagon & cart for rations, also A.M.S. called at this office this morning. Dismounted Div. coming back to mount. nevertur. surf. reserve all day.	
ST MARTIN D. HARDINGHEM				
	15th February		Still in same billet. 1 wagon & cart for rations. 1 wagon for hay rations & escorts. Major Craig went out to Q office meeting. from Mounted Div. returned to day	
ST MARTIN D. HARDINGHEM				
	16th February		Still in same billet. 1 wagon & cart for rations. 1 wagon & two carts for supper. Major Craig went out to office meeting & very attery wind. no O.C. CASC meeting to day. weather bad. received bill stay Raining	
ST MARTIN D. HARDINGHEM				
	17th February		Still in same billet. 1 wagon & cart for rations. 1 wagon for escort. Major Craig went to & office since the asses fix of the translation.	
ST MARTIN D. HARDINGHEM				

Army Form C. 2118

WAR DIARY
or
INTELLIGENCE SUMMARY
(Erase heading not required.)

Instructions regarding War Diaries and Intelligence Summaries are contained in F. S. Regs., Part II. and the Staff Manual respectively. Title Pages will be prepared in manuscript.

Place	Date	Hour	Summary of Events and Information	Remarks and references to Appendices
ST MARTIN D HARDINGHEM	18th February		Still in same billet. 1 wagon & cart parades. 1 wagon for wood. Cpl & officer Mess. Major Crag went to Q. office. Weather rained all day.	
ST MARTIN D HARDINGHEM	19th February		Still in same billet. 1 wagon & cart for rations. 1 wagon for wood. 2 cart to yp. Stables in the afternoon. Major Crag went to Q. office. weather showery.	
ST MARTIN D HARDINGHEM	20th February		Still in same billet. Major Crag went over to O. Q. & T. also 6 office. 1 wagon & cart for rations. weather fine.	
ST MARTIN D HARDINGHEM	21st February		Still in same billet. 1 wagon & cart for rations. 2 wagon Q. & T. wagon from adv. A. T. M. stores. Major Crag. went 8 office. weather fine, by rather cold.	
ST MARTIN D HARDINGHEM	22nd February		Still in same billet. 1 wagon & cart for rations. 1 wagon for pits use. 1 wagon Q. Q. & O. Q. T. wagon very cold snowing.	
ST MARTIN D HARDINGHEM	23rd February		Still in same billet. 1 wagon & cart for rations. 1 wagon for hay. horse up for tobacco. Major Crag and O. Q. office & stables at A. D. Q. & T. weather very cold & snowed most of the day.	

1875 Wt. W593/826 1,000,000 4/15 J.B.C. & A. A.D.S.S./Forms/C. 2118.

Army Form C. 2118

WAR DIARY
or
INTELLIGENCE SUMMARY
(Erase heading not required.)

Instructions regarding War Diaries and Intelligence Summaries are contained in F. S. Regs., Part II. and the Staff Manual respectively. Title Pages will be prepared in manuscript.

Place	Date	Hour	Summary of Events and Information	Remarks and references to Appendices
ST MARTIN D. HARDINGHEM	24th February		Still in same billet. 1 wagon sent for rations & wagon for hay & fodder. Wagon & cart went to O. officers. Weather very cold, still hard frost.	
ST MARTIN D. HARDINGHEM	25th February		Still in same billet. 1 wagon & cart for rations. Supply officers meeting. Weather very bad. Heavy fall of snow.	
ST MARTIN D. HARDINGHEM	26th February		Still in same billet. 1 wagon & cart for rations. Roads very bad. O.C. O.C. went to Q.G. Officers also S.M.D.R. + T. 3rd Reserve Park & Supply officers meeting. Thaw a little.	
ST MARTIN D. HARDINGHEM	27 February		Still in same billet. No rations delivered today. The one day rations in hand issued. A.M. consumed owing to the thaw. Weather fine, still thawing.	
ST MARTIN D. HARDINGHEM	28 February		Still in same billet. 2 wagon & cart to COYECQUE for rations. Rations been drawn to COYECQUE on account of the thaw. 1 wagon for wood at HODGES. Three running between O.C. O.C. went to S officers meeting. Fine still thawing.	
ST MARTIN D. HARDINGHEM	29th February		Still in same billet. 2 wagon to COYECQUE for rations. One wagon for hay. O.C. & S.O. went to M.O. officers. A special commander. Cart in the afternoon. Weather fine, snow nearly all gone.	

Confidential

War Diary

of 2nd Cavalry Divisional H.Q.

from 1/3/16 to 30/3/16

Volume XIX

Volume XIX

Army Form C. 2118

WAR DIARY
of
INTELLIGENCE SUMMARY
(Erase heading not required.)

Instructions regarding War Diaries and Intelligence Summaries are contained in F.S. Regs., Part II. and the Staff Manual respectively. Title Pages will be prepared in manuscript.

Place	Date	Hour	Summary of Events and Information	Remarks and references to Appendices
ST.MARTIN.D.HARDINGHEM	1st March 1916		Still in same billet. 1 wagon to GOYECOURT for rations. 1 cart for stores & 1 for S.A.A. O.C. went to G office. Also 6 H.Q. & S.S.T. in the afternoon up the avenue. Postal came today. Roads were open to M.T. again. Weather finer.	
ST.MARTIN.D.HARDINGHEM	2nd March		Still in same billet. 2 wagons to BOUT DELA VILLE for rations. O.C. went to G office. Weather fine much warmer.	
ST.MARTIN.D.HARDINGHEM	3rd March		Still in same billet. 2 wagons for rations. 1 for wood. O.C. also went to G office. Weather rained nearly all day.	
ST.MARTIN.D.HARDINGHEM	4th March		Still in same billet. 2 wagons for rations. 1 for wood. O.C. also went to G office. Weather showery.	
ST.MARTIN.D.HARDINGHEM	5th March		Still in same billet. 1 wagon & cart for rations 2 for coal at NIELLES.LEZ.BLEQUIN. 1 cart. 6. ORIONVILLE. Weather shower a little snow.	
ST.MARTIN.D.HARDINGHEM	6th March		Still in same billet. 1 wagon & cart for rations. O.C. went to G office. & him to inspect H. & L.T.A. Horses, some in poor condition. grooming not good. Harness notebook outpost whole found on top of arm. O.L.O. D.A.O went to O.C. D.A.O.S. of army. Weather fine. very cold. snowed hard last night.	

Army Form C. 2118

WAR DIARY
or
INTELLIGENCE SUMMARY

(Erase heading not required.)

Instructions regarding War Diaries and Intelligence Summaries are contained in F.S. Regs., Part II. and the Staff Manual respectively. Title Pages will be prepared in manuscript.

Place	Date	Hour	Summary of Events and Information	Remarks and references to Appendices
ST.MARTIN,D.HARDINGHEM	7th March		Still in same billet. 1 wagon & cart for rations. 1 wagon for hay. O.C. C.O.C. and 1 warrant officer. 12 Royal Engineers snooped. Horses good. Harness good & vehicles ground all day.	
ST.MARTIN,D.HARDINGHEM	8th March		Still in same billet. 1 wagon & cart for rations. 1 wagon for coal. 1 cart to R.E.M.Y. for schools. O.C. went inspected last preps. Harness good. Harness fair. Vehicles good. 6 men to B office. Weather. Heavy fall of snow about 6 inches on the ground. Strenuous work.	
ST.MARTIN,D.HARDINGHEM	9th March		Still in same billet. 1 wagon & cart for rations. 1 wagon to draw O.C. and 1 wagon & 2 ll horses. Horses good. Harness fair. Vehicles not very good. Weather cold. Thawing a little.	
ST.MARTIN,D.HARDINGHEM	10th March		Still in same billet. 1 wagon & cart for rations. 27 horses & limbers cart & wagon arrived & 2 men. O.C. arrived to A.S. O.C. arrived next to 8 officer not fell. N.S.S. Cav. New Transport. Weather fine able to do a little drill.	
ST.MARTIN,D.HARDINGHEM	11th March		Still in same billet. 1 wagon & cart for rations. 2 horses & limbers cart & wagon left for Abbeville at 9 o'clock this morning under the charge of 2nd Lt Lovett. Jun. 16 Horse H.T. Cony & O.C. able away to Q.Office. Weather fine. Still a bit of snow about.	
ST.MARTIN,D.HARDINGHEM	12th March		Still in same billet. 1 wagon & cart for rations. Weather fine. The men are always merry all day.	

1875 Wt. W593/826 1,000,000 4/15 J.B.C. & A. A.D.S.S./Forms/C. 2118.

WAR DIARY
INTELLIGENCE SUMMARY

(Erase heading not required.)

Army Form C. 2118

Instructions regarding War Diaries and Intelligence Summaries are contained in F. S. Regs., Part II. and the Staff Manual respectively. Title Pages will be prepared in manuscript.

Place	Date	Hour	Summary of Events and Information	Remarks and references to Appendices
	13th March		Still in same billet. 1 wagon & cart for rations. O.C. W.S.C. went to G. office, also inspected three H.S. Coys - everything very satisfactory - weather very fine.	
ST MARTIN D. HARDINGHEM				
	14th March		Still in same billet. 1 wagon & cart for rations 1 wagon for canteen. 1 wagon & cart for wood. O.C. W.S.C. went to G. office. Lt. P.Y. Earle R.E. Rev. Monty left for England. 2/Lt. Monckfort to take over any at M.P. Div. Supply. weather fine ceremony.	
ST MARTIN D. HARDINGHEM				
	15th March		Still in same billet. 1 wagon & cart for rations 1 wagon for rations - MCs also went out to G. office. weather fine.	
ST MARTIN D. HARDINGHEM				
	16th March		Still in same billet. 1 wagon & cart for rations. O.C. O.S.E. available to G.A. forwarded 6th D.J. forwarded G office. Also went to G. office. weather fine.	
ST MARTIN D. HARDINGHEM				
	17th March		Still in same billet. 1 wagon & cart for rations. 1 wagon for wood. O.C. W.S.C. inspected horses fair, wheels good. Supply Officer inspected wagon for rations.	
ST MARTIN D. HARDINGHEM			Q.O.H. horses good. Harness fair wheels good. Supply Officer inspected also inspected aviation gear.	

WAR DIARY
or
INTELLIGENCE SUMMARY

(Erase heading not required.)

Army Form C. 2118

Instructions regarding War Diaries and Intelligence Summaries are contained in F. S. Regs., Part II. and the Staff Manual respectively. Title Pages will be prepared in manuscript.

Place	Date	Hour	Summary of Events and Information	Remarks and references to Appendices
	18th March		Still in same billet. 1 wagon & cart for rations. O.C. & O.R. partake 3rd Homers. Horse pond damaged fair with cheer food. weather fine.	
ST MARTIN, D.HARDINGHEM	19th March		Still in same billet. 1 wagon & cart for rations. O.C. orr. & S.t.O. went to Rev Col. of Depot Horses. Horses fair. weather fine.	
ST MARTIN,D.HARDINGHEM	20th March		Still in same billet. 1 wagon & cart for rations. 2 wagons to THIEMBRONNE for wood. Horses put out on the line. weather fine & warm.	
ST MARTIN,D.HARDINGHEM	21st March		Still in same billet. 1 wagon & cart for rations. men working on stables. O.C. out & about. went up to Q.office. weather fine.	
ST MARTIN,D.HARDINGHEM	22nd March		Still in same billet. 1 wagon & cart for rations. 2 wagons & cart for wood at THIEMBRONNE. O.C. ors. E. went to Q.office. weather rained all day.	
ST MARTIN,P.HARDINGHEM.	23rd March		Still in same billet. 1 wagon & cart for rations. 1 wagon for hay. 1 cart for straw. O.C. orr. went to Q.office. weather fine but turning cold.	

Army Form C. 2118

WAR DIARY
or
INTELLIGENCE SUMMARY
(Erase heading not required.)

Instructions regarding War Diaries and Intelligence Summaries are contained in F. S. Regs., Part II. and the Staff Manual respectively. Title Pages will be prepared in manuscript.

Place	Date	Hour	Summary of Events and Information	Remarks and references to Appendices
ST MARTIN.D.HARDINGHEM	24th March		Still in same billet. 1 wagon & cart for rations. 2 wagons & cart for wood. Mess & potatoes. O.C. A.S.C. went to A.D. Office. Safety Officers meeting. extra ration drawn. cold night very cold today	
ST MARTIN.D.HARDINGHEM	25th March		Still in same billet. 1 wagon & cart for rations & carts to draw rations &c. cart went to Q Office. weather still snow falling. very cold.	
ST MARTIN.D.HARDINGHEM	26th March		Still in same billet. 1 wagon & cart for rations. weather showery. cold.	
ST MARTIN.D.HARDINGHEM	27th March		Still in same billet. 1 wagon & cart for rations. 1 cart for straw & one for carrots. O.C. A.S.C. went to A.D. Office. Received F.A.W.D. weather fine morning. Rained rest of day	
ST MARTIN.D.HARDINGHEM	28th March		Still in same billet. 1 wagon & cart for rations. O.C. A.S.C. went to A.D. Office. also went to O.C. 3rd Reserve Park. Called of 11 Lancers about coys. weather fine but cold	
ST MARTIN.D.HARDINGHEM	29th March		Still in same billet. 1 wagon & cart for rations. O.C. A.S.C. went to A.D. Office. Horses went out in to field for the day. weather fine morning. Part of afternoon still & bit cold.	

Army Form C. 2118

WAR DIARY
or
INTELLIGENCE SUMMARY
(Erase heading not required.)

Instructions regarding War Diaries and Intelligence Summaries are contained in F. S. Regs., Part II. and the Staff Manual respectively. Title Pages will be prepared in manuscript.

Place	Date	Hour	Summary of Events and Information	Remarks and references to Appendices
ST MARTIN D, HARDINGHEM	March 30th		Still in same billet. 1 wagon & cart for rations. 1 Lieut C. N. MARTIN od 2d Joined from 92nd Reserve Park & was posted to H.Q. 3rd Cav Bde for duty as T.O. to EWM R. Hutchinson transferred from T.D. to R.O. on arrival of 2t March. 1 H. Moon. being transferred of division HQ. weather fine & sunny	
	March 31st		Still in same billet. 1 wagon & cart for rations. wet morning fine rest of day.	

1875 Wt. W593/826 1,000,000 4/15 J.B.C. & A. A.D.S.S./Forms/C. 2118.

Confidential.

War Diary

of 2nd Cavalry Divisional A.S.C.

from 1/4/16 to 30/4/16

Volume XX.

Volume XX

Army Form C. 2118

WAR DIARY
or
INTELLIGENCE SUMMARY
(Erase heading not required.)

Instructions regarding War Diaries and Intelligence Summaries are contained in F. S. Regs., Part II. and the Staff Manual respectively. Title Pages will be prepared in manuscript.

Place	Date	Hour	Summary of Events and Information	Remarks and references to Appendices
ST. MARTIN, D. HARDINGHEM.	April 1st 1916		Still in same billet. 1 wagon & cart for rations & carts for canteen. Weather fine.	
ST. MARTIN, D. HARDINGHEM.	April 2nd		Still in same billet. 1 wagon & cart for rations. Weather fine morning, wet rest of day.	
ST. MARTIN, D. HARDINGHEM.	April 3rd		Still in same billet. 1 wagon & cart for rations. O.C. & S.C. inspected "H. Hereward" Horses & Transport. Also some returns from 1st Army might be better. Rations not very good. Shed completed with new Divisional Interpreter Marsh. Weather fine & warm.	abs. inspected H.Q.H.C.Ah
	April 4th		Still in same billet. 1 wagon & cart for rations. 1 charger arrived to replace H.Q.H.C. Also A.D. to A.G. wagon painted. Weather dull & cool.	O.C. can inspect 9 Laynes Horses good. Horses good. Names good which
ST. MARTIN, D. HARDINGHEM.	April 5th		Still in same billet. 1 wagon & cart for rations. Weather dull & cool. O.C. was inspected 16th Lancers. Horses good. Horses good, vehicles good.	
ST. MARTIN, D. HARDINGHEM.	April 6th		Still in same billet. 1 wagon & cart for rations. 1 wagon painted. Weather cool. Rain in the evening.	

WAR DIARY
or
INTELLIGENCE SUMMARY

(Erase heading not required.)

Army Form C. 2118

Instructions regarding War Diaries and Intelligence Summaries are contained in F.S. Regs., Part II. and the Staff Manual respectively. Title Pages will be prepared in manuscript.

Place	Date	Hour	Summary of Events and Information	Remarks and references to Appendices
	April 7th		Left for Rouen with 1 wagon & card intentions	
ST MARTIN D'HARDINGHEN				
	April 8th		Still in Rouen billet, having sent waggon to refitting workshops	
ST MARTIN D'HARDINGHEN			Ran down today for conversation & orders	
			in hand to No Commander. Nothing much to report	
	April 9th		Still in Rouen. Billet waggon & cart for return to Boulogne	
ST MARTIN D'HARDINGHEN			from Rouen in movement junction	
	April 10th		Still in Rouen billet. Began & cart to return to Boulogne the next day	
ST MARTIN D'HARDINGHEN			taking us & horse, the foreman Cpl Montagu and Cpl W.T.	
			to complete detachment into car load	
	April 11th		Still in Rouen billet, waggon & cart for return's journey in snow	
ST MARTIN D'HARDINGHEN			storm and morning, the rest of day	
	April 12th		Still in Rouen billet hospital & cart for return home stopped all day owing to snow	
ST MARTIN D'HARDINGHEN				

Army Form C. 2118

WAR DIARY
or
INTELLIGENCE SUMMARY
(Erase heading not required.)

Instructions regarding War Diaries and Intelligence Summaries are contained in F. S. Regs., Part II. and the Staff Manual respectively. Title Pages will be prepared in manuscript.

Place	Date	Hour	Summary of Events and Information	Remarks and references to Appendices
	April 13th		[illegible handwriting]	
ST MARTIN D HARDINGHEM	April 14th		[illegible handwriting]	
ST MARTIN D HARDINGHEM	April 15th		[illegible handwriting]	
ST MARTIN D HARDINGHEM	April 16th		[illegible handwriting]	
ST MARTIN D HARDINGHEM	April 17th		[illegible handwriting]	
ST MARTIN D HARDINGHEM	April 18th		[illegible handwriting]	
ST MARTIN D HARDINGHEM				

1875 Wt. W593/826 1,000,000 4/15, J.B.C. & A. A.D.S.S./Forms/C. 2118.

Army Form C. 2118

WAR DIARY
or
INTELLIGENCE SUMMARY
(Erase heading not required.)

Instructions regarding War Diaries and Intelligence Summaries are contained in F. S. Regs., Part II. and the Staff Manual respectively. Title Pages will be prepared in manuscript.

Place	Date	Hour	Summary of Events and Information	Remarks and references to Appendices
ST MARTIN D HARDINGHEM	April 19		fell in some killed wound & cart for...	
ST MARTIN D HARDINGHEM	April 20		fell in some kill wagon & cart for...	
ST MARTIN D HARDINGHEM	April 21		fell in some kill wagon & cart for...	
ST MARTIN D HARDINGHEM	April 22		fell in some kill wagon & cart for...	
ST MARTIN D HARDINGHEM	April 23		fell in some kill wagon & cart for...	
ST MARTIN D HARDINGHEM	April 24		fell in some kill wagon & cart for...	
ST MARTIN D HARDINGHEM	April 25		fell in some kill wagon & cart for...	

Army Form C. 2118

WAR DIARY
or
INTELLIGENCE SUMMARY
(Erase heading not required.)

Instructions regarding War Diaries and Intelligence Summaries are contained in F.S. Regs., Part II. and the Staff Manual respectively. Title Pages will be prepared in manuscript.

Place	Date	Hour	Summary of Events and Information	Remarks and references to Appendices
ST MARTIN D HARDINGHEM	26 April		[illegible handwriting]	
ST MARTIN D HARDINGHEM	27 April		[illegible handwriting]	
ST MARTIN D HARDINGHEM	28 April		[illegible handwriting]	
ST MARTIN D HARDINGHEM	29 April		[illegible handwriting]	
ST MARTIN D HARDINGHEM	30 April		[illegible handwriting]	

1875 Wt. W593/826 1,000,000 4/15 J.B.C. & A. A.D.S.S./Forms/C. 2118

Confidential.

War Diary.

of 2nd Cavalry Divisional A.S.C.

From 1/3/16 to 31/3/16

Volume XXII.

Volume XXI

Army Form C. 2118

WAR DIARY
or
INTELLIGENCE SUMMARY
(Erase heading not required.)

Instructions regarding War Diaries and Intelligence Summaries are contained in F. S. Regs., Part II. and the Staff Manual respectively. Title Pages will be prepared in manuscript.

Place	Date	Hour	Summary of Events and Information	Remarks and references to Appendices
ST MARTIN, D. HARDINGHEM	1st May		Still in same billet. 1 wagon & cart for rations. O.C. went to A.Q.Offices. 1st Cav Bde HQ & 3rd Hussars & moved to new billets. Weather fine	
ST MARTIN, D. HARDINGHEM	2nd May		Still in same billet. 1 wagon & cart for rations. O.C. went to A.Q. Offices. 1 Limber load Clearing of manure. Weather fine. Thunderstorm in the afternoon.	
ST MARTIN, D. HARDINGHEM	3rd May		Still in same billet. 1 wagon & cart for rations O.C went to A.Q. Office. 5 Car Bde moved today to new area. Finished clearing all manure. Escort of 150 S.O.C. 13th arrived at FAUQUEMBERGUES at 3 o'clock. rations by Div Trans. O.C. arr & SO Div Trans went to 4th Car Bde new area in the afternoon. Weather fine	
ST MARTIN, D. HARDINGHEM	4th May		Still in same billet. 1 wagon & two carts for rations. I went to Divl. Station. had word sent down Div Trans moving Saturday to LUMBRES. Wired over & got billets fixed for Recon. O.C. arr. went to A.Q. Offices. weather fine	
ST MARTIN, D. HARDINGHEM	5th May		Still in same billet. 1 wagon & two carts for rations. Orders came in to move tomorrow of S.S. H.Q. Signal Squadron. Sanitary Section. H.Q. R.H.A. 14 Q.A.S.C. to LUMBRES Weather fine	

WAR DIARY
or
INTELLIGENCE SUMMARY

(Erase heading not required.)

Army Form C. 2118

Instructions regarding War Diaries and Intelligence Summaries are contained in F.S. Regs., Part II. and the Staff Manual respectively. Title Pages will be prepared in manuscript.

Place	Date	Hour	Summary of Events and Information	Remarks and references to Appendices
LUMBRES	6th May		Moved to-day from ST MARTIN, D. HARDINGHEM, at 4.30 a.m. arriving at LUMBRES at 7.15 a.m. All settled in by 4 o'clock in the aftn. O.C. O.S.C. went round 4th & 5th Cav Bde. everything was alright. Ration wire delivered to Bdes to-day at 2 o'clock weather dull. Rained most of the afternoon.	
7th May LUMBRES			Still in same billet. 1 wagon & cart for rations. 12½ ton of potatoes bought over from ST MARTIN, D. HARDINGHEM. O.C. O.S.C. went to Q. Office. R.E. & Amm. Column musketmore weather fine	
8th May LUMBRES			Still in same billet. 1 wagon & cart for rations horse out exercising 1 wagon to ST MARTIN, D. HARDINGHEM. O.C. O.S.C. went to Q. Office weather rained nearly all day.	
9th May LUMBRES			Still in same billet. 1 wagon & cart for rations horses out exercising. 1 cart to ST MARTIN to clear up Billets. O.C. O.S.C. went to Q. Office weather rained hard all day.	
10th May LUMBRES			Still in same billet. 1 wagon & cart for rations 1 wagon for cinders Hoppen. O.C. O.S.C. went to Q. Office also went to advise H.T. Comp. team B. of Cav Bde — weather fine	
11th May LUMBRES			Still in same billet. 1 wagon & cart for rations. 1 cart went to Lumbres Station for the mornings 1 wagon to Stores for lanced cable. O.C. O.S.C. went to Q Office weather fine	

WAR DIARY
or
INTELLIGENCE SUMMARY

Army Form C. 2118

Place	Date	Hour	Summary of Events and Information	Remarks and references to Appendices
LUMBRES	12th May		Still in same billet. 1 wagon & cart for rations. 1 wagon to trip to Wisones with straw. O.C. cars went to Q. office. Weather fine	
LUMBRES	13th May		Still in same billet. 1 wagon & cart for rations. 1 wagon to WATTERDALE for wood. Supply officers meeting was held. H.Q. office. O.C. cars went to Q. office. Weather rained most of day	
LUMBRES	14th May		Still in same billet. 1 wagon & cart for rations. O.C. cars went to H.Q. office. Weather showery.	
LUMBRES	15th May		Still in same billet. 1 wagon & carts for rations. 1 cart to WESTECOURT for officers belongings to the Bath Cycle Coy. to transpt to LUMBRES station. 1 wagon on errands, one to WATTERDALE for wood. O.C. cars went to Q. office also went to 8th Reserve Park. Weather fine.	
LUMBRES	16th May		Still in same billet. 1 wagon & 2 carts for rations. 1 horse & man. to watch the street. O.C. cars went to Q. office "ANZAC" (av. 3 sergeants & 3 cycle (cars) arrived to day for training. Weather fine.	

Army Form C. 2118

WAR DIARY
or
INTELLIGENCE SUMMARY
(Erase heading not required.)

Instructions regarding War Diaries and Intelligence Summaries are contained in F. S. Regs., Part II. and the Staff Manual respectively. Title Pages will be prepared in manuscript.

Place	Date	Hour	Summary of Events and Information	Remarks and references to Appendices
LUMBRES	17th May		Still in same billet. 1 wagon & 2 carts for rations. 1 horse & man & water cart. 1 wagon to St Omer for Linseed Cake. O.C. ADC went to GQ office. Weather fine very warm.	
LUMBRES	18th May		Still in same billet. 1 wagon & 2 carts for rations. 1 wagon to Watendale for wood. O.C. ADSC went to G Office. 1 horse & man for the water cart. Weather fine very warm.	
LUMBRES	19th May		Still in same billet. 1 wagon & 2 carts for rations. 1 horse & man for water cart. O.C. case went to G Office. Supply Officers meeting. Weather fine very warm.	
LUMBRES.	20th May.		Still in same billet. 1 wagon & 2 carts for rations. 1 horse & man for water cart. O.C. case went to G Office. Aux H.T. Comp. Rail orders to move tomorrow. Weather fine very warm.	
LUMBRES	21st May		Still in same billet. 1 wagon & 2 carts for rations. 1 horse & man for water cart. Aux H.T. Comp. moved to-day from CLOQUANT to VAL-DE-LUMBRES. O.C. case went to G Office. Head word Railway to move back to WIZERN to-morrow. Weather fine very warm.	

1875. Wt. W593/826 1,000,000 4/15 J.B.C. & A. A.D.S.S./Forms/C. 2118.

WAR DIARY
or
INTELLIGENCE SUMMARY

(Erase heading not required.)

Army Form C. 2118

Place	Date	Hour	Summary of Events and Information	Remarks and references to Appendices
LUMBRES	22nd May		Still in same billet. 1 wagon & 2 carts for rations at WIZERNES Railhead. March today. O.C. cars went to 3rd officers mess. Weather fine very warm. a little shower in the evening.	
LUMBRES	23rd May		Still in same billet. 1 wagon & 2 carts for rations at WIZERNES Railhead. Horses & 2 men for water carts. O.C. cars went to O. Officer. 3rd Reserve Park loaded rations for the 5th Cav. Bde. & delivered same. Weather fine not quite so warm.	
LUMBRES	24th May		Still in same billet. 1 wagon & 2 carts for rations at WIZERNES Railhead. 2 horses & men for water carts. 3rd Reserve Park loaded rations of 5 Cav Bde supplies. O.C. Cars & OC Reserve Park went to dinner, everything alright. Weather fine not quite so warm.	
LUMBRES	25th May		Still in same billet. 1 wagon & 2 carts for rations at WIZERNES Railhead. O.C. cars went to O. Officer horses to have shoes on & harness & our cart. Rations issued in the morning but fine afternoon.	

Army Form C. 2118

WAR DIARY
or
INTELLIGENCE SUMMARY
(Erase heading not required.)

Instructions regarding War Diaries and Intelligence Summaries are contained in F. S. Regs., Part II. and the Staff Manual respectively. Title Pages will be prepared in manuscript.

Place	Date	Hour	Summary of Events and Information	Remarks and references to Appendices
LUMBRES	26th May		Still in same billet. 1 wagon & 2 carts for rations at WIZERNES. Supply Officers meeting. OC coast went to Q Office.	Spellhead weather fine and cloudy
LUMBRES	27th May		Still in same billet. Horses delivered D Sibbels today. the 2nd Squadron Lancashire horse show was a field day. Had orders about a detachment of men for digging trenches going on Monday 29th OC went to Q office.	
LUMBRES	28th May		Still in same billet. 1 wagon & 2 carts to draw rations from WIZERNES. OC coast went to Q Office. Weather fine quite warm.	Railhead
LUMBRES	29th May		Still in same billet. 1 wagon & 2 carts for rations from WIZERNES. railhead. In return carts OC coast went to Q Office. weather fine.	2 horses & 2 men
LUMBRES	30th May		Still in same billet. 2 wagons to WIZERNES railhead. ANZAC are due to leave for the new Area. Order cancelled. OC of C went to Q Office. weather fine all morning.	

1875 Wt. W593/826 1,000,000 4/15 J.B.C. & A. A.D.S.S./Forms/C. 2118.

Army Form C. 2118.

WAR DIARY
or
INTELLIGENCE SUMMARY

(Erase heading not required.)

Place	Date	Hour	Summary of Events and Information	Remarks and references to Appendices
LUMBRES	31st May.		Still in same billet. 2 wagons for relief, & TWO HORSES Railhead. 1 wagon & cart for green forage. 2 horses & men for ammunition cart. O.C. G.S.S. went to Ypres. Weather fine & quite warm.	

Confidential
War Diary
of 2nd Cavalry Divisional A.S.C.
from 1/6/16 to 30/6/16

Volume XXII.

Volume XXII

Army Form C. 2118

WAR DIARY
or
INTELLIGENCE SUMMARY
(Erase heading not required.)

Instructions regarding War Diaries and Intelligence Summaries are contained in F.S. Regs., Part II. and the Staff Manual respectively. Title Pages will be prepared in manuscript.

Place	Date	Hour	Summary of Events and Information	Remarks and references to Appendices
31st May LUMBRES			Still in same billet. 2 wagon for rations to WIZERNES. Railhead. 1 wagon & cart for green forage. 2 horses & men for water cart. O.C. sets. went to Q office, weather fine.	
1st June 1916 LUMBRES			Still in same billet. 2 wagon for rations to WIZERNES. Railhead. 2 horses came for water cart. O.C. sets. went to Q office. weather fine	
2nd June LUMBRES			Still in same billet. 2 wagon for rations to WIZERNES. Railhead. 1 wagon & cart for green forage with officers meeting. O.C. sets. went to Q office. weather fine.	
3rd June LUMBRES			Still in same billet. 2 wagon for rations to WIZERNES. Railhead. 2 horses came for water cart. 1 wagon & cart for green forage. Officer A.T. Corps. received 24 state Coats. weather fine.	
4th June LUMBRES			Still in same billet. 2 wagon for rations to WIZERNES. Railhead. 2 horses & men for water cart. O.C. sets. went to Q office. weather fine. morning. rained a little in the afternoon.	

Volume XXII

WAR DIARY
or
INTELLIGENCE SUMMARY
(Erase heading not required.)

Army Form C. 2118

Instructions regarding War Diaries and Intelligence Summaries are contained in F.S. Regs., Part II. and the Staff Manual respectively. Title Pages will be prepared in manuscript.

Place	Date	Hour	Summary of Events and Information	Remarks and references to Appendices
5th June LUMBRES		19/10	Still in same billets. 2 wagon to WIZERNES railhead for rations 1 wagon to St Omer for stores, 1 wagon sent for green forage in the afternoon. One officer & 30 other ranks came in. That the Machine Gun Section were going to the trenches on the 6th.	
6 June LUMBRES			Still in same billets. 2 wagon to WIZERNES railhead for rations 1 wagon for stores. 2 horses sent to the farm. One man from H.Q. & two other ranks were sent for offence. Recd orders that Dismounted Brigade Field Ambulance to concentrate & move by the evening.	
7th June LUMBRES			Still in same billets. 2 wagon to WIZERNES railhead for rations 1 wagon & 1 officer & two other ranks came. Dismounted Brigade 2 men off in the afternoon forage. One officer went to 2 officers arrived & 4 officers Dismounted Brigade all had gone natural at to be in-comm night weather fine by evening.	
8th June LUMBRES			Still in same billets. 2 wagon to WIZERNES railhead for rations 1 cart went to St Omer. 2 horses sent to Opal Hd. Lad men & officer reconnaissance all Brigade every thing a trip of weather fine & a little rain last night.	
9th June LUMBRES			Still in same billets. 2 wagon to WIZERNES railhead for rations. 1 cart 4 wagon for green forage.	

Army Form C. 2118

WAR DIARY
or
INTELLIGENCE SUMMARY
(Erase heading not required.)

Instructions regarding War Diaries and Intelligence Summaries are contained in F. S. Regs., Part II. and the Staff Manual respectively. Title Pages will be prepared in manuscript.

Place	Date	Hour	Summary of Events and Information	Remarks and references to Appendices
LUMBRES	10th June		Still in same billet & wagons to WIZERNES railhead for rations. 1 cart to Sa's trench to bring back empty cylinders. Weather fine.	
LUMBRES	11th June		Still in same billet & wagons to WIZERNES railhead for rations. Weather fine.	
LUMBRES	12th June		Still in same billet & wagons to WIZERNES railhead for rations. 1 wagon & cart for green forage. Weather rained all day very cold.	
LUMBRES	13th June		Still in same billet & wagons to WIZERNES railhead for rations. Second Army Hqrs "E" & "J" Batteries. R.H.A. H.Q. & Adjt & Brn. Amm Section (Amm Column) arr standing by to move off. Rain just off till to-morrow sure then very bad. Scarcel Rained all day & very cold.	
LUMBRES	14th June		Still in same billet & wagons to WIZERNES railhead for rations. 1 wagon to H.Q. UNITS on the road & sand. R.H.A. "E" & "J" Batteries light Amm Column also light Amm section of Amm Park moved off today. Rained at the nightfall 15th weather very bad. Rained all day.	

r875 Wt. W593/826 1,000,000 4/15 J.B.C. & A. A.D.S.S./Forms/C. 2118.

WAR DIARY
or
INTELLIGENCE SUMMARY

(Erase heading not required.)

Army Form C. 2118

Instructions regarding War Diaries and Intelligence Summaries are contained in F.S. Regs., Part II. and the Staff Manual respectively. Title Pages will be prepared in manuscript.

Place	Date	Hour	Summary of Events and Information	Remarks and references to Appendices
LUMBRES	15th June		Still in same billets. 2 wagons to WIZERNES railhead for rations, & 20 wagons for hay. New Batteries wore weather. Dull, still very cold.	
LUMBRES	16th June		Still in same billets. 2 wagons to WIZERNES railhead for rations. 1 wagon for fuel forage. Weather fine, still cold.	
LUMBRES	17th June		Still in same billets. 1 wagon to WIZERNES railhead for rations. 1 wagon to ALQUIN with coal & wood. Word came in a move is taking place. O.C. A.S.C. A.S.O. visited 4 & 5th Cav Bde. weather fine but still cold.	
LUMBRES	18th June		Still employed 3rd Battn d- Cav 7 Amb. Ammunition Column such billets. to be no sent to office	R Mallery orderly to Aux FT Complementation
LUMBRES	19th June		Still in same billets. 3 wagons to WIZERNES railhead. 1 wagon to STAPLE. O.C. A.S.C. went to a another gave. 3rd Cav Bde left tonight for _____ inspected albums for manage all supply	
LUMBRES	20th June		Still in same billets. 2 wagons to WIZERNES railhead for rations. Or. our went to Office. 3rd Cav Bde left last night for new billets. A Cav Bde moved back night & stayed the night for RENESCURE. Weather fine but still cold.	

WAR DIARY
or
INTELLIGENCE SUMMARY

(Erase heading not required.)

Army Form C. 2118

Place	Date	Hour	Summary of Events and Information	Remarks and references to Appendices
LUMBRES	21 June		Still in same billets. No serious work today. O.C. self went to D.O. Office. H. Campbell moved. Had night suit new billets. No Cars. moved too RENESCURE & EBBLINGHEM. Weather fine. turned much warmer.	
HAZEBROUCK	22nd June		H.Q. of 2 Cav. Div. & Div. Trans. moved today to HAZEBROUCK. H.A.S.C. left 10.30. arrived 20 hrs. left 5/6. 1 hour in it a full horses at FORT ROUGE arrived at HAZEBROUCK at 9 o'clock everything in good order. Hazebrouck weather fine. very hot. Capt. PRENDERGAST. reported to take over duties as D.D. Vet. in place of Captification.	
HAZEBROUCK	23rd June		Still in same billets. everybody in new billets today. O.C. spent to D. Office. St. Louis sent back for the Lambs of Aux. H.T. Coy. remaining the morning. very hot thunder in the afternoon. turn showery. am very fond of state.	
HAZEBROUCK	24th June		Still in same billets. obtained D.O. Office Aux. H.T. Conv. received all it hops. back weather very hot. seemed meal. all day.	
HAZEBROUCK	25th June		Still in same billets. Col. H.C. Beadon. left for No 2 Communication Park S.K.Q. O.C. O.C. self. went to D. Office. everything very quite. weather fine. pleasant.	

WAR DIARY
or
INTELLIGENCE SUMMARY

(Erase heading not required.)

Army Form C. 2118

Instructions regarding War Diaries and Intelligence Summaries are contained in F.S. Regs., Part II. and the Staff Manual respectively. Title Pages will be prepared in manuscript.

Place	Date	Hour	Summary of Events and Information	Remarks and references to Appendices
HAZEBROUCK.	26th June		Still in same billet. Others came in that Divisional HQ is going by 6 buses today. Supply Officers meeting. 1 wagon for Sub Qrs Rations /for green garage. Weather showery.	
HAZEBROUCK.	27th June.		Still in same billet. 1 wagon went to HQ to receive rations to be ready to move when wanted. S.C. Off. went to Q. office 1 wagon for supp & 1 for green garage orders came that Onpon party move today. Weather showery.	
HAZEBROUCK.	28th June.		Still in same billet. 1 wagon to STRAZEELE for cabbages. O.C. A.S.C. went to Q. office. A.S.O. went to decoard. Army Supplies party moved off yesterday. Weather some v hard last night, showery today.	
HAZEBROUCK.	29th June.		Still in same billet. 1 wagon for green forage. O.C. A.S.C. went to Q office. Weather dull. Rained a little. Scouts are running.	
HAZEBROUCK.	30th June.		Still in same billet. 1 wagon to STRAZEELE for cabbages. O.C. A.S.C. went to Q office. Supply Officers meeting. Everything very quiet. Weather still showery & warmer.	

CONFIDENTIAL.

WAR DIARY

of

2nd Cavalry Divisional A. S. C.

From: 1st July to 31st July. 1916.

(Volume XXIII.).

Army Form C. 2118

HEADQUARTERS,
2nd CAVALRY DIV.
A.S.O.
No. 1113/1
Date 3.8.16

WAR DIARY
or
INTELLIGENCE SUMMARY

Sheet No. 1.

(Erase heading not required.)

Instructions regarding War Diaries and Intelligence Summaries are contained in F.S. Regs., Part II. and the Staff Manual respectively. Title Pages will be prepared in manuscript.

Place	Date	Hour	Summary of Events and Information	Remarks and references to Appendices
HAZEBROUCK	1st July		Still in same billet. Wagon for wood at LA MOTTE. Bois as usual. D.O officer weather fine.	
HAZEBROUCK	2nd July		Still in same billet. O.C. & self went to D.B office very heavy thunderstorm last night. Started at 4 o'clock. Went on till about one in the morning. Weather fine.	
HAZEBROUCK	3rd July		Still in same billet as usual went to D.O office. 1 wagon out on hay & half great. Farmer weather fine & warm.	
HAZEBROUCK	4th July		Still in same billet. O.C. & self went to D.B office. 1 wagon out on wood. 6 horses turned suddenly lame had great deg. off morning field. One died. I hope Vet. arrived. 6 other horses not at all well. Bowels every bad. 4 under cover. 1 very bad. Weather fine in the morning. Rained all the afternoon.	
HAZEBROUCK	5th July		Still in same billet as usual went to D office in the morning. Vet. ordered 1 more horse to be shot in very great pain another one died in the afternoon. The remaining four sick are a little better. Weather fine.	

WAR DIARY
or
INTELLIGENCE SUMMARY

Army Form C. 2118

(Erase heading not required.)

Instructions regarding War Diaries and Intelligence Summaries are contained in F.S. Regs., Part II. and the Staff Manual respectively. Title Pages will be prepared in manuscript.

Place	Date	Hour	Summary of Events and Information	Remarks and references to Appendices
	6 July		Still in same billet. O.C. & 2/c went to B.Q. Office. 4 horses all sent out. Rain improved a lot. Wt. called this morning sent thine gas in overcoat weather - cloudy but fine.	
HAZEBROUCK.	7 July		Still in same billet. O.C. & 2/c went to B.Q. Office. 4 horses improved a lot. 1 wagon to wagon weather. Rained a little last night. fine to day.	
HAZEBROUCK	8 July		Still in same billet. O.C. & 2/c went to B.Q. Office. 4 remounts arrived & put in to 171 Bat. Res. 2 No H.Q. and C. 8" and to C. 8" Cav. Bde H.Q. & Bde Sig & Div. Sig. Company - moved to day to H.Q. Railway - fine weather Same very hot. 1 Remount not well bad cold	
HAZEBROUCK.	9 July		Still in same billet. O.C. & 2/c went to B.Q. Office. 1 wagon for (boy gun etrops) Remount much better and came back. 166 men from each Cav Bde Ego afficer on to 13th weather fine. a very hot day	
HAZEBROUCK	10 July		Still in same billet. O.C. & 2/c went to B.Q. Office. all remounts were found to be very good. Sent sick horses back on lorries again. weather fine.	
HAZEBROUCK	11 July		Still in same billet. O.C. & 2/c went to B.Q. Office. 1 wagon for wood all horses out exercise. A.D.V.S. inspected remounts weather fine.	

WAR DIARY
or
INTELLIGENCE SUMMARY Sheet No. 3

Army Form C. 2118

(Erase heading not required.)

Instructions regarding War Diaries and Intelligence Summaries are contained in F.S. Regs., Part II. and the Staff Manual respectively. Title Pages will be prepared in manuscript.

Place	Date	Hour	Summary of Events and Information	Remarks and references to Appendices
HAZEBROUCK	12th July		Still in same billet. 1 wagon for green forage. Rest of horses out exercising. O.C. with detacht to O. Office weather cloudy. T 2nd Lieut. R.D GODLEY arrived from Salt, detacht for dentist. Boulogne on relief of T. Lieut J.S. BACHIER, as R.O. & W.D.M., T. Lieut J.S. Bachier proceeded en to depot £0.05. C.T.D. ABBEVILLE on ceasing he of the SS	
HAZEBROUCK	13th July		Still in same billet. 1 wagon for green forage sent out exercising. Sergt. Major L.S.S. Office weather showery went cloudy, a slight	
HAZEBROUCK	14th July		Still in same billet. 1 wagon for green forage. Rest out exercising, orderly sergt 68 officers. O.C. Most Enfield Cadre H.T. Corps. weather fine.	
HAZEBROUCK	15th July		Still in same billet. 1 wagon for green forage. Rest out exercising a/c a/g went to office. weather fine. T Lieut. J.S. Bachier proceeded to ABBEVILLE in accordance with orders.	
HAZEBROUCK	16th July		Still in same billet. 1 wagon for green forage. Rest out exercising, o/c a/s went to office weather fine morning, showers rest of day.	
HAZEBROUCK	17th July		Still in same billet. 1 wagon for green forage. Rest out exercising. The RD GODLEY took over his duty as S.S.O. went on an enfield R.O. H.C. pb empd. The ph net were & two wagons clean washed & dust book & 46 H 1st Bn Rode Cpl Lewis S.O. of his Res. now put in charge of ... weather fine, sky cloudy.	

Army Form C. 2118.

WAR DIARY
or
INTELLIGENCE SUMMARY ̶C̶r̶u̶ M.4

(Erase heading not required.)

Instructions regarding War Diaries and Intelligence Summaries are contained in F. S. Regs., Part II. and the Staff Manual respectively. Title Pages will be prepared in manuscript.

Place	Date	Hour	Summary of Events and Information	Remarks and references to Appendices
HAZEBROUCK	18th July		Still in same billet. Route march of H.Q. coll. horses harness, prod. OC & S.O. went to "Car Pet" meeting June.	
HAZEBROUCK	19th July		Still in same billet. 1 wagon to Pradelles. OC a/c went to other unit from our west. S.O. went to Second Army Hd Qtrs. D.D.S.T.	
HAZEBROUCK	20th July		Still in same billet. 1 wagon for green forage OC a/c went to office. Weather fine.	
HAZEBROUCK	21st July		Still in same billet. 1 wagon for water OC a/c went to office. Weather fine.	
HAZEBROUCK	22nd July		Still in same billet. Sent to mend all wagons at H.Q. coll. OC coll. went to Q.T.F.C. Headqtrs. heavy rain in the morning, fine weather. Sent rest of day. took boy sick in Hazebrouck one of the remount received on the 9-7-16 who evacuated to Hy. to No. 1 Mobile Vet. Sec.	

Army Form C. 2118.

WAR DIARY
or
INTELLIGENCE SUMMARY Lieut. M.S.
(Erase heading not required.)

Instructions regarding War Diaries and Intelligence Summaries are contained in F. S. Regs., Part II. and the Staff Manual respectively. Title Pages will be prepared in manuscript.

Place	Date	Hour	Summary of Events and Information	Remarks and references to Appendices
HAZEBROUCK.	23rd July		Still in same billet OC ADC went to B office were for gave.	
HAZEBROUCK.	24th July		Still in same billet OC ASC went to B office. At about 10.30 last night a HSC Cpl Smith's name, Smith rushed over to Major Law's Engine, stated he was Carpho. Came. At about 4 PM N 2° line fire over the line, fifteen he exploded Capt Smith own. Antiaircraft Removed. Ext ranged on 28°th 9 Munition set of own Aeroplane com an esent. He soon observed to his own Smith his missing. with Capt Gammon and BSC	
HAZEBROUCK.	25th July		Still in same billet OC ASC went to B office. Also took three Germans & prisoners to the 9th Head Bgde. went to give a little benefit and lead.	
HAZEBROUCK.	26th July		Still in same billet OC ASC went to B office. Also inspected the whole corps of the 9th Head Bgde. went to OC Cavalry Saloon. Watching give ill. Crop was lead	
HAZEBROUCK.	27th July		Still in same billet OC ASC went to B office. Also inspected the whole cards of 10th Car. with OC Cavalry Saloon. Weather fine until Change over lead	
HAZEBROUCK.	28th July		Still in same billet OC ASC went to B offices alone as found in the Quart Master Halting. Weather fine Reinhamental and one 2-pay men to man defence of Ambulance. Capt Smith was one telet & LCM E day. OC 16 one of Horsier PCB to our armed training by night lable many, about 8000 about	
HAZEBROUCK.	29th July		Still in same billet. service men & B office also completed y.nc out. Sew Last to his Left with OC Sanity Section. Weather very hot	
HAZEBROUCK.	30th July		Still in same billet. OC ASC went to BC office 3th Bgde moving to morrow, than it can mount all the new tanks. weather fine very hot.	

Instructions regarding War Diaries and Intelligence Summaries are contained in F. S. Regs., Part II. and the Staff Manual respectively. Title Pages will be prepared in manuscript.

Army Form C. 2118.

WAR DIARY
or
~~INTELLIGENCE SUMMARY~~ Sheet No. 6

(Erase heading not required.)

Place	Date	Hour	Summary of Events and Information	Remarks and references to Appendices
HAZEBROUCK	31st July		Still in same billets. OC ASC went to [illegible] office also went to 3? Division in the afternoon. Weather fine very hot.	

[illegible] Lt & Adjt.
H.Q. A.S.C.
2nd Cav. Div.

3-8-16

2449 Wt. W14957/M90 750,000 1/16 J.B.C. & A. Forms/C.2118/12.

CONFIDENTIAL.

WAR DIARY OF

H.Q., A.S.C., 2nd CAV.DIV.

for August, 1916.

Vol XXIV

Army Form C. 2118.

WAR DIARY
or
INTELLIGENCE SUMMARY

(Erase heading not required.)

Place	Date	Hour	Summary of Events and Information	Remarks and references to Appendices
HAZEBROUCK	Tuesday 1st August 1916		Still in same billet. I.O.&C. went to R. office. The Assist. T.O. came in to see us & the Drawing Room. & home. Stanford weather very hot. JR	
HAZEBROUCK	Wednesday 2nd August 1916		Still in same billet. O.C. also went to D. office. Also promulgated Transfer of Capt Griffith was invalided. Ammunition Train from his truck on active service. He left HAZEBROUCK at 3-5 a.m. Passengers were taken to Rest Run to BOULOGNE & Rand Run over to the A.M.L.O. weather fine very hot. JR	BOULOGNE
HAZEBROUCK	Thursday 3rd August 1916		Still in same billet O.C. also went to D. office. Obtained O.O. for Journey to BEE DEPOT on application to A.F.D. 2132. Capt Pearson returned about 10.15 p.m. also cases put thro' Divl H.Q. Lieut. Allen left for 4 Car Pool. HQ MRC Ambee 2 Ambee motor June a BEE Depot Journey made to Base Shown. JR	
HAZEBROUCK	Friday 4th August 1916		Still in same billet. O.C. also went to D. office. Left Journey made to Base Shown. 6th time over. Same opened upon weather fine. A lot order. JR	
HAZEBROUCK	Saturday 5th August 1916		Still in same billet. O.C. also went to D. office. Working parties left below Rewaw Beach arrived & three. One weather fine. JR	
HAZEBROUCK	Sunday 6th August 1916		Still in same billet. O.C. also went to D. office. L. Carely Conroin observer & H.T. from Railhead. Ammunition Column + Suppl Colum. left for working parties was came. 8 Can Bde. Band men to music weather fine. JR	
HAZEBROUCK	Monday 7th August 1916		Still in same billet. O.C. also went to D. office. also Railhead. also taken away party at 5-30 his morning. Seeing to the 5 Can Bde working party morning off early. weather fine Morning worm - again. JR	

Army Form C. 2118.

Volume XXIV

WAR DIARY
or
INTELLIGENCE SUMMARY
(Erase heading not required.)

Sheet No 2.

Instructions regarding War Diaries and Intelligence Summaries are contained in F.S. Regs., Part II. and the Staff Manual respectively. Title Pages will be prepared in manuscript.

Place	Date	Hour	Summary of Events and Information	Remarks and references to Appendices
HAZEBROUCK	Tuesday 8th 1916		Still in same billet. O.C. cake went to Q Office weather fine very warm. J.F.	
HAZEBROUCK	Wednesday 9th 1916		Still in same billet O.C. adv went to Q Office Staff train this morning very late arriving, arrived at 6.20.a.m. D.A.D.T. called. Staff train O.C. etc. weather fine very warm J.F.	
HAZEBROUCK	Thursday 10th 1916		Still in same billet. O.C. cake went to Q Office horse very bad this morning. First Army O.C. Y.M.V.S. came over. Could not do all morning horses would not go in a coach presently A.D.V.S. came up in the evening Bravo very much better at 10.p.m another very hot day. The heat on	
HAZEBROUCK	Friday 11th 1916		Still in same billet O.C. cake sent to Q Office horses quiet alright to day. The feed on Green food 2 9am Staff Capt B Forrell joined to Supp Column for 6th division depth Officers meeting wednesday hrs — weather very hot J.F.	
HAZEBROUCK	Saturday 12th 1916		Still in same billet O.C. adv went to Q Office weather fine very hot J.F.	
HAZEBROUCK	Sunday 13th 1916		Still in same billet O.C. adv sent to Q Office weather fine much cooler J.F.	
HAZEBROUCK	Monday 14th 1916		Still in same billet O.C. adj Q went to Q Office weather fine morning rainy afternoon. Cpt J.R. Hawkins left for Ryland this day J.F.	

Army Form C. 2118.

WAR DIARY
or
INTELLIGENCE SUMMARY
(Erase heading not required.)

Sheet No. 3

Instructions regarding War Diaries and Intelligence Summaries are contained in F. S. Regs., Part II. and the Staff Manual respectively. Title Pages will be prepared in manuscript.

Place	Date	Hour	Summary of Events and Information	Remarks and references to Appendices
HAZEBROUCK	Tues Feb 15th 1916		Still in same billet. O.C. also went to B Office. weather showery, misty & dull.	
HAZEBROUCK	Wednesday 16th Feb		Still in same billet. O.C. also went to B Office, was out in afternoon. A.A. Rev. Tuck took service in morning 9 a.m. a few flakes of snow falling weather trim & cold.	
HAZEBROUCK	Thursday 17th 1916		Still in same billet. O.C. also went to B Office. weather frine morning turned to rain in afternoon. fine evening. R.	
HAZEBROUCK	Friday 18th 1916		Still in same billet. O.C. went to B Office. Also received 5 Court Martial forms in a.m. Staff officer meeting inspected and expected weather fine morning very cold after noon. R.	
HAZEBROUCK	Saturday 19th 1916		Still in same billet. O.C. also went to B Office. weather showery in morning fine in afternoon. R.	
HAZEBROUCK	Sunday 20th 1916		Still in same billet. O.C. also went to B Office. weather fine. R. Lieut P Oakenfield HQ. OS 2 p.m. at B. & T.D. HARVE	

Army Form C. 2118.

WAR DIARY
of
INTELLIGENCE SUMMARY

(Erase heading not required.)

Instructions regarding War Diaries and Intelligence Summaries are contained in F.S. Regs., Part II. and the Staff Manual respectively. Title Pages will be prepared in manuscript.

Place	Date	Hour	Summary of Events and Information	Remarks and references to Appendices
HAZEBROUCK	Monday 21st 1916.		Still in same billet. O.C. A.S.C. went to Q.M.H.C. One British aeroplane came down between HAZEBROUCK & HONDEGHEM. Both officers were killed. Much rain but a fine weather fine 2	
HAZEBROUCK	Tuesday 22nd 1916		Still in same billet. O.C. A.S.C. went to Q Office in the afternoon. Met Lieut. W. Carrington & Lieut Bright. Aeroplane at 30' about every very fast very. Both went East. 2 f 3 Cavalry Brigade. Transport good. Weather fine over Club.	
HAZEBROUCK	Wednesday 23rd 1916		Still in same billet. O.C. A.S.C went to Q Office. Lines were. I from was cloudy	
HAZEBROUCK	Thursday 24th 1916		Still in same billet. O.C. A.S.C. went to Q Office. Was invited for 5 horses in the Everything very good. Weather fine	
HAZEBROUCK	Friday 25th 1916		Still in same billet. O.C. A.S.C also went to Q Office. Supp. Officers meeting grown meeting a long pieces in the afternoon.	
HAZEBROUCK	Saturday 26th 1916		Still in same billet. O.C. A.S.C. went to Q Office weather fine sunny.	
HAZEBROUCK	Sunday 27th 1916		Still in same billet O.P. A.S.C. went to Q Office. Went to Church Morning Service 9.am. 2	

Army Form C. 2118.

WAR DIARY
or
INTELLIGENCE SUMMARY

(Erase heading not required.)

Shu m 5

Place	Date	Hour	Summary of Events and Information	Remarks and references to Appendices
HAZEBROUCK	Monday 29th 1916		Still in same billet. O.C. also went to O Officer stores in the morning. Fine afternoon & evening. 1.K.	
HAZEBROUCK	Tuesday 29th 1916		Still in same billet. O.C. also went to R Office also inspected Transport. Snow in Division area. Men kept employed. Rumour of being moved. K.	
HAZEBROUCK	Wednesday 30th 1916		Still in same billet. O.C. & two adjutants to Loytre went to B.H.Q. Some snow some rain and snow, also snow and sleet. K.	
HAZEBROUCK	Thursday 31st 1916		Still in same billet. O.C. &C. sent to Officer & Am O.C. 15 ebru weather fine. K.	

Signature
H.A.L.G.C.
O.C. Con Rev

SECRET.

Vol 3

WAR   DIARY

of

O.C., 2nd CAVALRY DIVISIONAL A.S.C.

for September, 1916.

VOLUME ~~XXXV~~.

******

WAR DIARY or INTELLIGENCE SUMMARY

Army Form C. 2118.

(Erase heading not required.)

HEADQUARTERS,
2ND CAVALRY DIVN.
A.S.C.

Sheet No 1.

Place	Date	Hour	Summary of Events and Information	Remarks and references to Appendices
HAZEBROUCK	September 1st 1916		Still in same billet as ordered to Office Suppy Mgrs Medical Mobile Supply Column. was brought up again by feeding the troops in the event of a move forward. Also went down in fact-digging parties with Moving Park on S.W. of 2nd September came up with 3" mortars & some of the batteries in reserve at Morbecq. Weather fine. YR.	
HAZEBROUCK	September 2nd 1916		Still in same billet as ABC sent to Office four things from HQ of Officer Commanding Divisional Dump. HAZEBROUCK steady fine YR.	
HAZEBROUCK	September 3rd 1916		Still in same billet as other sent to Office weather YR	
HAZEBROUCK	September 4th 1916		Still in same billet on our way to Office Divisional Dump. Moved from LEDGE BROUCK K LUMBRES. more movements of this Received 5 days rations sent morning & cup. Once shown in the afternoon YR	
HAZEBROUCK	September 5th 1916		Still in same billet as our sent to Officer order came more to move. Ste at Starling Bend STEENBECQUE STATION at 12 Noon, work B Echelon of Divisional transport UX HT Conf O.R.S. 245 came to Office with what the A.V.HT. Conf. orders to go & STRAZEELE STATION to load up. Return to this present billet & then follow on the next day soon for 2 days. Our Reserve Park. Weather raised all day. YR	

WAR DIARY
INTELLIGENCE SUMMARY
(Erase heading not required.)

Army Form C. 2118.

Sheet No. 2

Instructions regarding War Diaries and Intelligence Summaries are contained in F.S. Regs., Part II. and the Staff Manual respectively. Title Pages will be prepared in manuscript.

Place	Date	Hour	Summary of Events and Information	Remarks and references to Appendices
HAMET BILLET	September 6th 1916		O.C. & S.C. went to Q. office. Left HAMBROUCK at 10-45 a.m. and arrived at Harbey Dind-12 N°N. A.A. & Q.M.G. came with second part. the Aux.H.T. conf. Arrived 12 Rey 1.05. p.m. arrived. 4 more HAMET BILLET. 5. Marrow Divisional Bill. Dep. Lu. Starting point. 12.45 p.m. One Lall. rally the conf. 23 mile. March. H.R.& S.C. were in time present. billet at 2.20 p.m. everything in very good order. marched out in good order. 4.30 o'clock a Q.M.G's came down at 5 o'clock about rations for Reserve Park & Burnt H. Cony. O.C. & S.C. O.Q.M.G's. Came down at 5 o'clock about rations for Reserve Park & Burnt H. Army. went to Supply Column & made the arrangements. We returned to the Reserve Park later went at Aux.H. Army. everything alright. weather fine today. P.R.	
MONCHY CAYEUR	September 7th 1916		O.C. & S.C. went to R office. Left HAMET BILLET at 9.45 a.m. arrived at Billeting Area 11 a.m. Roads passing through the BUSNES & BURBURE-RAMBERT-PERNES-TANGRY-HESTRUS-MONCHY CAYEUR billet for one Row & 2 colour-left at RAMBERT at HESTRUS. R.E. & Postal Mounted to Billeting of Division. left Column at the first turning to the left of the flanning village of HESTRUS. H.R. case arrived Billet 5.20. O.C. 6.15 A.Q. & Q.M.G. came to see cadres and gave orders. He are in Billet Bivouac in Our field. 60 Lines for this night. one died of one reason. Fine. P.R.	
VACQUERIETTE	September 8th 1916		Left MONCHY CAYEUR at 9.30 a.m. & marched to at the X Road for MONCHY CAYEUR & FLEURY. ST. POL, HESDIN Sr. to the RE & heard at this point A.Q. & Q.M.G. & held to & old to S.C. of the Reserve Park & Aux.H.T. conf. were to remain in Rese Billet by R.B. 8th & RE further orders. Route taken FLEURY, BERMICOURT, HUMIERES, NOVELLE-LES-HUMIERES, WILLEMAN, WAIL. Road taken left to town of HUMIERES are also roads. New roads from the NUMIERES on the North Hy. Gurney arrived at manor BILLETS 3.40 p.m. the road from the NUMIERES on the North Hy. Gurney not good. Roads before and rough & hold. O.C. case went to Q office at 9 p.m. arrived Horse at. At Bruce. H.T. Conf. & Reserve Park R.E. Present Field to March. Weather during night overcast, rather then fine.	

2449 Wt W14957/Mgo 750,000 1/16 J.B.C. & A. Forms/C.2118/12.

WAR DIARY or INTELLIGENCE SUMMARY

Army Form C. 2118.

(Erase heading not required.)

Place	Date	Hour	Summary of Events and Information	Remarks and references to Appendices
VACQUERIETTE	September 9th 1916		Still in same billet as last & went to B.O. office noting by wireless noise & morse sigs. arrived by N-Debek?a. Posn & HQ of B.Cs VILLERS L'HOPITAL. A Divisional Review for Labour Corris to-morrow at X Ref M = MDK LEBLOND A HQ Conj: road Rubk. ??? = ABBEVILLE To-morrow 9.30 A.M. Inbad the tents at 9.0'clock. In afternoon Peter came - recreation fine. J.	
VILLERS L'HOPITAL	September 10th 1916		Left VACQUERIETTE at 2 a.m. Route taken Haye? ERQUIRES, QUOEU, HARIVESNES, BACHIMONT, BOIRE-AU-3015 NOEUX VILLERS L'HOPITAL. 10m 15 in 29th Division: 3 men of his Bill kd unhurt & halts for head & arrival of Batts 12.30 p.m. and 10 reason 9 Officer today unhurt & halts for head & arrival of Batts 12.30 p.m. and 10 reason 9 Officer mess to-morrow. weather fine. Steady up a little in the evening. J.K.	
VIGNACOURT	September 11th 1916		Left VILLERS L'HOPITAL at 7.30. Route taken FROHEN-LE-GRAND, FROHEN-LE-PETIT, LE MEILLARD, BERNAVILLE, CANAPLES, VIGNACOURT. 5 halts. each of CANAPLES 2 men had fits & unconfs one 2 cases sent to B.O Officer mess to-morrow. At 11.30 a.m. weather fair, quite hot. J.	
LAHOUSSOYE	September 12th 1916		Left VIGNACOURT at 11.30. Route taken VILLERS-BOCAGE-MOLLIENS-STAPTEN-QUERRIEU-PONT NOYELLES-LA NEUVILLE slashing hard. Road function ? mile N. of MOUTON VILLERS Arrived here at 1.30 p.m. on going through to villages of FLESSELLES HQ hard a narrow esc to water. One of the blasting paws/kicked & which Divisional 13th Echn music of off at 9 p.m. Post koll had as column was clear of VILLERS BOCAGE, a survey is not been allowed. At X 2000 6m R. M. of MOLLIENS a halt of ? how when ? taken. Roll ? taken - Road running ST ETIEN and had Still heavy wt. ?Koll??? ??? ?? QUERRIEU ??? ?? ?? ??? ??? ??? ???	

Army Form C. 2118.

WAR DIARY
INTELLIGENCE SUMMARY
(Erase heading not required.)

Sheet No. 4.

Instructions regarding War Diaries and Intelligence Summaries are contained in F.S. Regs., Part II. and the Staff Manual respectively. Title Pages will be prepared in manuscript.

Place	Date	Hour	Summary of Events and Information	Remarks and references to Appendices
LAHOUSSOYE	September 12th		After leaving diary to leave villages QUERRIEU & ONT-NOYEL E. came to a small tail on the way to LAMOTTE before entering the village. We halted & Major & myself went down a side lane to the hut to inspect possible guides for Brigades & returned. Was arrived at 8.15. at billet procured men horses all put & hut ½ 9.30. HQ. Q.M.S. & Qr at 9.m.I.O. cold wind & rain in place to chose "SAA" action & moved horses etc. to paddock. Quiet day. JR.	
LAHOUSSOYE	September 13th		Still in same billet. OC. OSC. went to Bd office. Came back with orders. Mentd. Staff & wrote more to be formed under R. Nevett & the 1st 33 Lancers. & & temps from Reserve Park were also brought to OC. OSC. & carry two days rations. Pack & Staff Officer ref 7.45 Q.M.S. 30 elect to day. Re Reserve Park & Ordered 9 S engr. repair at 9 a.m. Re OC & cyl. & used. to Q officer went text Ref "B" R.B. 4o & Cavalry Division would proceed in the morning. The next to meet tomorrow orders to move early to "B" R.B. at 7.45. All Ordnance sorts out. Sports to be given O. Mackenzie Capt OC. Mr Sherif C.S.O. R.A.V.C. ll. ad. S. O. about to office Supplies with orders 3rd & Cavalry Brigades & 10 Batten & all men to have in ordnance of any 5 days rations to be the cooked of tomorrow. To procure 16 horses ABEELE wagon etc. & Burkett & cyl. Quiet to day. JR.	
LAHOUSSOYE	September 14th		Still in same billet. OC & Sep. went to Bd office. Came out with more. Officer to tea & sort of Ordnance ret Oct. Officer from their afternoon orders one more to spread men lunch came & are got picks axes & the men to in 5.30 a.m. After Sunday we left to enchained from to men came back with orders at all men in to ordnance as some hence fall with one & wasn't good. JR.	

Instructions regarding War Diaries and Intelligence Summaries are contained in F. S. Regs., Part II. and the Staff Manual respectively. Title Pages will be prepared in manuscript.

WAR DIARY
or
~~INTELLIGENCE~~ SUMMARY

(Erase heading not required.)

Army Form C. 2118.

Sheet No 5.

Place	Date	Hour	Summary of Events and Information	Remarks and references to Appendices
September 15th 1916 ~~BILLET [illegible]~~ MEAULTE POSITION 50 yds N of C in VILLE-SOUS-CORBIE MAP Reference MAP 17 Scale 1/100,000			Left LAHOUSSOYE at 5-45 a.m. to follow 4th Cavalry Brigade [illegible] village [illegible] BONNAY. Lad [illegible] Machine Gun [illegible] while [illegible] ~~[illegible]~~ [illegible] ASC of we [illegible] Route taken. Starting Point [illegible] BONNAY [illegible] TREUX, VILLE-SOUS-CORBIE arriving at present billet 9.50. Mobile [illegible] also a small detachment of [illegible] Section. The Reserve [illegible] remained with "B" Echelon. After arriving in camp [illegible] camp. 9 Limbered G.S. wagon of S.A.A. Section Amm. Column [illegible] loaded with tents reported at 3 p.m. A.A. & Q.M.G. came [illegible] O.C. [illegible] issued to night as early as possible & cooks wagons to go back [illegible] night. rations were delivered to Divisional [illegible] 9 a.m. weather fine. [initials]	
September 16th 1916 POSITION 50 yds N of C in VILLE-SOUS-CORBIE MAP 17. Scale 1/100,000			Still in same billet. heavy bombardment last night & [illegible] most of the day. weather fine. [initials]	
September 17th 1916 POSITION 50 yds. N of C in VILLE-SOUS-CORBIE MAP 17. Scale 1/100,000			Still in same billet two German Aeroplanes came over the camp this morning. rations were delivered early & extra ½ rations of hay was ordered to be issued. O.C. [illegible] went to Railhead & Q office. A.A. & Q.M.G. was out. heavy bombardment last night. weather fine. towards evening looked like rain. [initials]	

2449 Wt. W14957/M90 750,000 1/16 J.B.C. & A. Forms/C.2118/12.

WAR DIARY or INTELLIGENCE SUMMARY

Army Form C. 2118.

Sheet No. 6.

(Erase heading not required.)

Place	Date	Hour	Summary of Events and Information	Remarks and references to Appendices
Position 30 yds N.W. of VILLE-SOUS-CORBIE. Map 17. Scale 100,000.	September 18th/1916		Still in same position, it started to rain last night & kept up all day attempts in a very bad state. No advance not to suppose as A & B Coys. Dug outs about 12.12 noon. The afternoon "B" Coy sent 4 reconnts. officers to move up to their positions to do.	Map 17. 33 x T. 30
Position 30 yds N.W. of VILLE-SOUS-CORBIE Map 17. Scale 100,000.	September 19th/1916		Still in same position. Several soft shells fell on my B.C. Coy's. position this morning. A.O.O.2 M.G. took over everything & arrived at position B.C.S. Nation's turn over down at 4-20 p.m. weather going from wet to day.	
Position 30 yds N.F. of VILLE-SOUS-CORBIE Map 17. Scale 100,000.	September 20th/1916		Still in same position. A heavy mist or [illegible] until 9-30 a.m. but would extend on to within 50 yds. went most of the day. No one [illegible] sent into front line to take by A. & [illegible] on the same day. Lost over two men wounded. Stations were relieved at 4.4.30 & been relieved relieving & finished 10.11.05	
Position 30 yds N.F. of VILLE-SOUS-CORBIE Map 17. Scale 100,000.	September 21st/1916		Still in same position. Heavy firing all going on. We will were in the up to left at 1 o'clock again. Batm'n. 3 been issued out 12:15 a.m. weather good.	

WAR DIARY
INTELLIGENCE SUMMARY

(Erase heading not required.)

Army Form C. 2118.

Place	Date	Hour	Summary of Events and Information	Remarks and references to Appendices
September 22 1916 Pozières N of G at VILLE-SOUS-CORBIE MAP 17 Sect 2			Still in same position. Very warm and sunny. Preparation to all the O.C.'s S.A.A. and 6 officers fall in for orders at day.	
September 23 1916 Pozières Sgym N & G VILLE S/S C. CORBIE MAP 17. Sect			Still in same position. 30 O.R.S. and 6 O Officer's attended divine services L. Return was hostile L.	
September 24 1916 Pozières Sgym N & C in VILLE-SOUS-CORBIE MAP 17. Sect	7/10 pm		Still in same position. Orders came about noon with new details of the movement. At left orders later about 4 o'clock. Self in readiness to move by 9.30 pm. 8. Q Office. Orders came at 8 p.m. for to leave A & 10.12.30 a.m for action. The ready to move in position Rolin a time, was near a fine, sent 8 & co to contact ...	
September 25 1916 Pozières Sgym N. G in VILLE-SOUS-CORBIE MAP 17 Sect	10/10 pm		Still in same position. At 6am Rev. T. Lunn 33 were summed services in small Square officers and men. Move from 12.30 pm. Bn. arrived 10.30 pm in Square. Bn spent 10.30 pm to 1 a.m. of C. got down to sleep in the camp. I dropped 4 bombs close to the O.C. Lt Q & a in Camp T.Q.& there is an drainage not however. The army coming went through & our artillery came out. To continue a night. & removed to Bill 11.30 p.m arm. Key was very good over to continue right. Raiders were released at 9.30 p.m on but short of far arm & sera. R.	

Army Form C. 2118.

WAR DIARY
or
INTELLIGENCE SUMMARY.

(Erase heading not required.)

Instructions regarding War Diaries and Intelligence Summaries are contained in F. S. Regs., Part II. and the Staff Manual respectively. Title Pages will be prepared in manuscript.

Place	Date	Hour	Summary of Events and Information	Remarks and references to Appendices
Left in Beaumetz-lès-Loges Position 57° to N.t.S. in VILLE-SUR-CORBIE MAP.17.d.0.6.	September 26th 1916.		Still in Beaumetz-lès-Loges. The March 8 hours - Intended halted at 4½ hours at remained for the night near GUEUDECOURT, LESBOEUFS, COMBLES & THIEPVAL taken maintained	Scheme No. 41 MORVAL &
Position 57° to N.t.S. in VILLE-SUR-CORBIE MAP.17.d.0.6.	September 27th 1916.		Still in same position. Lieut. Crosby marched each Group aircraft - Bulag of officer Suit of B officers to the machine & fitted adjusted the pilot to the afternoon word came last night that K.B. S Co. had one driver 5.7.24 (A short flag) of our advance are Corps had seen machine lives	
September 28th 1916 Position 57° to N.t.S. in VILLE-SUR-CORBIE MAP.17. d.0.6.			Still in same position. Returned his morning. 2 a.a.a to remove to see open at 10 o'clock. Lord Ronald & has written they leave on the leave manual J.S. & Selections parts & make arrangements for the following week. 3 great conversations came of Lieut. two officers moved a day so might be seen twelve aleman follows by Major Pridit. Lieut, Capt Kelly & Macefield the flying service were III Corps. Staff Lieut. & Major Capt) E.N.M BIRCH been to have the flight decons. pm III Corps Hor & Such Staff Sept 2nd & a.c.	
Left Ville-sur-Corbie Position 37° to N.t.S. in VILLE-SUR-CORBIE MAP.17.d.0.6.	Sept 29th 1916.		Lieutenant Landon Schwab for delivery Supplies & Reserves. Lt. Ord made of Aeroplane for part. Lt. N. yet our 1917/ph. Lt. 2nd Car made MORVAL beamed out & can but 2nd Lt. CORRIE Hq shown at the MORVAL beamed and Letter R.E. Ration from	

Army Form C. 2118.

WAR DIARY
INTELLIGENCE SUMMARY

(Erase heading not required.)

Place	Date	Hour	Summary of Events and Information	Remarks and references to Appendices
Anterior Royal N° 2 LUMELIE-SOUS-CORBIE Map M. Ref.	25th September	10 a.m.	[illegible handwritten entries]	

SECRET.

Vol 4

WAR DIARY.

of

H.Q. 2nd CAVALRY DIVL. A.S. CORPS.

OCTOBER, 1916.

VOL. XXVI.

VOL XXVI

Army Form C. 2118.

WAR DIARY
INTELLIGENCE SUMMARY
(Erase heading not required.)

Headquarters 2nd Cav. Div.

Instructions regarding War Diaries and Intelligence Summaries are contained in F. S. Regs., Part II. and the Staff Manual respectively. Title Pages will be prepared in manuscript.

Place	Date	Hour	Summary of Events and Information	Remarks and references to Appendices
	1st October Sunday			
Bouleux in VILLE-SUR-CARNE	5/7/16	m.p.e.	Still in same position. O.C. attd went to Brigade 2.0.3.4 a.m. Alright. 3rd & 5th Cavalry Bdes moved on to the line. O.O.302/16 when same was to Bielleuve Wood M 26/05 & 4	
Mot. M.T. Road		10.30 a.m	Proformer of 1st Cay Brigade moved tomorrow also Supply Column & relieved to LEDEGHEM to release rations moves also being made the great	f.R.
	2nd October Monday			
Bouleux in VILLE-SOUS-CORNE	5/12/N5.C		Still in same position. Os all mem as yesterday. 3rd & 5th Brigades drew rations O.O 302/16 & Supply Column moved to E.O.M. Hornsmate G.1.F.H &	f.R.
Mot M.T. Road		7.30 am		
			No 1 Gere M.T. Regt ADDED wire too arrived hard all low	f.R.
	3rd October Tuesday			
Bouleux in VILLE-SOUS-CORNE	5/12 N5 C		Still in same position. Os all men as yesterday & in office 2.0.3.4 & 5 on above & the 6 office Cmn of Comon date to O.O.R.A.S. all 3rd Brigades. Drew 6 Supply from arriving in the early morning 1 covered M.T. was also received Weather Shorny -	f.R.
Mot M.T. Ab 5		7.30 am		
	4th October Wednesday			
Bouleux in VILLE-SOUS-CORNE	5/12 N5 C		Still in same position 2.0.0.5. called in the afternoon. That cypring paries from Horrnilus.	
Mot M.T. Road		7.30 am	Orders in turn on returning to 61.45 M.T. Paper from Railroad II.1 moved Weather turned most all day.	f.R.

Army Form C. 2118.

WAR DIARY
INTELLIGENCE SUMMARY
(Erase heading not required.)

Lieut. W. R. [signature]

Instructions regarding War Diaries and Intelligence Summaries are contained in F.S. Regs., Part II. and the Staff Manual respectively. Title Pages will be prepared in manuscript.

Place	Date	Hour	Summary of Events and Information	Remarks and references to Appendices
Pavilion 597 MFC VILLE-SOUS-CORBIE Map 17. Scale 1/40000	5th October Thursday	2 a.m.	Still in 2 a.m. position. No alert. Sent B.Q. office into Bertrang. O.C. A.T. saw Gen. Portugal. 8 new alert. Surprise inventory. 47 Belgian soldiers to every day. Men weather shown in morning. Gave no infantry P.B.	
Pavilion 60yrs MFC VILLE-SOUS-CORBIE Map 17. Scale 1/40000	6th October Friday		Still in same position. O.C. & Staff went to Rainford. S.O.K. company meeting in mess. Gen. Shaw about Kerneny P.B.	
Pavilion 59th MFC VILLE-SOUS-CORBIE Map 17. Scale 1/40000	7th October Saturday		Still in same position. No other events. Went to B. Office. Some leave has been granted. "B" Division to draw stores from same northend at Reveren. Expected to start on the Yralenp weather fair. Gave surprise Reveren in a cordon. P.B.	
Pavilion 59th MFC VILLE-SOUS-CORBIE Map 17. Scale 1/40000	8th October Sunday		Still in same position. Infantry traim very late. Did not arrive until 2.30 a.m. Coal Div. Palat. About 4.30. owing to 2 Infantry Divisions having to load first. O.C. of S.C. went to Rainford. Road about here is being heavy traffic in afternoon. Weather broiling. Wet wind in night & a still wind tending to still traffic. day. P.B.	

WAR DIARY / INTELLIGENCE SUMMARY

Army Form C. 2118.

(Erase heading not required.)

Place	Date	Hour	Summary of Events and Information	Remarks and references to Appendices
9th October Monday Poulainville N.9.2. in VILLE-SOUS-CORBIE Map 17. Scale 1/100,000			Still in same position with train 3 hours late owing to morning. A.O. & A.V.S. called at 1.30 a.m. Reserve Park have 5 men in arrest, suspicions to mooring. Reserve Park Station in mess. Early and became fair. Ration to men & baking soap. Reserve Park sent Field Bakery to 12th Brigade 3rd Cavalry Brigade ration to Reserve Park to fr. 17 May orders received from Sure.	
10th October Tuesday Poulainville N.9.2. in VILLE-SOUS-CORBIE Map 17. Scale 1/100,000			Still in same position. Reserve Park moved off this morning straight to the [illegible] direction. 4th Cav. Brigade Supply Train arrived at 11 am. RHA HQ 3 Batteries RHA a Pontoon Column RHA (Sup'l Column of the light Column) moved to S.26.C.C. (A 18 Reims sheet plan) Weather fine.	
11th October Wednesday Poulainville N.9.2. in VILLE-SOUS-CORBIE Map 17. Scale 1/100,000			Still in same position. O.C.A.S.C. went to Q. Office SAA Section of ammunition column on Brigade of the HQ A.S.C. & Camp Commandant were morning June afternoon officers went again to the Car Brigade HQ at Beaupont.	
12th October Thursday Poulainville N.9.2. in VILLE-SOUS-CORBIE Map 17. Scale 1/100,000			Still in same position. O.C. A.S.C. went to ampere Divisional of the 3rd Cavalry Brigade Called this morning a fraud of about plan for railing a called again to operation about number of men to take over the June.	

Army Form C. 2118.

WAR DIARY
or
INTELLIGENCE SUMMARY
(Erase heading not required.)

Shut. No. 4

Instructions regarding War Diaries and Intelligence Summaries are contained in F.S. Regs., Part II. and the Staff Manual respectively. Title Pages will be prepared in manuscript.

Place	Date	Hour	Summary of Events and Information	Remarks and references to Appendices
Positions 5yds N of C. in VILLE-SOUS-CORBIE. Map.17. Scale 1/100,000	13th October Friday		Still in same position. O.C. A.S.C. went to R.R. office to have held in conference. Also supply officers meeting at H.Q. A.S.C. A.D.O.S. and Maj. G. H.Q. A.S.C. went to troops. weather fine. F.S.	1st 24-5th (?) Bde Brigade 11th 23rd & 24th H.Q. A.S.C. went to troops. All cleared by 12 a.m.
Positions 5yds N of C. in VILLE-SOUS-CORBIE. Map.17. Scale 1/100,000	14th October Saturday		Still in same position. O.C. A.S.C. went to Railhead. Supplies train arrived at 10 a.m. All cleared by 12 a.m. weather fine. F.S.	
Positions 5yds N of C. in VILLE-SOUS-CORBIE. Map.17. Scale 1/100,000	15th October Sunday		Still in same position. O.C. A.S.C. went to Q. office near our station. A.A. & Q.M.G. went to see us today. Place was chosen for railhead. weather fine. F.S.	
Positions 5yds N of C. in VILLE-SOUS-CORBIE. Map.17. Scale 1/100,000	16th October Monday		Still in same position. D.A.A. & Q.M.S. came to H.Q. A.S.C. in the office. to find out anything troops might wish for. Came our about half an hour. weather fine but very cold. Aeroplanes were our again last night. 9 fire but were driven off by ouy guns fire. F.S.	

WAR DIARY
INTELLIGENCE SUMMARY
(Erase heading not required.)

Army Form C. 2118.

Instructions regarding War Diaries and Intelligence Summaries are contained in F.S. Regs., Part II. and the Staff Manual respectively. Title Pages will be prepared in manuscript.

Place	Date	Hour	Summary of Events and Information	Remarks and references to Appendices
Position Boyde. N. of C. in VILLE-SOUS-CORBIE. Map 17. Scale 1/100,000	17th October Tuesday		Still in same position. An asst. and H.Q. officer was shown back area but line of movers, not known from schou corrected by to Reserve Park to be moved from the present billets to field units to A.R.A.C.B. Move to take place tomorrow see line shown on map.	
Position Boyde. N. of C. VILLE-SOUS-CORBIE Map 17 Scale 1/100,000	18th October Wednesday		Still in same position. Reserve Park moved on to field unit B.A.R.A.C.B. everything moved by 3.30 a.m. weather bad. Rained hard in the morning fairly fine in the afternoon. JR.	
Position Boyde. N. of C. in VILLE-SOUS-CORBIE Map 17. Scale 1/100,000	19th October Thursday		Still in same position. An asst. and H.Q. office had new area marked on map. weather very bad. Rained hard all day. JR.	
Position Boyde. A. N. of C. in VILLE-SOUS-CORBIE Map 17 Scale 1/100,000	20th October Friday		Still in same position. An asst. S.S.O. went to "H ARMY" Hrs AQHST. Sn/14 officers meeting held at H.A.A.C.C. H.Q. also held. Weather fine, very cold last night. JR.	
Position Boyde. N. of C. in VILLE-SOUS-CORBIE Map 17. Scale 1/100,000	21st October Saturday		Still in same position. An asst. H.Q. officer supt. shown to 6. stay. Army joining at aeroplane. but night weather fine very good. JR.	

Army Form C. 2118.

WAR DIARY
INTELLIGENCE SUMMARY
(Erase heading not required.)

Sheet No. 6

Instructions regarding War Diaries and Intelligence Summaries are contained in F. S. Regs., Part II. and the Staff Manual respectively. Title Pages will be prepared in manuscript.

Place	Date	Hour	Summary of Events and Information	Remarks and references to Appendices
Position Sqda No.1 C. in VILLE-SOUS-CORBIE. Map.17. Scale 1/10,000	22nd October Sunday		Still in same position. O.C. A.S.C. went forward the Supply Officer. Attempts 6 reinforcements arrived. Weather fine, still very cold. F.R.	
Position Sqda. N⁰ 1 C. in VILLE-SOUS-CORBIE. Map.17. Scale 1/10,000	23rd October Monday		Still in same position. O.C. A.S.C. went to H.Q. office. nothing to report. R.O.'s & go down to men. Area Morillon Ypres but very foggy in the morning. F.R.	
Position Sqda. N⁰ 1 C. in VILLE-SOUS-CORBIE. Map.17. Scale 1/10,000	24th October Tuesday	10p.m.	Still in same position. O.C. meeting. Held at 2 o'clock. Camp about R.O.S. parry. Orders to new area. O.C. A.S.C. went to 5 Cavalry Brigade all in the afternoon to Divisional Troops went to Mrs. area though high good report. Cancelled. R.O. party down from area. weather. Rained hard all day. F.	
Position Sqda. N⁰ 1 C. in VILLE-SOUS-CORBIE. Map.17. Scale 1/10,000	25th October Wednesday	10p.m.	Still in same position. O.C. A.S.C. went to Q office. everything in very good order. Heavy shelling by the germans this morning 9 of women & a Colonel. DERNANCOURT. Weather. Rained most of day. F.	

Army Form C. 2118.

WAR DIARY
or
INTELLIGENCE SUMMARY

(Erase heading not required.)

Sheet No. 7

Place	Date	Hour	Summary of Events and Information	Remarks and references to Appendices
Position 29910 M.4.e. in VILLE-SOUS-CORBIE Map. 17 Scale 1/10,000	26th October Thursday		Still in same position. O.C. O.S.C. went to Siege Offices & office. About other weather but rained most of day. Still very cold. R.	F.A.O.6. Q.705
2nd Bastion Infantry Position 29910 M.4.e. VILLE-SOUS-CORBIE Map. 17 Scale 1/10,000	27th Friday		Still in same position. O.C. O.S.C. went to D Office & Mess. Put on fires 15 minutes. S.S.O. went to new area. Suffy Column received a photo from army. Rat Ration coming Fair. Weather still too moist. B.W. moving. Siege mountain day. Still very cold. T & C. Lieutenant H. E. Perkin-Reynor A.S.C. joined 2 Car's Siege Suffy Column from Capt of Inventors Norton, to take place of Lt. C. Suell A.S.C. struck off strength of D.A.S.E. 7.15.10.16 transmitted to Paid. R.	
28th Saturday		Still in same position. Suffy Officer meeting held at H.Q. Office 2 Lieutenant. T. Land L. R.H. and S.A. left in England at 6 a.m. today. Report at war office. Weather though 3 Batteries + 3 Brigade BAC moved back into Here. also Battery area. "D" Battery and 6. 3" Can. Bde. to offices came that 2 "B" Car Seventh Ammunition Park move to move to R. 2. A.C.D. ALBERT, confirmed that. R.	
Position 29910 M.4.e. VILLE-SOUS-CORBIE Map. 17 Scale 1/10,000	29th October Sunday		Still in same position. O.C. O.S.C. went to D Office. Q. Office during morning & informed of R.F.2 A.C.&D. ALBERT confirmed that 2 enemy aeroplanes provionced most of day. Very cold. R. Suffy down about 1 p.m. later, weather.	

Army Form C. 2118.

WAR DIARY
INTELLIGENCE SUMMARY

Sheet No. 8.

(Erase heading not required.)

Instructions regarding War Diaries and Intelligence Summaries are contained in F. S. Regs., Part II. and the Staff Manual respectively. Title Pages will be prepared in manuscript.

Place	Date	Hour	Summary of Events and Information	Remarks and references to Appendices
Position 57yds N of C in VILLE-SOUS-CORBIE. Maf. M. Edel. 1/40,000	30th October Monday		Still in same position. OC A/C went to 6th Cavalry Brgde. weather showery in the morning. 2 heavy showers in the afternoon &c.	
Position 57yds N.E. in VILLE-SOUS-CORBIE. Maf. M. Edel. 1/40,000	31st October Tuesday		Still in same position. OC A/C went to DHQ office a.a. & m. aint. weather. yest. June ft. Grey Lt. Ag't H.Q. A.S.C. 2nd Cav. Div.	

SECRET.

Vol 5

WAR DIARY

of

HEADQUARTERS, 2nd CAVALRY DIVISIONAL A.S.C.

NOVEMBER, 1916.

VOL. XXVII.

WAR DIARY
INTELLIGENCE SUMMARY
(Erase heading not required.)

Army Form C. 2118.

Instructions regarding War Diaries and Intelligence Summaries are contained in F.S. Regs., Part II. and the Staff Manual respectively. Title Pages will be prepared in manuscript.

Sheet No. 1.   VOLUME XXVII

Place	Date	Hour	Summary of Events and Information	Remarks and references to Appendices
VILLE-SOUS-CORBIE Map. 17. Scale 100,000 Position 50yds N.of C.in	November 1st Wednesday		Still in same position. O.C. a.s.c. & S.S.O. went to Q office. a letter alluding in new area R.O. of Div. Insp. left for new area. They all leg for later of incoming weather. Phones quiet in the morning. T Lt. H. Pepper A.S.C. report to the acme H.T. Comp. to take the place of Lt. M (Read) J.A. Smith S.R. A.S.C. P.R.	
VILLE-SOUS-CORBIE Map. 17. Scale 100,000 Position 50yds N.of C.in	November 2nd Thursday		Still in same position. O.C. a.s.c. went to see Ammunition Park. Part of Divisional H.Q. moved to-day. Situation fair. much warmer. P.R.	
VILLE-SOUS-CORBIE Map. 17. Scale 100,000 Position 50yds N.of C.in	November 3rd Friday	(10/10/0)	Still in same position. O.C. a.s.c. went to Q office in the morning. 9 lorries & 1 box car (Seeley Bros) W.O. in charge of 2 men. Artr of H.R. moved today. A.a. & Q.M.G come over in the morning. see O.C. a.s.c. 10 Reserve Park. report to R. 2n Cavalry Division Y.M.R 4 lorries. 114 mules 53 horses. more details yet. still weather had rained most of day. P.R.	
VILLE-SOUS-CORBIE Map. 17. Scale 100,000 Position 50yds M/C in	November 4th Thursday	(10/10/0)	Still in same position. O.C. a.s.c. went to Q office. weather. had rained most of day.	

2449 Wt. W14957/M90 750,000 1/16 J.B.C. & A. Forms/C.2118/12.

WAR DIARY
INTELLIGENCE SUMMARY
(Erase heading not required.)

Army Form C. 2118.

Instructions regarding War Diaries and Intelligence Summaries are contained in F. S. Regs., Part II. and the Staff Manual respectively. Title Pages will be prepared in manuscript.

Place	Date	Hour	Summary of Events and Information	Remarks and references to Appendices
Position 57pk N.17.C. VILLE-SOUS-CORBIE. Map.57. Scale 1/40,000	November 5th Sunday		Still in same position. O.C. A.& Q., A.A. & Q.M.G. came to see O.C. A.S.C. Major Softly. Column left at 11.30am. Divisional Supply Division handed over. Rations this afternoon. Weather fair. Wind somewhat showery.	
Position 57pk N.17.C. VILLE-SOUS-CORBIE. Map.57. Scale 1/40,000	November 6th Monday		Still in same position. O.C. A.S.C. went to Q office attending the Division move on the 8th /Wednesday. H. sent of ration of the Motor Supply Column who sent out the 2nd Brigade & the Bristol lorries discharged at 7.30am. This afternoon. Ammn.H.T. received orders & Army Ammunition at VIGNIER MILL to Memonned & later packed as usual for weather fair.	
Position 50gm N.17.C. in VILLE-SOUS-CORBIE. Map.57. Scale 1/40,000	November 7th Tuesday		Still in same position. O.C. A.S.C. went to Q office. Orders arrived. The Division move tomorrow. "B" Ech. to send another O.C. A.S.C. weather fair morning, showery in the afternoon. J.	
BUSSY-LES-DAOURS.	November 8th Wednesday		Moved off this morning at 10 o'clock and started marking from 10.30. Held up for ½ hour owing to eighty German Prisoners. Route taken TREUX, MERICOURT, CORBIE, LA NEUVILLE-DAOURS, BUSSY. The roads were in a very bad condition, + the rain being against us that the Cavalry Brigade passing through MERICOURT + another just ahead BONNAY along, spoilt well. We got into BUSSY after leaving CORBIE & Chem arrived through marching + being late at night when the bombs were very thick for the H.T. to get safe but this were all clear to H.Q. are now an hour field by 6 p.m. but arrived at BUSSY at 14.45. The Germans came along very slick + another the road behind their Army to after we are prepared by	

2449 Wt. W14957/M90 750,000 1/16 J.B.C. & A. Forms/C.2118/22

WAR DIARY / INTELLIGENCE SUMMARY

Army Form C. 2118.

Sheet No. 3

Place	Date	Hour	Summary of Events and Information	Remarks and references to Appendices
BELLOY-SUR-SOMME	November 9th Thursday		Moved off this morning at 7 o'clock. "B" Echelon had long halts on the main road before getting to starting point 8.5 a.m. 3rd Cavalry Brigade moving off in front. Route taken: LAMOTTE, LA CHAUSSÉE, BELLOU-SUR-SOMME. Halts spent one of Artillery Journal, one Brigade entering AMIENS, one after passing through Artillery Column to clear up, one in AILLY-SUR-SOMME were part Regt of Column washed in ST SAUVEUR were the remainder of Column. Arrived at the entrance to BELLOY. "B" Ech of Brigade arrived Billeting Brigadier H.Q. arrived at 3.18 p.m. Have spent well ahead roads Routes bad on yesterday weather fine. J.R.	Starting point 1½ miles N of ST PIERRE, AMIENS, AILLY, ST SAUVEUR
BONNEVAL	November 10th Friday		Moved off this morning at 9 o'clock. Had long halt on the main road from BELLOY. Cavalry Brigade moving out. Arrived at starting point Cross roads 2 miles S.E of FLIXECOURT were the 3rd Cavalry Brigade. "B" Echelon ushered ahead H.Q. and 2 adv H.T.Coy and 4th Cavalry Brigade. "B" Echelon. Route taken FLIXECOURT, AILLY, ABBEVILLE ABBEY ≡ BUIGNY-ST-MACLOU, BONNEVAL. Halts spent Halt after entering MOUFLERS through FLIXECOURT. 4th Cavalry Brigade "B" on this halt. Halt become public entering MOUFLERS. Kits were not long on account of H. Cav Bde. "A" Echelon arriving 2 Bde of C. Billy moved H.Q Car & adv. H.T Conf ordered ahead of Bde. Yn. 1 hour. 5 of Cavalry Bgd. "B" spent on the Am Brigades H. K of? Pref Duranville. ABBEVILLE. 5th. after training through entrance at the ABBEY. Found narrow. new billets ordered at new billets 6.30 p.m. also had another long halt at BUIGNY and somebody sent out order after the arrival at new Billets of BONNEVAL. road from post — 3 very bad hills. Horses going well. Weather fine. J.R.	Starting point 2 miles S.E of FLIXECOURT
DOMPIERRE	November 11th Saturday		Moved off this morning at 8 o'clock. H.Q. and 4 Cav. adv H.T. Conf arrived at starting point 8.30. Four miles N of BUIGNY. ST MACLOU. Route taken. HAUTVILLERS, LAMOTTE-BULEUX FOREST-LA BOAYE, CRECY, NADICOURT, DOMPIERRE. Halt at starting one before entering CRECY, one at CRECY were the Column attacked. Column commanded of Space Q Cart H.T.Conf. One first after leaving WADICOURT. Some horses of H.Q. Conf were tired but the rest came along very well. Roads quite good. Arrived in billets at 12 W A.M. weather fine J.R.	Starting point 4 miles N of BUIGNY

Army Form C. 2118.

WAR DIARY
INTELLIGENCE SUMMARY
(Erase heading not required.)

Shrut. N.H.

Place	Date	Hour	Summary of Events and Information	Remarks and references to Appendices
DOMPIERRE	November 12th Sunday		Still in same billet. O.C. A.S.C. went to Q offices next holiday spent in firing up horses & mens of H.Q. A.S.C. & Assoc. H.T. Comp. weather fine. Cloudy overhead. JR	the RC wagn
DOMPIERRE	November 13th Monday		Still in same billet. O.C. Assoc H.T. Comp. came over about mess billets. Spent evening [?] Entrait [?] map offices to Qu Base A.D.& D.M.S. & attempted for their anoure [?] horses weather fine cloudy overhead. JR	
DOMPIERRE	November 14th Tuesday		Still in same billet. O.C. are went to Q. offices. Assoc H.T. Comp. fixed up with new billets. G.O.I.m of cycle arrived last night for C.O. Divisional train. weather fine. Shans of Quarter. JR	
DOMPIERRE	November 15th Wednesday		Still in same billet. O.C. A.S.C. went to refinement at 3rd Cavalry Brigade rec a few funs leaving coys. JR	
DOMPIERRE	November 16th Thursday		Still in same billet. O.C. arc as S.S.O. went to Q. offices when on leave about the arrival from the base McCREDY. S.S.O. went to Cavalry Corps in the afternoon. weather fine. Little frost last night. JR	
DOMPIERRE	November 17th Friday		Still in same billet. Supply Officer meeting held at H.Q. A.S.C. offices at 8.a.m. weather fine gentle a hard frost last night. JR	
DOMPIERRE	November 18th Saturday		Still in same billet. O.C. are went to Q. offices. Divisional troops started to leave heating up billets for mounted Infantry & the S.O. Arrived & reheired to railhead. putting the first on [?]. Section. The new S.O.C. arrived att S. Divisional troops from his morning. Divisional troops were all ehear by dep. atten very bad in the morning. Road post last night a driving blizzard which was very trying to Kaplin. [?]	

WAR DIARY or INTELLIGENCE SUMMARY

Army Form C. 2118.

Sheet No. 3

Place	Date	Hour	Summary of Events and Information	Remarks and references to Appendices
DOMPIERRE.	November 19th Sunday.		Still in same billet. 20.3rd Cavalry Brigade came over see about bay for his Brigade arranged for him to draw from 3rd Cavalry Brigade area. Tomorrow weather fine much milder. J.R.	
DOMPIERRE.	November 20th Monday.		Still in same billet. A.D. A.S.C. went to Q. office weather fine J.R.	
DOMPIERRE.	November 21st Tuesday.		Still in same billet. O.C. A.C. went to see wood delivered to Brigades Col. Duffy Colonel Parker this morning weather fine J.R.	
DOMPIERRE.	November 22nd Wednesday.		Still in same billet. O.C. A.C. went to R office weather fine J.R.	
DOMPIERRE.	November 23rd Thursday.		Still in same billet 6 wagons of A.C.C. H.T. Coy. dispatched Armoy to satisfying requirements of 3rd Cav. Bde. for a Tarrant weather fine J.R.	
DOMPIERRE.	November 24th Friday.		Still in same billet. O.C. A.S.C. went to Q. office. 4 officers meeting held at H.Q. office at F.P.M. weather fine morning rain rest of day. J.R.	
DOMPIERRE.	November 25th Saturday.		Still in same billet. O.C. A.C. went to Q. office. A.D.S.T. Col. Col. called this morning 6 wagons J.S. of Ammunition Column placed at disposal of M.E. and S.Q. weather very mild J.R.	

2449 Wt. W14957/M90 750,000 1/16 J.B.C. & A. Forms/C.2118/12.

WAR DIARY. Sheet No. 6.

Army Form C. 2118.

INTELLIGENCE SUMMARY
(Erase heading not required.)

Place	Date	Hour	Summary of Events and Information	Remarks and references to Appendices
DOMPIERRE	November 26 Sunday		Still in same billet. 1 wagon sent by Aux. M.T. Coy. to attend to Divisional School. weather wet all day. JR.	
DOMPIERRE	November 27 Monday		Still in same billet OC a.e. sent to B office weather fine & party JR.	
DOMPIERRE	November 28 Tuesday		Still in same billet. detachment of 1st & 5th Car Res Park from Hd Qr Car Res Park. 1 officer Lieut. L. Russe. Major, A.S.C. HE Other Ranks H. motor Lorries, 34 L.D. & 13 wagons 5 x 3 pr. Ac Car Res Park. 1 officer 2nd Lieut. A.W.R. Miller A.V.C., 4 Other Ranks 4 motor Lorries 69 L.D. & 13 wagons Hk. detachment arrived Dist at 9 a.m. having been at hour billets MARICOURT and now Hk. attached to the 2nd Cavalry Division OC a.e. & Lieuten. or the post detachment 2 now billeted in same house & party JR.	
DOMPIERRE	November 29 Wednesday		Still in same billet OC a.e. sent to B office officers of the Reserve Parks called at Hk. office weather fine JR.	
DOMPIERRE	November 30 Thursday		Still in same billet. One one wagon detailed from our HK coy. for Divisional School as usual weather. JR.	

Diary Pt & 4 9t
H.Q. a.s.c.
2n Car Div.

CONFIDENTIAL.

WAR DIARY

of

HEADQUARTERS, 2nd CAVALRY DIVISIONAL A.S.C.

DECEMBER, 1916.

VOL. XXVIII.

Army Form C. 2118.

WAR DIARY
INTELLIGENCE SUMMARY

(Erase heading not required.)

HEADQUARTERS,
2nd CAVALRY DIVN.
A.S.C.

Vol. XXVIII

Instructions regarding War Diaries and Intelligence Summaries are contained in F. S. Regs., Part II and the Staff Manual respectively. Title Pages will be prepared in manuscript.

Place	Date	Hour	Summary of Events and Information	Remarks and references to Appendices
DOMPIERRE.	December 1st Friday.		Still in same billet. O.C. A.S.C. to Q office. Supply officers meeting held at H.Q. a.a.o. office weather fine. JR.	
DOMPIERRE.	December 2nd Saturday.		Still in same billet. O.C. A.S.C. went to Q office on Cavalry Corps instructions. Fine. JR.	
DOMPIERRE.	December 3rd Sunday.		Still in same billet. A.R. Supply Column called in the afternoon. Weather fine JR.	
DOMPIERRE.	December 4th Monday.		Still in same billet. O.C. a.a.c. went to Q officers on absence Capt Bamber on sick to be attached temporary to Cavalry Corp. weather fine JR.	
DOMPIERRE.	December 5th Tuesday.		Still in same billet. O.C. a.a.c. went to Q office in forenoon. Capt H.W. Bridgard went to said of Capt. on temporary duty. Pack Rations arrived late kept out up till 9pm. the A.D.M.E. weather fine morning less officers in the afternoon. JR.	
DOMPIERRE.	December 6th Wednesday		Still in same billet. O.C. a.a.c & A.D.O. went to Q office. D.C. & Rly. journal H.Q. came to temporary duty with Capt W. Bridgard during a weather fine JR.	
DOMPIERRE.	December 7th Thursday		Still in same billet. O.C. a.a.c. went to Q office. also went to MEADICOURT for stables 2 P.G. of Res Parks weather fine turning cold again JR.	

Army Form C. 2118.

WAR DIARY
or
INTELLIGENCE SUMMARY

(Erase heading not required.)

Instructions regarding War Diaries and Intelligence Summaries are contained in F.S. Regs., Part II. and the Staff Manual respectively. Title Pages will be prepared in manuscript.

HEADQUARTERS
2ND CAVALRY DIV.
A.S.C.
VOL XXVIII

Place	Date	Hour	Summary of Events and Information	Remarks and references to Appendices
DOMPIERRE.	December 8th Friday		Still in same billet. O.C. A.S.C. went to Q office. Supply officers meeting held at H.Q A.S.C. office at 6.30 p.m. Baggage fresh details settled re day sweating arrangement of day. J.R.	
DOMPIERRE.	December 9th Saturday		Still in same billet. O.C. A.S.C. went to Q office. O.C. Supply column talked over arrangements for a conf. re meet of Supply column. No news the bus arranged that the last reinforcement of Supply 75 has arrived. J.R.	
DOMPIERRE.	December 10th Sunday		Still in same billet. O.C. A.S.C. went to Q office, and went round infantry lines. 11, 2, & 6 R.F. talked to morning, wire secured last night. The Div staff they will likely be moving up from here before X-mas. J.R.	
DOMPIERRE.	December 11th Monday		Still in same billet. O.C. A.S.C. went to Q office and to S.C.O & Bill Post, the Div will probably be in-Crops states Q offr, arrived on to Div & weather showery. J.R.	
DOMPIERRE.	December 12th Tuesday		Still in same billet. O.C. A.S.C. went to see the Lt Col at H.Q Bde. Perkins, no sick & stormy weather, snowing part of the morning, worked with him & continued part of day. J.R.	
DOMPIERRE	December 13th Wednesday		Still in same billet. O.C. A.R.C. went to Q in the morning, Mr Supply between guard & Squadron parade, fairly fine, a little rain. J.R.	
DOMPIERRE	December 14th Thursday		Still in same billet. O.C. A.S.C. went to Q office & then on to Railhead, O.C. Supply Column called in the morning, weather had cold & snowed most of day. J.R.	
DOMPIERRE	December 15th Friday		Still in same billet. An O.C. went to Q office. O.C. Supply Column came over to Spm. Supply Officers meeting held at H.Q at 5 p.m. was fair. Snow covered all day. J.R.	

WAR DIARY
INTELLIGENCE SUMMARY

(Erase heading not required.)

Army Form C. 2118.

Place	Date	Hour	Summary of Events and Information	Remarks and references to Appendices
DOMPIERRE	December 16th Saturday		Still in same billet. OC ASC went to R. office this morning. Weather fine. F.L.	
DOMPIERRE	December 17th Sunday		Still in same billet. in the infantry weather fine. Intercept. F.L.	
DOMPIERRE	December 18th Monday		Still in same billet. OC ASC went to R office. Weather fine. Intercept. F.L.	
DOMPIERRE	December 19th Tuesday		Still in same billet. OC ASC went in the afternoon here. the distance of the platoon in my good order was for for morning a little dinner fell in the afternoon F.L.	
DOMPIERRE	December 20th Wednesday		Still in same billet. OC ASC went to R office this morning. Snow was trying the evening with SLO weather fine very cold. F.L.	
DOMPIERRE	December 21st Thursday		Still in same billet. OC Coffy Officer called at HQ on office this morning. weather fine quite mild again F.L.	
DOMPIERRE	December 22nd Friday		Still in same billet. OC ASC went to R office. New sport scheme was sought out also again. weather Shower quite mild. F.L.	
DOMPIERRE	December 23rd Saturday		Still in same billet. OC ASC went to Q office in the morning and inspected for the parks in the afternoon. weather rained most of day. F.L.	

WAR DIARY
or
INTELLIGENCE SUMMARY
(Erase heading not required.)

Army Form C. 2118.

Sheet No. 4

Place	Date	Hour	Summary of Events and Information	Remarks and references to Appendices
DOMPIERRE	December 24th Saturday		Still in same billet. Two convoys of rations to-day. Rebellion known on ammo. colony weather fairly fine a little rain. JF	
DOMPIERRE	December 25th Monday		Still in same billet. O.C. A.S.C. went to H.Q. Officer, word came that Christmas escort went off on the A.S.C. weather fine. JF	
DOMPIERRE	December 26th Sunday		Still in same billet. O.C. A.S.C. went to "A" office in the morning. D.A.A. & Q.M.G. called this morning. Weather gone very dismal rest of day. JF.	
DOMPIERRE	December 27th Wednesday		Still in same billet. O.C. A.S.C. went to "A" office in the morning. Heavy fall of snow last night. JF	
DOMPIERRE	December 28th Thursday		Still in same billet. A.A. & Q.M.G. called in this morning also O.C. Supply Column. weather very cold morning. Hard frost last night, started train in afternoon. JF.	
DOMPIERRE	December 29th Friday		Still in same billet. O.C. A.S.C. went to "A" office, snowing hard this morning. JF	
DOMPIERRE	December 30th Saturday		Still in same billet. O.C. A.S.C. went to "A" office. O.C. Ammunition Park called this afternoon. weather fine. JF.	
DOMPIERRE	December 31st Sunday		Still in same billet. O.C. A.S.C. went there. Rev Parks O.C. Ammunition Park came over this morning, a motor cycle accident which had happened an 1 his own O.C. men killed 6 wounded how man and trucks working on sick. R. to sick. JF.	Every 7 days etc 1 H.Q. A.S.C. 2nd Cav. Div.

CONFIDENTIAL.

WAR DIARY

of

H.Q., 2nd CAVALRY DIVISIONAL A.S.C.

JANUARY, ~~1916.~~ 1917

VOL. XXIX.

Army Form C. 2118.

WAR DIARY
INTELLIGENCE SUMMARY
(Erase heading not required.)

[illegible] per Cavalry Divn Sheet No. 1 VOLUME XXIX

Place	Date	Hour	Summary of Events and Information	Remarks and references to Appendices
DOMPIERRE	January 1st Monday		Still in same billet. O.C. A.S.C. went "Q" office B'g A.S.C. was going to train went to bring the bus [illegible] make up a line lay round for the Division. Weather fine a little misty seen in the afternoon. J.R.	
DOMPIERRE	January 2nd Tuesday		Still in same billet. S.O. B'g. went to "Cav. Bde. to see S.O. & passed on the transport to division ration from HESDIN rather warmer fine. J.R.	
DOMPIERRE	January 3rd Wednesday		Still in same billet. O.C. A.S.C. went to "Q" office. weather misty rain most of day. J.R.	
DOMPIERRE	January 4th Thursday		Still in same billet. O.C. A.S.C. went to Cav. Corps. Hd. quarters — one other horse [illegible] in 2 morning — fine afternoon. J.R.	
DOMPIERRE	January 5th Friday		Still in same billet. O.C. A.S.C. went to "Q" office this morning. Also the H.Q.S. & G.H.Q. collection this morning with Lieut. J.R.	
DOMPIERRE	January 6th Saturday		Still in same billet. O.C. A.S.C. went to Q office this morning wind in [illegible]. J.R.	
DOMPIERRE	January 7th Sunday		Still in same billet. O.C. Supply Column came over this morning. casualties fine J.R.	
DOMPIERRE	January 8th Monday		Still in same billet. O.C. A.S.C. went to "B" office this morning. water fine morning rain & showed rest of day. J.R.	

Army Form C. 2118.

WAR DIARY
or
INTELLIGENCE SUMMARY

(Erase heading not required.)

Shut. No. 2

Instructions regarding War Diaries and Intelligence Summaries are contained in F. S. Regs., Part II. and the Staff Manual respectively. Title Pages will be prepared in manuscript.

Place	Date	Hour	Summary of Events and Information	Remarks and references to Appendices
DOMPIERRE	9th January Wednesday		Still in same billet. Detachment of No 4 Cavalry Remount Park att. to this Division are moving to morrow. The att. to 6 Coy No. R.H. in exchange/relieve. The reserve ration were moved by lorry to the units. Several men off duty. R	
DOMPIERRE	10th January Wednesday		Still in same billet. O.C. R & C went to F.R. office the attachment of No 4 Cavalry Remount Park moved out to F.R. this morning & the Supply Column is/were now from R. an SB line lorry.	
DOMPIERRE	11th January Thursday		Still in same billet. O.C. Ammunition Park called in this morning weather somewhat a little on the morning. Snow west of cosy. R.	
DOMPIERRE	12th January Friday		Still in same billet. O.C. Supp Column came over this morning. Supply Officers meeting held. H.R.C. ... weather finer. R	
DOMPIERRE	13th January Saturday		Still in same billet. O.C. Supp Column came over the morning. had lunch of 3 lunch & drove to H.T. van. Received on Monday anecdote fine. open little Ottoma R	
DOMPIERRE	14th January Sunday		Still in same billet. O.C. Ammunition Park came over this morning. weather snow till hot and grew rapide R	
DOMPIERRE	15th January Monday		Still ... billet. O.C. Adj ... present - E.G. officers. O.C. Supp Column. came over to ... ... moon fair by ... open and overhead. ... weather fine & cold R.	

2449 Wt. W14957/M90 750,000 1/16 J.B.C. & A. Forms/C.2118/12.

Army Form C. 2118.

WAR DIARY
or
INTELLIGENCE SUMMARY
(Erase heading not required.)

Instructions regarding War Diaries and Intelligence Summaries are contained in F. S. Regs., Part II. and the Staff Manual respectively. Title Pages will be prepared in manuscript.

Shef-My-3

Place	Date	Hour	Summary of Events and Information	Remarks and references to Appendices
DOMPIERRE	16th January Tuesday		Still in same billet. C.C.O. went to R. Office. Lieut. T.C. Mallet returned today from Cavalry Depot at Rouen. 2 Cavalry Divisional A.S.C. weather fine boisterous cold. J.R.	
DOMPIERRE	17th January Wednesday		Still in same billet. 2 Lieut J.E. Bowden Benjamin returned to the South Coleman hunt L.C. Mallet and C.O. to ordnance Stores Senarpont on return from ones full ordnance Lorry will register J.R.	
DOMPIERRE	18th January Thursday		Still in same billet. C.C.O. went to "A" office this morning. Re A.A. & D.R.G. came down in the afternoon to see about transport scheme. weather raining a little. Still snow & slight frosts in the P.M. JR.	
DOMPIERRE	19th January Friday		Still in same billet. Supply Officers meeting held at H.Q.A.S.C. office. Snow upon ground some 10th inch weather fine still lots of snow on the ground & hard frost JR.	
DOMPIERRE	20th January Saturday		Still in same billet. C.C.O. went to "E" "Q" office. Re Supply returns. 20 la cl. A.S. improving weather fine. Still hard frost JR.	
DOMPIERRE	21st January Sunday		Still in same billet. Capt. Pendergart came over from Cav. Cav. with word that 5 Car Div & Red Cross are going through gave orders that all forage in GSL horse areas to be bought into our command Cav & Horses over area. also M.T. Still hard frost JR.	
DOMPIERRE	22nd January Monday		Still in same billet. Lieut. L.C. Mallet Bgt B.S.A.S.C. perfect to 4th Cam Bde for Cavalry 2nd Lieut R.P.C. Hewit with the Belgian Surport. R. H.Q. Suppy 2/Lt Have. Lieut A.P. Edwards came over to R.O. Cav & bombed in Lo. unport with several smaller dine. Still hard frost. JR	

2449 Wt. W14957/M90 750,000 1/16 J.B.C. & A. Forms/C.2118/12.

Army Form C. 2118.

WAR DIARY
or
INTELLIGENCE SUMMARY
(Erase heading not required.)

Instructions regarding War Diaries and Intelligence Summaries are contained in F. S. Regs., Part II. and the Staff Manual respectively. Title Pages will be prepared in manuscript.

Sheet No. 4.

Place	Date	Hour	Summary of Events and Information	Remarks and references to Appendices
DOMPIERRE	23rd January. Sunday.		Still in same billet. S.S.O. went to "Q" office this morning. 2/Lt. Pickles rejoined H.Q.R.A.S.C. for duty as S.O. Supply Troops. One day reserve holding. Two drawn advance of supply indents from Supply Column another three still very hard frost. J.G.	
DOMPIERRE	24th January. Monday.		Still in same billet. Lieut. R.A.S. came up. Left for Bruno this day. Weather still cold & hard frost. J.G.	
DOMPIERRE.	25th January. Thursday.		Still in same billet. L.S.O. went to "Q" office this morning. Nevers Ray 2 2nd came out. Very hard frost. Officers Mess. Ration issued as usual. Some still hard frost. J.G.	
DOMPIERRE	26th January. Friday.		Still in same billet. Supply Officers once in billet — H.Q. A.S.C. Office. Cook supply officers came up for duty. Reserve ration for man & horses of two brigades arrived today. Some still hard frost. J.G.	
DOMPIERRE	27th January. Saturday.		Still in same billet. S.S.O. went to "R" office. Advance party of 5th Cavalry came to moving in. We were still hard frost. J.G.	
DOMPIERRE	28th January. Sunday.		Still in same billet. 3 remount came up to H.Q. A.S.C. also for "reinforcement". We were still hard frost. J.G.	
DOMPIERRE	29th January. Monday.		Still in same billet. O.C. O.C. went to "Q" also O.C. Ammunition Park. O.C. Supply Column came on this morning. A.D.M.S. also came to see. We are weather still hard frost. J.G.	

Army Form C. 2118.

WAR DIARY
or
INTELLIGENCE SUMMARY
(Erase heading not required.)

Place	Date	Hour	Summary of Events and Information	Remarks and references to Appendices
DOMPIERRE	30th January Tuesday		Still in same billet. O.C. A.S.C. went to our H.Q. also to our S.P.O. Hospital & little umfest. day	J.R.
DOMPIERRE	31st January Wednesday		Still in same billet. O.C. A.S.C. went to D.O. office also to H.Q. Heavy frost, fine & very cold. snowed last night.	J.R.

Every M4 Capt.
H.Q. A.S.C.
2nd Cav. Div.

CONFIDENTIAL.

WAR   DIARY

of

O.C. A.S.C., 2nd CAVALRY DIVISION.

FEBRUARY, 1917.
VOL. XXX.
===========

Army Form C. 2118.

WAR DIARY
INTELLIGENCE SUMMARY
(Erase heading not required.)

HEADQUARTERS,
1ST CAVALRY DIVL.
A.S.C.

Instructions regarding War Diaries and Intelligence Summaries are contained in F. S. Regs., Part II. and the Staff Manual respectively. Title Pages will be prepared in manuscript.

Place	Date	Hour	Summary of Events and Information	Remarks and references to Appendices
DOMPIERRE	February 1st Thursday		Still in same billet. OC QMC H.T. Coln. called in the evening, also O.C. Ammunition Sub & Oil Sub & Cov. train, intended to & C.C.C. Francis wrote letter to friend, walked into village & back.	
DOMPIERRE	February 2nd Friday		Still in same billet. O.C. A.S.C. went to R.H.Q. this morning. Left Sykes reconnecting. Major Ashby O.C. 11 Cavalry Reserve Park came in & inspected his detachment will be relieved by one to-night. O.C. A.S.C. returned in the aftn. 2 C.P.C. Furs Park came. JR.	
DOMPIERRE	February 3rd Saturday		Still in same billet. O.C. Supply Coln. in called in this morning, weather fine, still bright front JR.	
DOMPIERRE	February 4th Sunday		Still in same billet. weather still hard frost. Gun Fire. JR.	
DOMPIERRE	February 5th Monday		Still in same billet. A.C. A.S.C. went to "Q" office weather still hard frost. Gun JR.	
DOMPIERRE	February 6th Tuesday		Still in same billet. Bt/Col. W. Scott Elliot went to District Hd. Qrs. Major R.T. Gray but was taken ill. The Major A.O. 5th Cav Bde. called in on his way over, & one new ASC. Gun about seven distinct shocks than a hay tale of men Bd-night weather still hard frost. Gun JR.	

2449 Wt. W14957/M90 750,000 1/16 J.B.C. & A. Forms/C.2118/12.

WAR DIARY
or
INTELLIGENCE SUMMARY

Army Form C. 2118.

(Erase heading not required.)

Place	Date	Hour	Summary of Events and Information	Remarks and references to Appendices
DOMPIERRE	February 7th Wednesday		Still in same billet. S.S.O. went to "Q" office. Also went to Supply 4 km or so ft. S.O. & 2nd R.E. Our forces into more of 5th Car Bole weather still hard frost. Fine J.R.	
DOMPIERRE	February 8th Thursday		Still in same billet. O.C. Supply Column is Col. this morning was tortake Out partice J.R.	
DOMPIERRE	February 9th Friday		Still in same billet. S.S.O. went ft S. & "Q" re. ft Car Bole Animal. Rations. P.O. that duc. Division to this evening that everything was alright weather thaw little hard post. J.R	
DOMPIERRE	February 10th Saturday		Still in same billet. S.S.O. went to Montreuil when to build them this rations alright everything alright weather fine still hard post. J.R	
DOMPIERRE	February 11th Sunday		Still in same billet. S.S.O. went to "Q" office this morning weather still hard thaw a little day the day. J.R	
DOMPIERRE	February 12th Monday		Still in same billet. Lt. A.D. Cooper reported to H.Q. O.R.S. officer his missing. Reported at the Divisional H.Q. Came Pigeon Park on Saturday 10/10th 9 to h over from 2nd L.T. L.L. Thompson on Sunrise 11th 2 at 2nd L.L. Thompson dept this day for Pai. H.Q. weather fine. Still hard post; but fine a little down day J.R	
DOMPIERRE	February 13th Tuesday		Still in same billet. S.S.O. went to "Q" office. Also went to Mackay Regt at H.Q. Rations at 2.30 p.m. this alknown. weather 2 L.M. hard ground fine J.R	

Army Form C. 2118.

WAR DIARY
or
INTELLIGENCE SUMMARY

(Erase heading not required.)

HEADQUARTERS,
CAVALRY DIVL.
A.S.O.

Shel. N° 3

Instructions regarding War Diaries and Intelligence Summaries are contained in F. S. Regs., Part II. and the Staff Manual respectively. Title Pages will be prepared in manuscript.

Place	Date	Hour	Summary of Events and Information	Remarks and references to Appendices
DOMPIERRE	February 14th Wednesday		Still in same billet. T.O. 4th Cav. Bde. came over here about transport returns for 3rd Cav. Bde. JB	
DOMPIERRE	February 15th Thursday		Still in same billet. S.S.O. went to Q' offices this morning. S.O. borrowed 2 books sent out to 2nd & 3rd Cav. Bde. Park JB. Came about lorries on the return from Gare Pilot Rail Head. JB	
DOMPIERRE	February 16th Friday		Still in same billet. Supply Officers made S.Col. of H.Q. O.&C. today. He came forward. Talked over a few staff issues master their training front this afternoon. JB.	
DOMPIERRE	February 17th Saturday		Still in same billet. At 11.30 a.m. Lieut. was going to H of the Motor Rail returned no lorries to be on the S.S.O. went to their monies. Their special day's Reserve Rations, late on in the day the lorries were allowed to travel ready. Supply Officer returned. 3.D. 3rd Cav. Bde. on the afternoon 2nd R.B. lightly R.B on the roads. So the Supply Column arrived to S.O. Dumps in the afternoon. 3rd Cav. Bde. left. This day. No report. When the training was front, a little more is the JB.	
DOMPIERRE	February 18th Sunday		Still in same billet. Went some colonel this of Division S. 3rd Cav. Bde. a Divl. trans. Arrived from 3 R & 3rd Bde the this arrived. In no training from Rations on Sunday. Sunday & Wednesday, Monday, Tuesday, Wednesday. JB.	
DOMPIERRE	February 19th Monday		Still in same billet. S.S.O. went to "Q" offices this morning. Was to the Cav. Bde. on the Supply Column about same arrival to the 3rd Cav. Bde. × Divl. Transport lorries by Lorries on Sunday. Arrived in Monday evening. Started by H.T. Rates to DEVONPORT All Rations front. JB. Rides for SUPPLY change is ETIENNE Monday train. JB	

2449. Wt. W14957/M90 750,000 1/16 J.B.C. & A. Forms/C.2118/12.

Army Form C. 2118.

WAR DIARY
or
INTELLIGENCE SUMMARY
(Erase heading not required.)

Instructions regarding War Diaries and Intelligence Summaries are contained in F. S. Regs., Part II. and the Staff Manual respectively. Title Pages will be prepared in manuscript.

Place	Date	Hour	Summary of Events and Information	Remarks and references to Appendices
DOMPIERRE	February 20th Tuesday		Still in same billet. No lorries out today. Nissen ration issued. Meat ration every 4th day. F.R.	
DOMPIERRE	February 21st Wednesday		Still in same billet. No lorries out today. Nissen ration issued. Weather very quite warm. F.R.	
DOMPIERRE	February 22nd Thursday		Still in same billet. Lorries detailed to stay 2 to 3 days. Rations gun received. Weather fine. F.R.	
DOMPIERRE	February 23rd Friday		Still in same billet. No lorries on the road today. Rations drawn by A.T. from the 61/19 Column A.D.O.S. 69th Canadian. Reported to D.D. 14 Can. Rr. Park this morning at 11.30. Having no leslie & few ambulance lorries was not just S.S.O. Adjutant went to "A" & then on to his respective location. Weather fine, many all day. F.R.	
DOMPIERRE	February 24th Saturday		Still in same billet. Lorries detailed today. A.D.O.S. 69th consulted the D.D.S. at the Park at 11.30 asked for a fresh supply. Sent to Canc. A.T. Col. at 4 o'clock. Traffic convoy very good, weather fine. F.R.	
DOMPIERRE	February 25th Sunday		Still in same billet. Rations are now being issued in the ordinary way. 2 each S.S.O. Dumps weather fine. F.R.	
DOMPIERRE	February 26th Monday		Still in same billet. S.A.O. went to "Q" office. Weather fine. F.R.	

Army Form C. 2118.

WAR DIARY
or
INTELLIGENCE SUMMARY
(Erase heading not required.)

Instructions regarding War Diaries and Intelligence Summaries are contained in F. S. Regs., Part II. and the Staff Manual respectively. Title Pages will be prepared in manuscript.

Sheet No. 6

Place	Date	Hour	Summary of Events and Information	Remarks and references to Appendices
DOMPIERRE	February 27 Tuesday		Still in same billet. S.S.O. & Adjutant went to "Q" office this morning. Supply Column Park at Pte Col. This morning. Dinner as after fame. J.R.	
DOMPIERRE	February 28 Wednesday		Still in same billet. "A" Supply Brigade Supply Column went to new area. Ammunition Park moved to OUDENY. Adjutant went to gave H.Q A.S.C. weather fine J.R.	H.Q. A.S.C. 2nd Cav. Div.

2449 Wt. W14957/M90 750,000 1/16 J.B.C. & A. Forms/C.2118/12.

CONFIDENTIAL.

Vol 9

WAR   DIARY

of

HEADQUARTERS, 2nd CAVALRY DIVISIONAL A.S.C.

MARCH, 1917.

VOL. XXXI.

Army Form C. 2118.

WAR DIARY
or
INTELLIGENCE SUMMARY

(Erase heading not required.)

HEADQUARTERS,
2nd CAVALRY DIVL.
A.S.C.

Volume XXXI   Sheet No 1.

Place	Date	Hour	Summary of Events and Information	Remarks and references to Appendices
DOMPIERRE	March 1st Thursday		Still in same billet. S.E.O. went to "Q" office for on to 4th Cav. Bde. reveals to best on bills to 5th Cav Bde. Park. but was unable to find any on account of some savage horses. Bed horses sent thro' to A.F.G.	
DOMPIERRE	March 2nd Friday		Still in same billet. N.O. of General troops inspected all the horses of the 5th Cav. Bn. Park unable to A.F.G.	
DOMPIERRE	March 3rd Saturday		Still in same billet. S.E.O. went to "Q" office. M.O.V.S. went to inspect horses of the 5th Cav. Bn. Park. 3 horses sent to Mobile Vet. Section. Genie quite a heavy frost last night. A.F.G.	
DOMPIERRE	March 4th Sunday		Still in same billet. Adjutant H.Q. A.S.C. went to "Q" office this morning. weather fine. F.G.	
DOMPIERRE	March 5th Monday		Still in same billet. H. [?] Major Zemoil. M.H. Gridsonly S.O.O. of 2nd Bde. Div. A.A.Q.R.G. H.Q.C.'s A.S.C. left office in charge. R.A.O.S. left officer in charge for detail conference this afternoon. Lieutenant F.H. of 5th Bn Horses Park 9.O.C. 6S for horse called in on bn. been lost no. his uniform was his calisher sword surrendered by him. Large field of horses seen going to A.F.G.	
DOMPIERRE	March 6th Tuesday		Still in same billet. S.E.O. & Adjutant of H.Q. A.S.C. went to "Q" office this morning. the Commander in Park march from GUIGNY to WADICOURT, 9 Kms. Arrival - H.Q. 5 Cav. Bde. Park from WADICOURT to VIRONCHEAUX. weather fine. F.G.	
DOMPIERRE	March 7th Wednesday		Still in same billet. Adjutant went over to VIRONCHEAUX, a no 5th Bn Cav. Park Billets met general march to inspect quarters gave a few of the park details been slant on account of transporters in the ... going to ...	

2449 Wt. W14957/M90 750,000 1/16 J.B.C. & A. Forms/C.2118/12.

WAR DIARY or INTELLIGENCE SUMMARY

Army Form C. 2118.

HEADQUARTERS,
2nd CAVALRY DIVL.
A.S.C.

Sheet No 2.

Place	Date	Hour	Summary of Events and Information	Remarks and references to Appendices
DOMPIERRE.	March 8th Thursday		Still in same billet. S.S.O. went to "Q" Office & then on to see the 5th Lancers Park who were billeted at Chaulny west from Casey forest. for the 43rd (an Ind. mounted Bgde.) & heard some interesting PR.	
DOMPIERRE.	March 9th Friday.		Still in same billet. One day puncture rations on S.O. Shown "Q" Office agreed the permanent standing orders for division & typed from R.O. his Army arrangement made for the second day resume meeting and the army would not properly the army would not properly the army would not properly thing.	
DOMPIERRE.	March 10th Saturday.		Still in same billet. S.S.O. Adjutant and I saw 2nd Can Pusher Park and then to lunch at 5th Lancers weather gone snow all gone. heavy frost. PR.	
DOMPIERRE.	March 11th Sunday.		Still in same billet. Adjutant went to "Q" Office this morning. The Division Service to "Q" that 5th as second day have been cancelled today, as the weather has changed, weather fine. sun & PR.	
DOMPIERRE.	March 12th Monday.		Still in same billet. S.S.O. went to "Q" Office after an brilliant weather mostly sunny most of day. PR.	
DOMPIERRE.	March 13th Tuesday.		Adjutant same Lifthate Col Scott Ellis returned to duty today from Hospital. Lt. Ball & Major Lufthate same Lifthate of Colonel left to proceed but left now coming back tomorrow. weather there sunny frosty PR. nice & sunny that the 3rd Cavalry Division.	
DOMPIERRE	March 14th Wednesday		Still in same billet. A.O & O.M.S. Chart the army office but sunny fresh are O.P. all days but cold weather had some of Prisoners. Sunny afternoon. PR.	

WAR DIARY
or
INTELLIGENCE SUMMARY

(Erase heading not required.)

Army Form C. 2118.

HEADQUARTERS,
2nd CAVALRY DIVL.
A.S.C.

Place	Date	Hour	Summary of Events and Information	Remarks and references to Appendices
DOMPIERRE	15th March. Thursday		Still in same billet. O.C. A.S.C. went to "B" Squadrons Horse Show. Officers arrived from Divisional Weather fine. FR	
DOMPIERRE	16th March. Friday		Still in same billet. O.C. Supply Column called this morning. S.O. meets R.A.S.C. of H in today. Weather fine. FR	
DOMPIERRE	17th March. Saturday		Still in same billet. O.C. A.S.C. went to "D" Officers this morning. No show at the HESDIN show. Weather fine. FR	
DOMPIERRE	18th March. Sunday		Still in same billet. O.C. A.S.C. went to ADRIFT Covent. went at Once Majors Regiment of the rank and file of the Rifles. 2nd by men taken & next drawn billy from Rouxmil. Weather fine. FR	
DOMPIERRE	19th March. Monday		Still in same billet. O.C. A.S.C. went to "R" Officers also to the H + L Cav. Res. Park as their Comm over for he has detachments sent to both these shows. Arrange to ready to move off tomorrow a.m. The Sapr. Sections were drawn today & issued at the Divnl. H.T. Comp Sections the morning. Starts & hour of 4 p.m. + Lancl Res. of Vl. tomorrow. FR	
DOMPIERRE	20th March. Tuesday		Still in same billet. H.Q. Cav Res Park moved to WADICOURT today. O.C. A.S.C. rode to WADICOURT in afternoon from the Reserve Park. Weather changed much colder a little snow & little rain. FR	
DOMPIERRE	21st March. Wednesday		Still in same billet. O.C. A.S.C. went to "B" Officers in the afternoon went to see the extreme of 6th Bn. Reserve Park at WADICOURT. Weather much colder & a little rain. FR	

Army Form C. 2118.

WAR DIARY
or
INTELLIGENCE SUMMARY

(Erase heading not required.)

HEADQUARTERS,
2nd CAVALRY DIVL.
A. S. C.

Place	Date	Hour	Summary of Events and Information	Remarks and references to Appendices
DOMPIERRE	22nd March Thursday		Still in same billet. Have obtained 4 & 5 Reserve Parks moved from WADI COURT to [illegible]. They are situated off the outskirts of the 2nd Cavalry Division. His Majesty's ships were inspected at [illegible] 4 Cow Ambce for Vet Fees & the delegated of the [illegible] Park, O.C. A.S.C. went to see them on the evening. Everything alright. G. Savage, gun. Lt. A.H.T. Corp officers driven today. O.C. Supply Officer called on his afternoon, weather very cold & some snowfall.	
DOMPIERRE	23rd March Friday		Still in same billet. O.C. went to "Q" office in early hrs with the Ammunition Park horses weather fine, very cold. Yet [illegible] from 3 Cavalry Brigade (5 Ammunition) reported his [illegible]	
DOMPIERRE	24th March Saturday		Still in same billet. Two wagons left for the Ammunition Park early today to bring in belongings [illegible] Rations sent to the 26 Horse. Maj. Brown & 2 officers in the afternoon. O.C. A.S.C. Park [illegible] free shoot. Got rations from for 4 Cavalry Division and areas.	
DOMPIERRE	25th March Sunday		Still [illegible] Capt. [illegible] (RAMC) attached from Hospital went to 3 Cav Corps Installation fine.	
DOMPIERRE	26th March Monday		Still in same billet. O.C. A.S.C. went to Inspect the 2 Cavalry Reserve Park with an Ordnance Officer today. Supplies and [illegible] at condition and no complaints. They have been [illegible] [illegible] weather fine very cold.	

WAR DIARY
or
INTELLIGENCE SUMMARY

Army Form C. 2118.

(Erase heading not required.)

HEADQUARTERS,
2nd CAVALRY DIVL
A.S.C.

Place	Date	Hour	Summary of Events and Information	Remarks and references to Appendices
DOMPIERRE	27th March Tuesday		Still in same billet. O.C. A.S.C. went to "B" Sqdn: also Capt Bernard O.C. Aux H.T. Coy. O.C. Ammunition Park called this evening; weather fine; fairly day. P.F.	
DOMPIERRE	28th March Wednesday		Still in same billet. O.C. Aux H.T. Coy. came here; O.C. A.S.C. departing. Cap't O'Neil & prison arrangements; have been made 4 P.M. 2" Car. Regs. Rec'd 1 day's sup. Odm Unit Sub at night. weather warm. P.F.	
DOMPIERRE	29th March Thursday		Still in same billet. O.C. A.S.C. went to "B" office in the afternoon. 2 General G.S. wagons arrived to A.B.H.Comp. to be overhauled as follows; 1 ex R.H.A.Bde. 1 ex Brigade H.Q. Fine warm overcast day. P.F.	
DOMPIERRE	30th March Friday		Still in same billet. S.S.O. went to MONTREUIL to see abo't Cars. Lieut. Alexander 2nd, 3rd, 4th Cav. Regts. came to H.Q. re. supply arrangts. to be made; all the Landed G.Scoys. were out to-day. Rec'd in from H.Q. weather cold snowy all day. P.F.	
DOMPIERRE	31st March Saturday		Still in same billet. O.C. A.S.C. went to "B" office. S.S.O. went to BEDDIN to think abo't it. Cold damp. weather showery P.F.	

Rosy Sus Copt.
H.Q. A.S.C.
2nd Cav. Div.

CONFIDENTIAL.

WAR   DIARY

of

HEADQUARTERS, 2nd CAVALRY DIVISIONAL A.S.C.

APRIL, 1917.

VOL. XXXII.

Army Form C. 2118.

WAR DIARY
INTELLIGENCE SUMMARY
(Erase heading not required.)

HEADQUARTERS, 2nd CAVALRY DIVL. A.S.C.

No. ....
Date ....

Somme XXII Chief ?

Instructions regarding War Diaries and Intelligence Summaries are contained in F.S. Regs, Part II. and the Staff Manual respectively. Title Pages will be prepared in manuscript.

Place	Date	Hour	Summary of Events and Information	Remarks and references to Appendices
DOMPIERRE	April 1st Sunday		Still in same billet. Occupied N.E. event A.R. office this morning. Weather fairly fine. JB	
DOMPIERRE	April 2nd Monday		Still in same billet. O.C. A.S.C. went to "Q" office this morning & leave, and to deliver to billets. Omesseux. So turned out S. sweeper from the 10 Bryan Park arrived at WADICOURT today. O.C. A.S.P. went to airfield. Weather much cooler, rather showery, cold. JB	
DOMPIERRE	April 3rd Tuesday		Still in same billet. O.C. A.S.C. went to "Q" office in the evening. Lorries delivered to the heavy R.E & O. tops, and to dump of the Safety Steam Coy. O.C. Supply Column came here. O.C. A.S.C. is back. Arrived at... D.A.O. went to A.D.M.S.T. & on coal. Horses about pack in forward area. O.C. A.S.P. on delivery from 10 squad brought back 2 mules. Also the 3 police move on 3rd. Weather keeps ? of answer. Last night half moon all gone by the morning. JB	
DOMPIERRE	"April 4th Wednesday"		Still in same billet. O.C. A.S.C. went to "Q" office this morning. Mobile Supply Steam Bakers sent 555 sacks of flour to R.S.T. loaded. 131 came of emb? rations. 6 3 tracks of oats. Also R.T. bent 1 leach. 36 wagons with ammunition for the Divisional Park moved tomorrow 3 Am Bde. Remember Park of WADICOURT. Ammunition ? was sent up today. JB	
DOMPIERRE	April 5th Thursday		Still in same billet. O.C. A.S.C. went to "Q" office. You ? orders taken for the move to the divisions for lack of Albn of oats per horse were received & they go with L Bn & Bn's American Horses. O.C. A.S.C. went to See Mobile Supply Steam & to the Mobile Supply Column Park AA Moure Somewhere. Weather fine. Except wind. Morning slight rr. ? Shower fell. 11 wounded. Arrangements were completed for a 4 Bourne. JB	

2449 Wt. W14957/M90 750,000 1/16 J.B.C. & A. Forms/C.2118/12.

Army Form C. 2118.

WAR DIARY
INTELLIGENCE SUMMARY
(Erase heading not required.)

HEADQUARTERS, 2nd CAVALRY DIVL. A.S.C.

Instructions regarding War Diaries and Intelligence Summaries are contained in F.S. Regs., Part II. and the Staff Manual respectively. Title Pages will be prepared in manuscript.

Place	Date	Hour	Summary of Events and Information	Remarks and references to Appendices
DOMPIERRE	6th April Friday		Still in same billet. Letter in writing comes about 2230 of Major O.C. Supply Colm. called in on the way back. He supply column marched today to Arras. He regt. & four BARLY & NEUVILLETTE. The railhead now for HEDIN & BOURGE MAISON. A.S.C. went to railhead. Weather showery most of day. Y.R.	
DOMPIERRE / WAVAN.	7th April Saturday		March to day leaving DOMPIERRE at 11 am. March taken LE BOISLE, WILLENCOURT, RUE-LE-CHATEAU, WAVAN. Horse Pack Coy. left 10.0 & I.C.C. (camping at WILLENCOURT) ... on way at the head of the main body. ... & ballooning team followed half way ... at WAVAN 6.3.20 pm. ... new billet at WAVAN 6.3.20 pm. Motor Lorries arrived at 6 pm & main time. Y.R.	
WAVAN / HENU	8th April Sunday		Rather heavy last night. Snow tomorrow ... 2.0412m. ... HENU came to be lyg. ... DOULLENS, POMMERA, GRENAS, 243, & NU. NARAY ... Supply Colm arr. ... arrived at 10.30. Namela very bad ... ... owing to only having 2 marks to finish which is...	
HENU	9th April Monday		Still in same billet. Dr. 49. KARHA small smart Coy. Colm. Mobile Supply Colm. moved from HENU this afternoon. The remainder of HENU stiffish ... orders today. The balloon & HENU coy left ... weather showery, very cold.	
HENU	10th April Sunday		Still in same billet. Motor camp in Rest-rations still to be obtained to supply Dept today. Order to fill our balloon 13th regty. Dept. moved from HENU & Colm leaving about 6 p.m. to BEAUMETZ LES LODES & will move from Beat Manual Place brigade from WAILLY Weather showery quite a lot ...	

WAR DIARY
or
INTELLIGENCE SUMMARY

Army Form C. 2118.

HEADQUARTERS,
2nd CAVALRY DIVL.
A.S.C.

No. ....
Date ....

About No. 3

Place	Date	Hour	Summary of Events and Information	Remarks and references to Appendices
HENU.	11th April. Wednesday.		Still in same billet. The entire Division ordered to move off tomorrow. Orders they left out by on road arrays being so slack as to the One Section of Supply Column arrived here at 6.30 p.m. to look for the supply of Column called in, weather improved most of day. J.P.	Issued with Supply
HENU.	12th April. Thursday.		Still in same billet. Word came in that the whole Division was not to billets ------ if possible. On the strength B.G. Orders were altered & all troops to ------ again at night. Detachments of troops were all in billets by 10 p.m. Owing to scarcity of ------ forage & having to ------ up the Horse lines to take all our ------ they were very ------ to the Supply Column. ------ sent to if no means of communication with the Supply Column at 1 R.h.in. & statements from "B" Echelon were dumped & sent to be ------ Battery showing Sup Rqmt to Brands. As above & 24 hours ration to RAS's owing to the Scarcity of Materials Supply Column being with 4th Car Bde. at 9 h.m. several days ration ------ ------ a more Serviced at ------ troops in HENU were Bruns & Pol. Camp, 12 Pvt. Bde for Ronunion- ------ Weather. Rained most of day. J.P.	
HENU.	13th April. Friday.		Still in same billet. Rations arrived from the ------ depot at 4 p.m. 9.B Echelon 4 days rations for "B" Echelon were dispatched to 4th Cav Bde to ------ one day 1 & 3 Cav Bde, 13 Rinser Park ------ to HENU today. Weather fine J.P.	
HENU.	14th April. Saturday		Still in same billet. Rations were delivered for the whole of Government today ------ ------ to all units by ------ L.G.S & Pol. Same ------ advance party in Adv. HENU in ------ & "B" Echelon to locate ------ ------ & to the 14th C.S.S. Can Bde. are over for the "D" Echelon Rations & 3 days supply sent off this afternoon for their ------ out of ------ 2 days rations which were sent up by & bn. of 3 days for ------ Bde. to ------ the ------ delivery in feed up to Midnight Weather fine J.P.	

2449 Wt. W14957/Mp0 759,000 1/16 J.B.C. & A. Forms/C.2118/12.

WAR DIARY
or
INTELLIGENCE SUMMARY

Army Form C. 2118.

HEADQUARTERS,
2nd CAVALRY DIVL.
A.S.C.

Place	Date	Hour	Summary of Events and Information	Remarks and references to Appendices
HENU.	15th April Sunday		Still in same billet, ration for Divisional Troops received in bulk today. O.C. A.S.C. went to "A" Офис from H.Q. Divnl. train. Arrangements made for same Divisional Train Coy. from H.Q. Divnl. Train to run. Cancelled, ration served for Details H. Divisional Troops in bulk. No A.S.C. A.S.P. офис matter form. K.	
HENU.	16th April Monday		Still in same billet. O.C. A.S.C. went to "A" Офис. Royal Field Army 3rd "A" Brigade for permission. Moved Withing to GROUCHES. to tours of H.Q. 3 Cav.Bde. Rd. to comp. west of village HUMEROEUIL to own billet. Left by the train at 8 Cav. Bde. moved same. From Супп. Colln. train this S.A.L. Oats dock arrived 9pm plus. Sups. had to be delivered at Supp. Colon during next day to be issued at the rate H. Hom. per horse. per Feld. ration issued for one day will sent form. K.	
HENU.	17th April Tuesday		Still in same billet. O.C. A.S.C. went to "A" Офис. 20th Car. Bde. could not be about. Lieut Col. to "B" Office. Had taken over & understand men moved the evening to HQ Divn. O.C. deposit to "Q". That to move to Labeflyre from there as far as for Brigade of the Division Divisional Train Divnl. A.S.C. Rd. pre rang & Labeflyre sam a half horses billets by the night Divnl. Troops weather came most of day. K.	
HENU.	18th April Tuesday		Still in same billet. O.C. A.S.C. went to "A" Офис. Pte. E.W. Hutchinson went to hospital this At Aylore, same to Vith care the Mobile Supp. Colon. About 6 a.m. men was consulted but stayed till later morn same moved that 3 Cav Bde more morning however. O.C. Supp. Colon on a fast Sring found with for the delivery of rations H.T. was going to be used as possible more quite a lot & cold.	
HENU.	19th April Wednesday		Still in same billet. O.C. A.S.C. went to "A" Офис. 3 Car. Bde. moved today, the move for 5 Car.Bde & Divisional Troops to be cancelled for Divnl. Troops but 3 Car. Bde. more tomorrow & later Div. the one attached Divn.Troops moves as well as the once already attend them, O.C. Supp. Colon called the next morn. Arranged Divnl. Train Misch form. K.	

Army Form C. 2118.

WAR DIARY
or
INTELLIGENCE SUMMARY
(Erase heading not required.)

HEADQUARTERS,
2nd CAVALRY DIVL.
A.S.C.

April 1915

Place	Date	Hour	Summary of Events and Information	Remarks and references to Appendices
HENU	20th April Friday		Still in same billet. O.C. A.S.C. went to "Q" Office. 5th Cav. Bde. moved Billets also the 3rd Cav. Bde. sent on Billeting Party. Flash'' Party to draw new Rolls at HESDIN. Tomorrow the Ammunition Park moved to HENU today. Rather quiet front. Village on fire. P.A.S. Quite weather fine. P.R.	
HENU	21st April Saturday		Still in same billet. O.C. A.S.C. went to "B" Office. new from Details Supply about [illegible] to Postal went to Pte Mitchell Supply Store 3 H.Q. C.T.O. together with his mare for remounts. 2.2 Funks Q.S. 18.S wagons & carts to draw at 1 pm, 8 one from ALBRINGHEM, water Coy had a bath a yard up to prices but H.T. seemed to perhaps water to burstle words of Coy's away. heavy to have to cool as for remount horses about 10.30am weather fine. P.R.	
HENU	22nd April Sunday		Still in same billet. O.C. A.S.C. went to "Q" Office. Q.M.S. went [illegible] to the 10th Ro Park Lorries arrived rather very late owing to the heavy rain & bad roads. to LIGNY-FLOCHEL to make up weather fine. P.R.	WAR A COURT
HENU	23rd April Monday		Still in same billet. O.C. A.S.C. went to "B" Office. Lorries on as before weather fine. P.R.	
HENU	24th April Tuesday		Still in same billet. O.C. A.S.P. went to "Q" Office. 3 old 4" cost change this afternoon meeting for Divn Coat. supplied with quarter from P.R.	

2449 Wt. W14957/Mgo. 750,000 1/16 J.B.C. & A. Forms/C.2118/12.

WAR DIARY
INTELLIGENCE SUMMARY

(Erase heading not required.)

Army Form C. 2118.

HEADQUARTERS,
2nd CAVALRY DIVL.
A.S.C.

No. ....
Date ....

Instructions regarding War Diaries and Intelligence Summaries are contained in F. S. Regs., Part II. and the Staff Manual respectively. Title Pages will be prepared in manuscript.

Place	Date	Hour	Summary of Events and Information	Remarks and references to Appendices
HENU	25th April Wednesday		Still in same billet. O.C. A.S.C. went to "Q" office. 1st & 2nd Lines Supply Columns C. Roth mot. packed & out for the Supply Column, A.D.V.S. came round & inspected horses of the H.Q. A.S.C. all very good. weather fine. quiet day. J.R.	April No 6
HENU.	26th April Thursday		Still in same billet. O.C. A.S.C. went to "Q" office. G.O.C. inspected the Mobile Supply Column this afternoon. Was out for the weather fine. Game Corners. J.R.	
HENU.	27th April Friday		Still in same billet O.C. A.S.C. went to "A" office. A.D.V.S. inspected the 1st & 2nd Cavalry Brigade. The Veterinary Officers turn out formation through have been doing all under out the Somme. weather fine. J.R.	
FROHEN-LE-GRAND	28th April Saturday		March orders. HENU to the Divisional H.Q. Signal Depot at HENU 5.0. & Divisional Hosp. & Reserve Park of Div. Sup. Col. HENU at 9 a.m. arriving at FROHEN-LE-GRAND 3-15 p.m. arriving head before leaving Road & Supp. not used before arriving Ammunition heads hitting railway sidings heads hitting on the AUXI-LE-CHATEAU. side & munition head. Park. Bs. S.R.	
FROHEN-LE-GRAND	29th April Sunday		Still in same billet O.C. Div. went out to "Q" office. S.O. 3rd Can. R.S. & 5.S. 3 Can.Br. Called in today have about 9 rations. weather fine. J.R.	
FROHEN-LE-GRAND	30th April Monday		Still in same billet. O.C. A.S.C. went to "Q" office. weather fine June 79.	

Frew Lieut Col
H.Q. A.S.C.
2nd Cav. Div.

CONFIDENTIAL.

WAR   DIARY

of

HEADQUARTERS, 2nd CAVALRY DIVL. A.S.C.

MAY, 1917   -   COL. XXXIII.

Army Form C. 2118.

WAR DIARY
or
INTELLIGENCE SUMMARY. VOLUME XXIII.
(Erase heading not required.)

Instructions regarding War Diaries and Intelligence
Summaries are contained in F. S. Regs., Part II.
and the Staff Manual respectively. Title pages
will be prepared in manuscript.

Place	Date	Hour	Summary of Events and Information	Remarks and references to Appendices
FROHEN-LE-GRAND.	1st May 1917 Tuesday.		Still in same billet. O.C. A.S.C. went to "Q" office. O.M. also came in from the Supply Column. A.D.V.S. and O.C. on leave - see note Gen. F.	
FROHEN-LE-GRAND.	2nd May Wednesday.		Still in same billet. O.C. A.S.C. went to "Q" office. Arrangements being made to move H.T. Coys. Lieut. Sheet. A.V.C. 4 to inspect Coys. Horses Gen. F.2.	
FROHEN-LE-GRAND.	3rd May Thursday.		Still in same billet. O.C. A.S.C. went to "Q" office. D.S.O. went to R.H.Q.S. to see about holding Divan. Gen. Cavalry Corps. and to Divnl. H.Q. regarding new officer in charge of very little information on received weather Gen. F.2.	
FROHEN-LE-GRAND. MÉZEROLLES.	4th May Friday.		Still in same billet. O.C. A.S.C. went to "Q" office. Also went to C Cav.Bde. Supply Column or weather Gen. F.2.	
FROHEN-LE-GRAND.	5th May Saturday.		Still in same billet. O.C. A.S.C. went to "Q" office. Arrangements to see S.O. & Car.Bde. weather Gen. F.2.	

2353 Wt. W2544/1454 700,000 5/15 D. D. & L. A.D.S.S./Forms/C. 2118.

Army Form C. 2118.

WAR DIARY
or
INTELLIGENCE SUMMARY.
(Erase heading not required.)

Instructions regarding War Diaries and Intelligence Summaries are contained in F.S. Regs., Part II. and the Staff Manual respectively. Title pages will be prepared in manuscript.

Place	Date	Hour	Summary of Events and Information	Remarks and references to Appendices
FROHEN-LE-GRAND.	6th May. Sunday.		Still in same billet. O.C. O.S.C. went to "Q" office & O.C. A.S.C. went to HEND with O.C. A.S.C. Park. Reconne of H Horse Park. Weather fine. F.	
FROHEN-LE-GRAND.	7th May. Monday.		Still in same billet. O.C. O.S.C went to "Q" office. Weather fine. F.	
FROHEN-LE-GRAND.	8th May. Tuesday.		Still in same billet. O.C. A.S.C. went to "Q" Office & A.D. of S&T Park Corps called in afternoon. Weather fine. F.	
FROHEN-LE-GRAND.	9th May Wednesday.		Still in same billet. O.C. A.S.C. went to Q Office. D.A. & Q.M.G. Senior & Lees Sen & O.C. Supply Park & one A.D.M.S. Brig. Roberts and the O.C. A.S. Park Weather fine. F.	
FROHEN-LE-GRAND.	10th May. Thursday.		Still in same billet. O.C. A.S. went to "Q" Office. O.C. Supply O.C. Lofty Oleum called. Weather fine. F.	
FROHEN-LE-GRAND.	11th May. Friday.		Still in same billet. O.C. A.S.C. Supt. of "Q" Office. 2.30 p.m. Lees & O.C. A.S.C. Park left at 2:30 & arrived to H.Q. Bolivia B.E. Office. The [illegible] left to [illegible] for [illegible] London. Weather fine. F.	

Army Form C. 2118.

WAR DIARY
or
INTELLIGENCE SUMMARY.
(Erase heading not required.)

Place	Date	Hour	Summary of Events and Information	Remarks and references to Appendices
ST. OUEN	12th May Saturday		Left FROHEN-LE-GRAND at 7.15 a.m. Arrived at/Sch. Echn. BERNAVILLE 10.0 a.m. ST. LEW POLES. DOMART. Arrived at Route very good. Arrived ST. OUEN 1245 p.m. 20 mile short halt B. Echelon 2h. had Half Rations for & went on. B & Q offrs. of FROHEN-LE-GRAND. Rations were secured. Breakfast at ST. OUEN at 3 p.m. O.C. ever under "A" "Q" offrs. weather fine. rug Ref. 28.	Arrived ST. OUEN 1.15 a.m.
BUSSY-LES-D...	13th May Sunday		Left ST OUEN at 8 a.m. Arrived at BUSSY-LES-DAOURS at 4 p.m. Route taken VIGNACOURT, ST VAST. BUSSY. roads good. push a few small hills some Cold wind at ST VAST. not got permits - Yesterday called & 1 Corps dept. Info. Railway crossing "0" Supply Column called and in today & info. that Can M 68 had been in an accident on ST the front spring broke & car burned over. Can taken out. Supply Column. O.C. one went "A" "Q" offrs. in the evening at new billets. weather fine. rug Ref. 28 & 29 or rain or enemy. JF	Aubrite AMIENS
LAMOTTE-EN-SANTERRE	14th May Monday		Left BUSSY-LES-DAOURS at 8 a.m. Arrived at LAMOTTE-EN-SANTERRE 12 noon. Route taken DAOURS, AUBIGNY, FOUILLOY. Whole road over very bad after passing through FOUILLOY. O.C. Supply Column called in today. O.C. O.C. went to "Q" office speaking fine matty. day & rest. Lt Reav. Phoenix & McPherson	DAOURS FOUILLOY

Army Form C. 2118.

Instructions regarding War Diaries and Intelligence Summaries are contained in F.S. Regs., Part II and the Staff Manual respectively. Title pages will be prepared in manuscript.

WAR DIARY
INTELLIGENCE SUMMARY
(Erase heading not required.)

Army Form C. 2118.

Place	Date	Hour	Summary of Events and Information	Remarks and references to Appendices
ROISEL	15th May Tuesday		Left LAMOTTE-EN-SANTERRE at 7.20 a.m. Arrived at ROISEL 7.30 p.m. Route - along main road to PONT-LES-BRIE, 15m N/ORPE, LE MESNIL, CARTIGNY, BUIRE, TINCOURT, MICQRAIN, ROISEL. Roads good except for bad patches between 2 & 3 miles S. East of Amiens on the O.C. arrived 1.45 & after seeing the Landing G. moved my long division thus fr.	
ROISEL	16th May Wednesday		Still at same place. This day spent in arranging details & getting [illegible] settled. O.C. all went to [illegible] Anti the [illegible] C[illegible] Special Public assembly [illegible] at 11/30 [illegible] [illegible] also present from Capt. [illegible] W.B. Nicholls & C.O. Roscanon 2nd [illegible] A.Liegt General 7th Divisional [illegible] Divn. & the [illegible] Captain.	
ROISEL	17th May Thursday		Still at same place. Rations were drawn by M.T. This morning for the whole Division every thing went very well. Escort by the Escort have yesterday Branard [illegible] back. Weather clear, F.	
ROISEL	18th May Friday		Still in same place. Rations were still drawn by M.T. from [illegible] & [illegible] supply dump [illegible] to St. Pulaine. & [illegible] dump & [illegible] [illegible].	
ROISEL	19th May Saturday		Still in same place. Ration still drawn by M.T. in 2. Section 11 Pds. Park. arrived last night suddenly at no notice F.S. very night fr. R.E. dump, arrived at 7 a.m. a return about 2 a.m. were in fr. F.	

2353 Wt. W2544/1454 700,000 5/15 D.D. & L. A.D.S.S./Forms/C. 2118.

Army Form C. 2118.

WAR DIARY
or
INTELLIGENCE SUMMARY.
(Erase heading not required.)

Instructions regarding War Diaries and Intelligence
Summaries are contained in F.S. Regs., Part II.
and the Staff Manual respectively. Title pages
will be prepared in manuscript.

Book 3

Place	Date	Hour	Summary of Events and Information	Remarks and references to Appendices
ROISEL.	20th May. Sunday.		Still in same place. Orders to cease to empty petrol tins have been countermanded from the Brigade as the trench the bodies of this petrol tin can be trench. The shortage of such tins to come has been supplied. Requirements OC ASC went to 2/3rd & 4th Supply offices down another.	
ROISEL.	21st May. Monday.		Still in same place. OC ASC visits DAQ offices. Nothing to report. Drew rations from FP.	
ROISEL.	22nd May. Tuesday.		Still in same place. OC ASC went to 5th office & S OS Retmas BSA & Ball Supplies. Going well. Weather ranged all day. Left to anon today hut at an QM HQ.	
ROISEL. 23rd May. Wednesday.			Still in same place. OC ASR went to "A" office & S.A. Dump. 2nd Lieut (T/Capt) H.W. Bundegast R.A.S.C. V. Attached off. His strength of this unit this day. On attachment to A.D.H.S. & T Corps Corp. Temp. 2nd Lt RASCV. Shoppy Queen ASC. Joined HQ ASC from Base Depot HAVRE. Strain same SC.	
ROISEL.	24th May. Thursday.		Still in same place. OC ASC went to "A" office. The Ball Supplies Section today. a Brigade from the 5 Car Div 10th Fan Don North.	

2353 Wt. W2544/1454 700,000 5/15 D.D. & L. A.D.S.S./Forms/C. 2118.

Army Form C. 2118.

Sheet No 7

WAR DIARY
OR
INTELLIGENCE SUMMARY.
(Erase heading not required.)

Instructions regarding War Diaries and Intelligence Summaries are contained in F. S. Regs., Part II and the Staff Manual respectively. Title pages will be prepared in manuscript.

Place	Date	Hour	Summary of Events and Information	Remarks and references to Appendices
ROISEL.	25th May Friday		Still in same place OC A.S.C sent to B. office L.O. Division Report sent in as usual. Go to send for Co to same. weather fine very warm ft.	
ROISEL.	26th May Saturday		Still in same place. OC A.S.C sent to "B" office in "A" person A.S.C taken as rest break at Lavel. A.P.O. F.O.B with O/O continue till further notice. O Division N? were to sent & go to remove subalterns G.J.O. Rob Lt. F. Webb RAMC. weather fine very warm ft.	
ROISEL.	27th May Sunday		Still in same place. OC A.S.C sent to "B" office OC Supply Column came over today. Reinforcements arrived C.O.R for A.S.C. 3 NCOs for Division which were sent out by lorries for the three Brigades artillery heavy guns. Early this morning a landed for one hour nectar guns ft.	
ROISEL.	28th May Monday.		Still in same place OC A.S.C sent to B. office as usual. Still to remain here ft.	
ROISEL.	29th May Tuesday.		Still in same place OC ASC sent to "B" office Division Report sent in as usual. Lieut Brown Leave wish Leave to the 25th 3rd Sanitary Section returned with a Thes of dinner amp to Oisly Division. Lasual Return as usual at noon Our Detail sent to Leave Gravel at Roum lever camp ft.	

2353 Wt. W2544/1454 700,000 5/15 D. D. & L. A.D.S.S./Forms/C. 2118.

Army Form C. 2118.

WAR DIARY
or
INTELLIGENCE SUMMARY
(Erase heading not required.)

Instructions regarding War Diaries and Intelligence
Summaries are contained in F. S. Regs., Part II
and the Staff Manual respectively. Title pages
will be prepared in manuscript.

Place	Date	Hour	Summary of Events and Information	Remarks and references to Appendices
ROISEL	30 May Wednesday		Still in same place. O.C. A.S.C. went to D.R. office, inspected Ambs. took him June 7?.	Lists No. 7.
ROISEL	31 May Thursday		Still in same place. O.C. A.S.C. went to "A" office. J.O.C. 5" Can. Div took over command from Lieut Colen. Field General Court Martial held at H.Q. 2 S.C., the Court, on M. Tw/10/175, Driver D.L. Prese 3 A.C. 10th Reserve Park. President Major W. v. Ameen D.S.O, 16th Canners. Members Capt. D.J. Ratts M.C. and Lieut T Copper A.S.C. prosecuter Capt. Hood A.R.C. 16th Pion Park. Proceedings were taken to be sent 2nd Canadian Division. Weather fine. L.	

Supp H5 Adjt
H.Q. A.S.C.
2nd Can. Div.

CONFIDENTIAL

War Diary
of

HEADQUARTERS, 2nd Cavalry Divisional A.S.C.

from 1st June, 1917 to 30th June, 1917.

(VOLUME XXXIV)

Army Form C. 2118.

[Stamp: HEADQUARTERS, 2nd CAVALRY DIVL. A.D.C.]

WAR DIARY
or
INTELLIGENCE SUMMARY.
(Erase heading not required.)

VOLUME XXIV April-May

Instructions regarding War Diaries and Intelligence Summaries are contained in F. S. Regs., Part II and the Staff Manual respectively. Title pages will be prepared in manuscript.

Place	Date	Hour	Summary of Events and Information	Remarks and references to Appendices
ROISEL	1st June 1917 Friday		Still in same place. O.C. A.D.C. went K.G. officer mess. Fine weather. Low K.E.	
ROISEL	2nd June 1917 Saturday		Still in same place. O.C. A.D.C. went to "B" office. Several advance guns were an x r. A.L.K.	
ROISEL	3rd June Sunday		Still in same place. O.C. A.D.C. went to "B" office. 3 shells dropped quite close to Roisel this morning. A man went off several details over tea time K.E.	
ROISEL	4th June Monday		Still in same place. O.C. A.L.E. went to "Q" office. W.O. 9. 5 a.m. German aeroplane flew over H.Q. A.D.C. office, where our men were being fired at all round at low burned meant to machine for its own line, at 10.15 the German destroy machines 9.E. group of animals T. S. O. 2 "Ca. Bat (Bhal.Bot.) about 10 shells were slipped for about 2 hours, 3 shells again this time dropping shells allocated on fell within myles of H.A.L.E. office, 2 in the village of ROISEL, yours on R.E. dump, again at about ell about to hr men to 2nd 6 mor shells over 3 grubs near H.Q. A.D.C. & the next R.E. dump a part of evening aright gate weather fine very hot. K.E.	

Army Form 2118.

**HEADQUARTERS,
2nd CAVALRY DIVN**

WAR DIARY
of
INTELLIGENCE SUMMARY
(Erase heading not required.)

Sheet No. I

Place	Date	Hour	Summary of Events and Information	Remarks and references to Appendices
ROISEL	5th June Tuesday		Still in same place. O.C. A.S.C. went H.Q. office usual details gen reg. Pt. fg.	
ROISEL	6th June Wednesday		Still in same place. O.C. A.S.C. went to "Q" office usual detail weather fine very hot. F.	
ROISEL	7th June Thursday		Still in same place. Major Odin made A.R.C. limit 07.1st Can Div. egan some very good points on enters every train. Still in same place, usual detail not after firm morning, a very bad thunder storm in the afternoon F.	
ROISEL	8th June Friday		Still in same place. O.C. A.S.C. went to Q office, formin soldiers buried. St Emile	
FAUCON	9th June Saturday		weather fine Clouds towards evening F.	
ROISEL	10th June Sunday		Still in same place. O.C. A.S.C. went to Q office usual detail weather fine F.	
ROISEL	11th June Monday		Still in same place. O.C. A.L.C. went to "Q" office, usual detail, weather fine F.	
ROISEL			Still in same place. O.C. A.L.C. went to "Q" office Last night heavy firing started on our front at 10 P.M. & lasted for an hour, after that it still continue but not good heavy firing. Field General Court Martial, assembl. of H.Q. A.L.C. by M. T.S/ 116 Lt. Morris I.M. C. & C. of 1st Can H.T. Cpt. Provost Mason A. Soller C.P.S., Creator R.S. Wood A.C. No. Pro Pak. 2nd K.C. Hatter A.C.R.H.A. 2r. & Officer Cap. Barratt the Prisoner the person accused sumando hill brown shirt hammock come weather showery very heavy thunderstorm last night F.	

Army Form 2118.

HEADQUARTERS,
2nd CAVALRY DIVL.
A.S.C.

Sheet N 3

WAR DIARY
INTELLIGENCE SUMMARY

(Erase heading not required.)

Instructions regarding War Diaries and Intelligence Summaries are contained in F. S. Regs, Part II. and the Staff Manual respectively. Title pages will be prepared in manuscript.

Place	Date	Hour	Summary of Events and Information	Remarks and references to Appendices
ROISEL.	12th June. Tuesday.		Still in same place. O.C. A.S.C. went to "Q" office. Lt. Kidd, General Court Martial appeared to give evidence at 10 a.m. duration June Y.S.	
ROISEL.	13th June. Wednesday.		Still in same place. O.C. A.S.C. went to "Q" office. Supply Officers meeting held at H.Q. A.S.C. office 6.15 p.m. Several details weather fine. Y.S.	
ROISEL.	14th June. Thursday.		Still in same place. O.C. A.S.C. went to "Q" office. 5th Lan Rele S.O. changed over with 1st 3rd Cav Rele. Several details weather fine. Y.S.	
ROISEL.	15th June. Friday.		Still in same place. O.C. A.S.C. went to "Q" office. Several details weather fine. Y.S.	
ROISEL.	16th June. Saturday.		Still in same place. O.C. A.S.C. went to "Q" office. A.D.F.& T. Sen Cav. called. Today sick off head o.s. on the transport of A.S.C. officers & supply units weather fine. very hot. Y.S.	
ROISEL.	17th June. Sunday.		Still in same place. O.C. A.S.C. went to "Q" office. Several details. weather fine. very hot. Y.S.	

Army Form C. 2118.

HEADQUARTERS,
2nd CAVALRY DIVL.
A.S.C.

No. ....
Date ....

Sheet No. 3

WAR DIARY
or
INTELLIGENCE SUMMARY.
(Erase heading not required.)

Instructions regarding War Diaries and Intelligence Summaries are contained in F. S. Regs., Part II. and the Staff Manual respectively. Title pages will be prepared in manuscript.

Place	Date	Hour	Summary of Events and Information	Remarks and references to Appendices
ROISEL	18th June. Monday.		Still in same place. O.C. A.S.C. went to "Q" Office. Heavy thunderstorm with rain and movement of enemy in afternoon. F2.	
ROISEL	19th June. Tuesday.		Still in same place. O.C. A.S.C. went to "Q" Office. 7.9. Divin. & Cavalry went to PERONNE LA CHAPELLETTE which assuming them mules taken sent to troops drawn from supply depot. Begin issuing interlope of light draught horses. Have mules. am. & to issue and to mules in am. about 1/2 an hour done at 6 p.m. today. weather very heavy thunderstorm in the morning. sent F1 & F2, June 18.	
ROISEL	20th June. Wednesday.		Still in same place. O.C. A.S.C. usual visit. weather very heavy showers. F2.	
ROISEL	21st June. Thursday.		Still in same place. O.C. A.S.C. went & inspected Transport of H.Q. 3rd Cavalry Brigade this morning. On the whole turn out fair. Horses about 70% of the H.Q. Details & 1st Dragoon Guards. 135% robinson dram. from LA CHAPELLE to H.Q. No.1 Section. 3rd Cav Reserve Park. weather showery. F2.	
ROISEL	22nd June. Friday.		Still in same place. O.C. A.S.C. went to "Q" Office. Lastly Officers meeting held at H.Q. at 6.15 Officers 6 p.m. today. weather showery several cool. F2.	

WAR DIARY
INTELLIGENCE SUMMARY

(Erase heading not required.)

Army Form 2118

HEADQUARTERS,
2nd CAVALRY DIV'L
A.S.C.

Instructions regarding War Diaries and Intelligence Summaries are contained in F.S. Regs., Part II. and the Staff Manual respectively. Title pages will be prepared in manuscript.

Place	Date	Hour	Summary of Events and Information
ROISEL	23rd June. Saturday		Still in same place. O.C. A.S.C. went to "B" Offices. Usual cold weather. Shower R.
ROISEL	24th June. Sunday.		Still in same place. ROISEL Railhead & H.Q. A.S.C. Arr. H. Comp. + 11th Bn Bn. were all badly shelled. This morning the shelling started at 9.20 & Repeated between 2 & 4.20 shells were shot over. 0.9.0 A.S., came over at 12 noon & aimed at Gun Pits on German Aeroplane over here was Railway at 5 p.m. & not at the guns. weather fine F.
ROISEL	25th June. Monday.		Still in same place. O.C. 3 Cav. Bde will be attached to H.Q. A.S.C. moved forward by the 4th Div. Cav. at 1215 R&A.S.C. K10.c.3.5. to R.M.P. K10.c.3.5. near the Junction. Usual cold weather. Shower R.
ROISEL K10.c.3.5.	26th June. Tuesday.		Still in same place O.C. A.S.C. went "A" Offices. Sale last night. S.O.3rd Cavalry Brigade came over to say that his Brigade were coming out of trenches & going in the next night. John noted that H.Van Doris Again & that H.Van Doris would take over good. Orders received that night from H.Q. 2nd Cav. Div. that the Division will exclude the Mont Kentucky & will take over ground near R.M. by 8th Cavalry Division. One Shell was been thrown South of ROISEL village this afternoon. weather fine R.
ROISEL K10.c.3.5.	27th June. Wednesday.		Still in same place. O.C. A.S.C. went to "B" Offices. Usual cold weather. Shower R.

Army Form C. 2118.

HEADQUARTERS,
2nd CAVALRY DIVN.
A.S.C.

No. ....
Date ....

Remarks and references to Appendices

Sheet 6

WAR DIARY
INTELLIGENCE SUMMARY.
(Erase heading not required.)

Instructions regarding War Diaries and Intelligence Summaries are contained in F. S. Regs., Part II. and the Staff Manual respectively. Title pages will be prepared in manuscript.

Place	Date	Hour	Summary of Events and Information
ROISEL R.10.c.8.5.	29th June Thursday		Still in same place. O.C. A.S.C. went to "Q" office. Several detail meeting — day of the entry. A very heavy thunderstorm to-night. JG.
ROISEL R.10.c.9.5.	29th June Friday		Still in same place. O.C. A.S.C. went to "Q" office all morning, left point 6, 3 Car Div. were taken over 6, 2 Ca Ba. weather fine. JG.
ROISEL R.10.c.8.5.	30th June Saturday		Still in same place. O.C. A.S.C. went to "Q" office several detail. weather rain all day. JG.

Jury. Capt. & Adjt.
H.Q. A.S.C.
2nd Cav. Div.

CONFIDENTIAL

War Diary
of
Headquarters 2nd Cavalry Divisional A.S.C.

From 1st July 1917 to 31st July 1917.

(VOLUME XXXV)

WAR DIARY
or
INTELLIGENCE SUMMARY.
(Erase heading not required.)

Army Form C. 2118.

VOLUME XXXV

HEADQUARTERS,
2nd CAVALRY DIV.
A.D.S.S.

Instructions regarding War Diaries and Intelligence Summaries are contained in F.S. Regs., Part II and the Staff Manual respectively. Title pages will be prepared in manuscript.

Place	Date	Hour	Summary of Events and Information	Remarks and references to Appendices
	1st July. Sunday.		Still in same place. Usual detail. Weather rained most of day. fr.	
ROISEL.	K.10.c.3.5.			
	2nd July. Monday.		Still in same place. O.C. A.S.C. went to "B" office. Usual detail weather fine fr.	
ROISEL	K.10.c.3.5.			
	3rd July. Tuesday.		Still in same place. O.C. A.S.C. went to "Q" office. Usual detail weather showery fr.	
ROISEL	K.10.c.3.5.			
	4th July. Wednesday.		Still in same place. O.C. A.S.C. visited "B" "Q" offices. Orders came that Railhead for 2nd Cav Div. would be TINCOURT for 6.5.17 onwards. weather fine fr.	
ROISEL	K.10.c.3.5.			
	5th July. Thursday.		[illegible]	
ROISEL	K.10.c.3.5.		Still in same place. O.C. A.S.C. went to "B" office about [illegible] matter [illegible] fr.	
	6th July. Friday.		Still in same place. O.C. A.S.C. went to "Q" office, Q.M.G. off "B" office & on to [illegible] 3rd [illegible] [illegible] morning & got on at attached work cards fr.	
ROISEL	K.10.c.3.5.			
	7th July. Saturday.		Still in same place. fr.	
ROISEL	K.10.c.3.5.		Still in same place. O.C. A.S.C. went to "B" office. Usual K.10.c detail weather fine fr.	

Army Form C. 2118.

WAR DIARY
or
INTELLIGENCE SUMMARY
(Erase heading not required.)

Instructions regarding War Diaries and Intelligence Summaries are contained in F. S. Regs., Part II. and the Staff Manual respectively. Title pages will be prepared in manuscript.

HEADQUARTERS, 2nd CAVALRY DIVN.

Vol XXXI
Sheet No. V

Place	Date	Hour	Summary of Events and Information	Remarks and references to Appendices
ROISEL K.10.c.3.5.	8th July. Sunday.		Still in same place. OC. A.S.C. and 1st H.Q. officer, Supply Officer & Divisional Interpreter to Supply dump today to BUIRE. D.A.Q.M.G. called No. 6 platoon A.S.C. Supply column. Weather very bad. Thunderstorm early PM. Morning & two evening. Not very heavy. Storms in between. JL	
BUIRE	9th July. Monday.		A.S.C. H.Q. & transport move from ROISEL today. All came at 9.5 am. O.C. A.S.C. went to "Q" office in the morning & evening. Thunderstorm in evening, rain seemed to have driven air somewhat fresher. Not heavy storms. JL	
BUIRE	10th July. Tuesday.		Still in same place. O.C. A.S.C. went to "Q" office in morning. Also again in the evening. D.A.A.Q.M.G. called this evening just after June. JL	
BUIRE	11th July. Wednesday.		Still in same place. OC. A.S.C. went to "Q" office in morning. Usual detail working JL	
BUIRE	12th July. Thursday.		Still in same place. O.C. A.S.C. went to "Q" office in morning & evening. 4 & 5" cavalry Bdes moved today. Usual detail weather fine JL	

2353 Wt W2544/1454 700,000 5/15 D. D. & L. A.D.S.S./Forms/C. 2118.

WAR DIARY or INTELLIGENCE SUMMARY

Army Form C. 2118.

Vol XXXV

(Erase heading not required.)

Place	Date	Hour	Summary of Events and Information	Remarks and references to Appendices
SUZANNE.	13th July. Friday.		Divisional troops & 3rd Cavalry Brigade moved today. H.Q. 2nd Cav left BUIRE at 8.30 through MÉRICOURT, QUINTON, CLERY, MARICOURT, SUZANNE. C.H. A.S.C. units moved in by A.A.M. road. Very good. Div. rec Rifles. O.C. A.S.C. went to "Q" office. D.A.Q. 9 A.M. called on his Excellency & cancelled ordnance. Junior meeting here at Arch TREUX presentation. Very hot place. JR.	
TREUX	14th July. Saturday.		Divisional troops & 3rd Cavalry Brigade move today. H.Q. 2nd Cav. left SUZANNE at 7.30 a.m. through BRAY, MORLANCOURT, TREUX. Arrived 9 a.m. in billets — W.P.F. & A.P.M. moved into billets. Also some details. Aid to "Q" office 4th / 7th Car. Rifles. BRAY very bad place. O.C. A.S.C. went to "Q" office. Weather fine. JR.	
THIEVRES.	15th July. Sunday.		Divisional troops & 3rd Cav. Bde moved today. H.Q. 2nd Cav. left TREUX at 6.30 a.m. sunlit. Stanley. Paid: Church St. LAVIEVILLE, HENENCILLE, FORCEVILLE, LOUVENCOURT, THIEVRES. Roads bad. From TREUX to LAVIEVILLE. Church. Used of roads good, but quite a number of long hills. Off. A.S.C. lunch (H.T.) and G. 1.30 p.m. H. & 5th Car Bgdes moved today. O.C. A.S.C. went to "Q" office just after arriving & opened at 5 p.m. weather moved. Road all last night. Quite today. JR.	

Army Form C. 2118.

WAR DIARY
INTELLIGENCE SUMMARY.
(Erase heading not required.)

Instructions regarding War Diaries and Intelligence Summaries are contained in F.S. Regs., Part II. and the Staff Manual respectively. Title pages will be prepared in manuscript.

HEADQUARTERS,
2nd CAVALRY DIVL.
A.S.C.

Place	Date	Hour	Summary of Events and Information	Remarks and references to Appendices
HOUVIGNEUL	16th July Sunday		Divisional troops & 3rd Cav Bde. moved today. H.Q. A.S.C. left THIEVRES at 9.20 A.M. via Acheux, Harbonnières, Pont, T. Noyelle, THIEBS, BEAURICOURT, MARIEUX, HALLOY, LUCHEUX, IVERGNY, HOUVIGNEUL. Arriving at HOUVIGNEUL 3.30 P.M. Roads proved unsatisfactory. FR	
HOUVIGNEUL	17th July Monday		Still in same place. O.C. A.S.C. spent S & Q. officers evening to make arrangements for horses. Have to go 2 miles kiosk in regard details weather fine FR	
HOUVIGNEUL	18th July Tuesday		Still in same place O.C. A.S.C. went to "Q" office. weak. actual weather showery FR	
HOUVIGNEUL	19th July Wednesday		Still in same place. O.C. A.S.C. went to "Q" office. Class in afternoon to 2nd Line #7 2nd Ammunition Park. Reserve Park. weather rained most of today. FR	
HOUVIGNEUL	20th July Thursday		Still in same place O.C. A.S.C. went to "Q" office weather fine FR	
HOUVIGNEUL	21st July Friday		Still in same place. O.C. A.S.C. went to "Q" office weather rainy. FR	
HOUVIGNEUL	22nd July Saturday		Still in same place O.C. A.S.C. went to "Q" office Maj. N. McCrae departed for civil leave to BOULOGNE. A.Q.M.Q.M.S. called. Weather fine FR	

WAR DIARY or INTELLIGENCE SUMMARY

Army Form C. 2118.

Vol XXXI Sheet No. 5

HEADQUARTERS, 2nd CAVALRY DIVL. A.S.C.

Place	Date	Hour	Summary of Events and Information	Remarks and references to Appendices
HOUVIGNEUL	23rd July. Monday.		Still in same place. O.C. A.S.C. went to "A" Office. O.C. Cattle Purchase Board called. weather fine. ft.	
HOUVIGNEUL	24th July. Tuesday.		Still in same place. O.C. A.S.C. went to "Q" Office. A.A. & Q.M.G. called. also O.C. Aux. H.T. Coy. O.C. Supply Colm. weather fine. ft.	
HOUVIGNEUL	25th July. Wednesday.		Still in same place O.C. A.S.C. went to "Q" Office weather showery. ft.	
HOUVIGNEUL	26th July. Thursday.		Still in same place. O.C. D.S.C. went to "Q" Office. weather fine. ft.	
HOUVIGNEUL	27th July. Friday.		Still in same place. O.C. A.S.C. went to "Q" Office. 1st day of Divisional Horse Show. weather fine. ft.	
HOUVIGNEUL	28th July. Saturday.		Still in same place. O.C. A.S.C. went to "Q" Office. 2nd day of Divisional Horse Show. weather fine. ft.	
HOUVIGNEUL	29th July. Sunday.		Still in same place. O.C. A.S.C. went to "Q" Office. weather very hot. Thunderstorm evening fol. by heavy ft.	

Army Form C. 2118.

WAR DIARY
or
INTELLIGENCE SUMMARY.
(Erase heading not required.)

Instructions regarding War Diaries and Intelligence Summaries are contained in F. S. Regs., Part II. and the Staff Manual respectively. Title pages will be prepared in manuscript.

HEADQUARTERS, 2nd CAVALRY DIVL. A.S.C.
No. ....

Place	Date	Hour	Summary of Events and Information	Remarks and references to Appendices
HOUVIGNEUL	30th July. Monday		Still in same place. O.C. A.S.C. went to "Q" office. O.C. Supply Column collected his morning 2nd Cavalry Reserve Park. D. Assot. A.T. Comp. moved to-day to ETREE WAMIN. Mobile Supply Column forwt today as usual. Capt. C.C. Aylmer A.S.C. at ETREE WAMIN awaiting the moment for transfer to A.S.C. reinforcements. The afternoon's mail'd kall. 3 remits and found. Bells the obergue's excell. in Mobile Supply Column. 1 Lce/Sjt 5. appointed from 5th Lancers. Lt. C.P. Bloodworth A.S.C. joined from A.S.C. Base Depot & appointed to H.Q. 2nd Car. Bde. as T.O. vice Lt. P. Whittome. 4 mules arrived from Reserve Park to replace 4 T.D. of the Divisional reinforcements. All mares sent to SILVELIN as Brood mares now accepted from this unit. Supply Column drew the following Reserve Ration today from H.Q. Field Supply. Depot. DOULLENS Iron ration. 15,440. Oats. 130,566 lbs. in 2 lb sacks = 1632 sacks. These are now stored at the Supply Column. Weather fine. F	
HOUVIGNEUL	31st July. Tuesday		Still in same place. O.C. A.S.C. went to "Q" office. Lt. P.E. Whittome left for No. 2 School Bedford, England. He attached to the Infantry meanwhile from his first arrival in Brig. as empland. Hereinafter taken. F.	

Every. Capt & Adjt.
H.Q. O.A.C.
2nd Cavalry Division

Vol. 14

WAR DIARY
OF.
HEAD QUARTERS, A.S.C., 2nd CAVALRY DIVISION
FOR
AUGUST 1917.

(VOLUME XXXVI)

Army Form C. 2118.

WAR DIARY

INTELLIGENCE SUMMARY.

(Erase heading not required.)

Instructions regarding War Diaries and Intelligence
Summaries are contained in F. S. Regs., Part II.
and the Staff Manual respectively. Title pages
will be prepared in manuscript.

HEADQUARTERS,
2nd CAVALRY DIVL.
A.S.C.

VOLUME XXVI

Sheet No. 1

Place	Date	Hour	Summary of Events and Information	Remarks and references to Appendices
HOUVIGNEUL.	1st August 1917.		Still in same place. O.C. A.S.C. went to "A" Office. O.C. Supply Column called. I.D. from FREVENT there but will not till about with the Division. Weather rained all day.	
HOUVIGNEUL.	2nd August 1917.		Still in same place. O.C. A.S.C. went to "Q" Office with O.C. Supply Column. D.A.Q.M.G. called at morning. D.A.Q.M.G. called at mid-day. O.C. A.S.C. went to see Reserve Park, Amm. & T Coy & Mobile Supply Column everything alright. Weather rained all day.	
HOUVIGNEUL.	3rd August 1917.		Still in same place. O.C. A.S.C. went to "A" Office. O.C. Supply Column called this morning. O.C. D.L.C. went to inspect transport of the 3rd Cavalry Brigade & Divisional's good allround. Weather rained most day.	
HOUVIGNEUL.	4th August 1917.		Still in same place. O.C. A.S.C. went to inspect transport of 1st & 4th Cavalry Brigade. Himself liked. O.C. Res. Park & O.C. Amm. & T Coy. called this morning. D.A.Q.M.G. came to "A" Office. Weather fine.	
HOUVIGNEUL.	5th August 1917.		Still in same place. O.C. A.S.C. went to "Q" Office also a Mobile Supply Column inspection general.	
HOUVIGNEUL.	6th August 1917.		Still in same place. O.C. A.S.C. went to "Q" Office also to the Ammunition Park. Weather fine. Major R.J. Davis A.S.C. 10 days leave to England.	

Army Form C. 2118.

WAR DIARY

INTELLIGENCE SUMMARY.
(Erase heading not required.)

Instructions regarding War Diaries and Intelligence Summaries are contained in F.S. Regs., Part II. and the Staff Manual respectively. Title pages will be prepared in manuscript.

[Stamp: HEADQUARTERS, 2nd CAVALRY DIVL. A.S.C.]

Sheet No. II

Place	Date	Hour	Summary of Events and Information	Remarks and references to Appendices
HOUVIGNEUL	7th August 1917		Still in same place. O.C. A.S.C. went to "Q" Office. In the afternoon went to inspect supply section of the 8th Hussars. Weather fine. JR.	
HOUVIGNEUL	8th August 1917		Still in same place. O.C. A.S.C. went to "Q" office also went to inspected the Mobile Supply Officer. Weather fine all day. Two small thunderstorms in the evening. JR.	
HOUVIGNEUL	9th August 1917		Still in same place. O.C. A.S.C. went to "Q" office. O.C. Supply Column called in the morning. Weather fine morning, showery rest of day. JR.	
HOUVIGNEUL	10th August 1917		Still in same place. O.C. A.S.C. went to "Q" Office. 2i/c Cavalry Corps Sup. Column etc. pm. The Assoc. H.T. Cont. everything in good order. Weather showery. JR.	
HOUVIGNEUL	11th August 1917		Still in same place. O.C. A.S.C. went to "Q" Office. O.C. Supply Column called this morning. Weather fine morning, rained all afternoon & heavy thunderstorm in the evening. JR.	
HOUVIGNEUL	12th August 1917		Still in same place. O.C. A.S.C. went to "Q" Office. Lt. Colonel W. Scott Elliot O.C. A.S.C. went on leave to the United Kingdom this day. Major J. Murphy will take over command of the section of the A.S.C. at. weather. June JR.	

Army Form C. 2118.

WAR DIARY
INTELLIGENCE SUMMARY
(Erase heading not required.)

Instructions regarding War Diaries and Intelligence Summaries are contained in F. S. Regs., Part II. and the Staff Manual respectively. Title pages will be prepared in manuscript.

Chief. No. III

HEADQUARTERS,
2nd CAVALRY DIVL.
A.S.C.

Place	Date	Hour	Summary of Events and Information	Remarks and references to Appendices
HOUVIGNEUL	13th August 1917		Still in same place. Adjutant H.Q. a.s.c. went to "Q" Office. O.C. Supply Column here this morning. Weather fine J.R.	
HOUVIGNEUL	14th August 1917		Still in same place. Adjutant H.Q.a.s.c. went to "Q" Office. O.C. Supply Column called this morning. Weather fine also thunderstorm in the evening J.R.	
HOUVIGNEUL	15th August 1917		Still in same place. Adjutant H.Q.a.s.c. went to "Q" Office. O.C. Supply Column called this morning. Weather fine, morning showery afternoon J.R.	
HOUVIGNEUL	16th August 1917		Still in same place. Adjutant H.Q. A.S.C. went to "Q" Office. O.C. Supply Column called this morning. Weather fine J.R.	
HOUVIGNEUL	17th August 1917		Still in same place. Adjutant H.Q. a.s.c. went to "Q" Office. O.C. Supply Column called this morning. Weather fine J.R.	
HOUVIGNEUL	18th August 1917		Still in same place. Adjutant H.Q. A.S.C. went to "Q" Office. (all know are reporting Division on the 24th) O.C. Supply Column called this morning. weather showery J.R.	

Army Form C. 2118.

WAR DIARY
INTELLIGENCE SUMMARY
(Erase heading not required.)

Instructions regarding War Diaries and Intelligence Summaries are contained in F. S. Regs., Part II. and the Staff Manual respectively. Title pages will be prepared in manuscript.

HEADQUARTERS,
2nd CAVALRY DIVL
A.S.C.
Date..................

Sheet No. IV.

Place	Date	Hour	Summary of Events and Information	Remarks and references to Appendices
HOUVIGNUEL	19th August 1917		Still in same place. Adjutant H.Q. A.S.C. went to "A" Office. O.C. Supply Column called this morning, weather fine. J.E.	
HOUVIGNUEL	20th August 1917		Still in same place. J.O.C. 2nd Cavalry Division inspected the Convoy at 10 o'clock. Also 6 Supply Column, Ammn. H.T. Coy., R.A. Park, "S.A.P. Section of Ammunition Column, Mobile Supply Column. Very well turned out. Gave an order. He would inspect them again in the near future. Seems pleased for appearance. All an improvement of some sort of the journals. Good. Batteries returned today. O.C. Supply Column called in this morning, weather fine. J.E.	
HOUVIGNUEL	21st August 1917		Still in same place. Adjutant H.Q. A.S.C. went to "Q" Office, also to inspection of the Reserve of Mobile Supply Column by A.D.V.S. 6 horses to be evacuated & the sent through the regiment for them to be checked. Also strongest horses. O.C. Supply Column here in the morning. Weather fine. J.E.	
HOUVIGNUEL	22nd August 1917		Still in same place. Adjutant H.Q. A.S.C. went to "B" Office. O.C. Supply Column called this morning. Also O.C. Amn H.T. Coy., J.O.C. 3rd Cavalry Brigade inspected the 3rd Cavalry Brigade Ammn Column of the Mobile Supply Column. Weather fine. J.E.	

2353 Wt. W2544/1454 700,000 5/15 D. D. & L. A.D.S.S./Forms/C. 2118.

Army Form C. 2118.

WAR DIARY
or
INTELLIGENCE SUMMARY.
(Erase heading not required.)

Instructions regarding War Diaries and Intelligence Summaries are contained in F. S. Regs., Part II. and the Staff Manual respectively. Title pages will be prepared in manuscript.

HEADQUARTERS,
2nd CAVALRY DIVL.
A.S.C.

Place	Date	Hour	Summary of Events and Information	Remarks and references to Appendices
HOUVIGNEUL	23rd August 1917		Still in same place. Adjutant + H.Q. O.I.C. went to "Q" office. O.C. Supply Column called this morning. L.O.C. 1.8th Cavalry Brigade inspected the Brigade section of Mobile Supply Column. Fine day. Heavy showers in the evening. J.R.	
HOUVIGNEUL	24th August 1917.		Still in same place. Adjutant + H.Q. O.I.C. went to "Q" office. O.C. Supply Column called this morning. Lieut J. 4th Cavalry Brigade inspected the Brigade section of Mobile Supply Column. Lt-Col W. Scott Elliot returned from leave this day. weather fine. J.R.	
HOUVIGNEUL	25th August 1917.		Still in same place. O.C. O.I.C. went to "Q" office. S.S.O. went to inspect the advance Dump. Orders been taken. D.O.I.S. adjutant. Brown return to tea & bicycles. fine day. Good starting trip. weather fine. J.R.	
HOUVIGNEUL	26th August 1917.		Still in same place. O.C. O.I.C. went to "Q" office. weather fine. J.R.	
HOUVIGNEUL	27th August 1917.		Still in same place. O.C. O.I.C. went to "Q" office. O.C. Res Park & O.C. Divn AT cant called this afternoon. weather fine. morning. rained rest of day & all night. J.R.	

Army Form C. 2118.

WAR DIARY
INTELLIGENCE SUMMARY.
(Erase heading not required.)

Instructions regarding War Diaries and Intelligence Summaries are contained in F. S. Regs., Part II. and the Staff Manual respectively. Title pages will be prepared in manuscript.

HEADQUARTERS, 2nd CAVALRY DIVL A.S.C.

Sheet No. VI

Place	Date	Hour	Summary of Events and Information	Remarks and references to Appendices
HOUVIGNEUL	28th August 1917.		Still in same place. O.C. A.S.C. went to "B" Office. also went to Supply Column in the afternoon. weather fine. FE	see MTAR
HOUVIGNEUL	29th August 1917.		Still in same place. O.C. A.S.C. went to "B" Office. weather rained hard all day. FE	
HOUVIGNEUL	30th August 1917.		Still in same place. O.C. A.S.C. went to "B" Office. also to A.D.S. & T. Corps by Corps. in the afternoon. weather showery. FE	
HOUVIGNEUL	31st August 1917.		Still in same place. O.C. A.S.C. went to "B" Office. also to Gd.S. 5th Cavalry Brigade & A.Squad. Brigade H.Q. weather fine. FE	

Evans. Capt. & Adjt.
H.Q. A.S.C.
2nd Cavalry Division

> HEADQUARTERS,
> 2nd CAVALRY DIVL.
> A.S.C.
>
> No.
> Date

CONFIDENTIAL

War Diary

of

Headquarters 2nd Cavalry Divisional A.S.C.

from 1st September 1917 to 30th September 1917.

VOLUME XXXVII.

Army Form C. 2118.

WAR DIARY
INTELLIGENCE SUMMARY.
(Erase heading not required.)

VOLUME XXXVII Sheet No 1

HEADQUARTERS,
2nd CAVALRY DIV.
A.S.C.

Instructions regarding War Diaries and Intelligence Summaries are contained in F. S. Regs., Part II. and the Staff Manual respectively. Title pages will be prepared in manuscript.

Place	Date	Hour	Summary of Events and Information	Remarks and references to Appendices
HOUVIGNEUL.	1st September 1917.		Still in same place. O.C. A.S.C. went to "Q" Office. Cavalry Corps. Horse Show. Weather fine morning. Showery & cold rest of day. P.L.	
HOUVIGNEUL.	2nd September 1917.		Still in same place. O.C. A.S.C. went to "Q" Office. Weather fine P.L.	
HOUVIGNEUL.	3rd September 1917.		Still in same place. O.C. A.S.C. went to "Q" Office. All wagons & carts belonging to H.Q. A.S.C. went out. Relieving teams in A.C. & M.S. called. weather fine P.L.	
HOUVIGNEUL.	4th September 1917.		Still in same place. O.C. A.S.C. went to "Q" Office. All wagons & carts still on farm work. weather fine. P.L.	
HOUVIGNEUL	5th September 1917.		Still in same place. O.C. A.S.C. went to "Q" Office. O.C. Res. Park called this morning. All wagons on farm work. weather fine. P.L.	
HOUVIGNEUL.	6th September 1917.		Still in same place. O.C. A.S.C. went to "Q" Office. O.C. Supply Column called this morning. A.D.V.S & A.D.? Sgt Cavalry Corps. lunch at H.Q. A.C. & in the afternoon inspected 1st & 2nd Cavalry Divisions Res. Park & Amm. H.T. Carts. 6th note will handed with demands. weather fine. Very heavy shower in the evening P.L. Major R.J. Cox's relieve (other than Farrier & m.n.) Bain P.L.	

Army Form C. 2118.

WAR DIARY
INTELLIGENCE SUMMARY

(Erase heading not required.)

HEADQUARTERS,
2nd CAVALRY DIV'L A.S.C.

Sheet No. II

Place	Date	Hour	Summary of Events and Information	Remarks and references to Appendices
HOUVIGNEUL	7th September 1917		Still in same place. O.C. A.S.C. went to "Q" office weather F.	
HOUVIGNEUL	8th September 1917		Still in same place. A.A. & Q.M.G. called this morning, also O.C. Supply Column. Some M.T. cars washed. Fine F.	
HOUVIGNEUL	9th September 1917		Still in same place. O.C. A.C. went to "Q" office, also to Medical Dept. to supply Column. Wood Merrier called last night. 3rd & 4th Brigades money some of their unit. Issued a lorries for 5th Cavalry Bde. O.C. A.S.C. went to see 3rd & 4th Can Bde. L.O. Thin afternoon weather fine F.P.	
HOUVIGNEUL	10th September 1917		Still in same place. O.C. A.S.C. went to "Q" office's 4th Can Brigade. Moved some of its units. Weather fine F.	
HOUVIGNEUL	11th September 1917		Still in same place. O.C. A.S.C. went to "Q" office. O.C. Supply Column called this morning. Also went with D.A.D. & Q.M.G. Bus for billets of Can. H.T. Coms weather fine F.P.	
HOUVIGNEUL	12th September 1917		Still in same place. O.C. A.S.C. went to "Q" office. Part H.T. Coms moved from ETRÉE WAMIN to MONCHEL also got in to Bedevn and green 3 Can Bde + one for 4 Can Bde. Weather fine. F.P.	
HOUVIGNEUL	13th September 1917		Still in same place. O.C. A.S.C. went to "Q" office. Also H.T. Coms. started today to bring rations from Railhead at "Pool" + "Can Bde." Weather fine F.P.	

WAR DIARY.

INTELLIGENCE SUMMARY.

(Erase heading not required.)

Army Form C. 2118.

HEADQUARTERS,
2nd CAVALRY DIVL.
A.S.C.

Instructions regarding War Diaries and Intelligence Summaries are contained in F. S. Regs., Part II. and the Staff Manual respectively. Title pages will be prepared in manuscript.

Appx. No. III.

Place	Date	Hour	Summary of Events and Information	Remarks and references to Appendices
HOUVIGNEUL	14th September 1917		Still in same place. O.C. A.S.C. went to "Q" office. O.C. Supply Column called this morning. O.C. A.S.C. went to see Mobile Supply Column in afternoon. weather fine. F.R.	
HOUVIGNEUL	15th September 1917		Still in same place. O.C. A.S.C. went to "Q" office. O.C. Supply Column called this morning. O.C. Ant. Interview with O.C. Supply Column at the Supply Column from 10 to 6 CIVs an hour. Road & horse petrol dump of the Main Reserve left in good order. O.C. Mobile Supply Column called this morning. weather fine. F.R.	
HOUVIGNEUL	16th September 1917		Still in same place. O.C. A.S.C. went to "Q" office. O.C. Supply Column called this morning. weather fine. F.R.	
HOUVIGNEUL	17th September 1917		Still in same place. O.C. A.S.C. went to "Q" office. Also to see Ammunition Park in K afternoon. O.C. Supply Column called this morning. weather fine. F.R.	
HOUVIGNEUL	18th September 1917		Still in same place. O.C. A.S.C. went A.D. office. O.C. Supply Column called this morning. weather fine. F.R.	
HOUVIGNEUL	19th September 1917		Still in same place. O.C. A.S.C. went to "A" office. J.O.C. inspected Horses & Supply Column this afternoon. O.C. A.S.C. passed everything good. weather fine. F.R.	

Army Form C. 2118.

Sheet No. IV

WAR DIARY

INTELLIGENCE SUMMARY.

(Erase heading not required.)

Instructions regarding War Diaries and Intelligence Summaries are contained in F.S. Regs., Part II. and the Staff Manual respectively. Title pages will be prepared in manuscript.

HEADQUARTERS, 2nd CAVALRY DIVL. A.S.C.

Date........................

Place	Date	Hour	Summary of Events and Information	Remarks and references to Appendices
HOUVIGNEUL	20th September 1917		Still in same place. O.C. asc. went to "S" office. Work carried on until 12. Remainder afternoon men at ex. M.O. & D.S. on transport of M.T. Accounts party. K. Weather fine.	
HOUVIGNEUL	21st September 1917		Still in same place. O.C. asc. went to "D" office. Word came more of remounted cancelled for 2 days but transport moved to day to receive two days rations above 102. Men on parade at 23. Weather fine. K.	
HOUVIGNEUL	22nd September 1917		Still in same place. O.C. O.C. went to "D" office. Thompson promoted 2 Lieut K JOURDAIN in command to be attached to A6 Supply Column for [?] remounts or arrival in advance [?] two horses which are [?]. Weather fine. K.	
HOUVIGNEUL	23rd September 1917		Still in same place. O.C. O.C.S. saw a "D" office. Remounts finally arrived 177 horses of the Thomson.	
HOUVIGNEUL	24th September 1917		Still in same place. O.C. asc. went to a "B" office. Lieut. O.H. Hayhurst-Hayward to the Supply Column. Moved with S.S.O. to see. Saw a fifty horses worked on the ground wanting of surplus. Weather fine. K.	
HOUVIGNEUL	25th September 1917		Still in same place. O.C. asc. went to "S" office. Lieut. Appointment to Railway unit. S.S.O. Lieut. on a [?] at Supply Officer's [?] to attend. S.S.O. going to give a [?] pass on 6 Company transports. Weather fine. K.	

Army Form C. 2118.

WAR DIARY
or
INTELLIGENCE SUMMARY.
(Erase heading not required.)

HEADQUARTERS,
2nd CAVALRY DIVL.
A. S. C.

Instructions regarding War Diaries and Intelligence Summaries are contained in F. S. Regs., Part II. and the Staff Manual respectively. Title pages will be prepared in manuscript.

Place	Date	Hour	Summary of Events and Information	Remarks and references to Appendices
HOUVIGNEUL	26th September 1917		Still in same place. O.C. A.S.C. went to "Q" office. Also went to Sec. Quart. H.T. Coy. Afternoon weather fine rainy. Work afternoon. JR	
HOUVIGNEUL	27th September 1917		Still in same place. O.C. A.S.C. went to "Q" office. O.C. Supply Column called this morning also O.C. Res. Park. O.C. O.R.C. & S.t.O went to 5th Cavalry Brigade H.Q. also to HQ. O.C. 17-18 Royal Hussars XX Hussars On account of short-weight 17 oats & Hay. Everything arranged & settled weather fine. Rain shower last night JR	
HOUVIGNEUL	28th September 1917		Still in same place. O.C. A.S.C. went to "Q" office. O.C. Supply Column called this morning, O.C. A.S.E. went to Mobile Supply Column weather fine JR	
HOUVIGNEUL	29th September 1917		Still in same place. O.C. A.S.C. went to "Q" & "R" office. O.C. Supply Column called this morning also. O.C. Ammunition Park the afternoon. weather fine JR	
HOUVIGNEUL	30th September 1917		Still in same place. O.C. Supply Column called this morning, also A.C.G.M.G. O.C. A.S.C. went to "Q" office. this evening on the perform the Supply Column & O.C. Section weather fine JR	

Sirur Coff a Capt.
H.Q. A.S.C.
2nd Cavalry Division

CONFIDENTIAL.

WAR DIARY.

of

H.Q., 2nd Cavalry Divisional

Army Service Corps.

From 1st October 1917, To 31st October 1917.

(Volume. XXXVIII)

HEADQUARTERS,
2nd CAVALRY DIVL
A.S.C. Army Form C. 2118.

No..........
Date..........

VOLUME XVIII Sheet No 1

WAR DIARY
or
INTELLIGENCE SUMMARY.
(Erase heading not required.)

Instructions regarding War Diaries and Intelligence Summaries are contained in F. S. Regs., Part II. and the Staff Manual respectively. Title pages will be prepared in manuscript.

Place	Date	Hour	Summary of Events and Information	Remarks and references to Appendices
HOUVIGNEUL.	1st October 1917.		Still in same place. O.C. A.S.C. went to "B" & "Q" Office. O.C. Mobile Supply Column called this morning also Temm'l. Supply Officer and Supervising Veter. Surgeon. Weather fine. J.R.	
HOUVIGNEUL.	2nd October 1917.		Still in same place. O.C. A.S.C. went to "Q" Office. O.C. Supply Column as not this morning. O.C. A.S.C. went to see of Ammunition Park. O.C. Mobile Supply Column called this morning to say that all Vehicles had returned to their Brigades. Weather fine. J.R.	
HOUVIGNEUL.	3rd October 1917.		Still in same place. O.C. A.S.C. went to "Q" Office. O.C. Supply Column called this morning. The O.C. of the Mobile Supply Column moved into grounds for old chail in a decent of H.Q.C.M.C. Weather changed. Rain. J.R.	
HOUVIGNEUL.	4th October 1917.		Still in same place. O.C. A.S.C. went to "B" & "Q" Office. O.C. Supply Column called this morning also Temm'l. Supply Officer. Programme received today for O.C. Division Ammunition to move on 9 & 10 J. October. Changed in morning, fine in afternoon. Quiet enemy. J.R.	
HOUVIGNEUL.	5th October 1917.		Still in same place. O.C. A.S.C. went to "Q" Office. O.C. Supply Column called this morning. Transport of 15 Lancashire retired today. Weather cold autumn. J.R.	
HOUVIGNEUL.	6th October 1917.		Still in same place. O.C. A.S.C. went to "B" & "Q" Office. O.C. Supply Column called this morning. Orders received today. Division move on 9th but detrained but will call a limit. Weather fined and clearing. Enemy in splendid. J.R.	
HOUVIGNEUL.	7th October 1917.		Still in same place. O.C. A.S.C. went to "Q" Office. O.C. Supply Column called this morning. All supplies according to Mobile Supply Column now being loaded up to go with train. Orders at lunch from Division. J.R.	

WAR DIARY
INTELLIGENCE SUMMARY
(Erase heading not required.)

HEADQUARTERS,
2nd CAVALRY DIVL.
A.S. Army. Form C. 2118.

Instructions regarding War Diaries and Intelligence Summaries are contained in F. S. Regs., Part II. and the Staff Manual respectively. Title pages will be prepared in manuscript.

Place	Date	Hour	Summary of Events and Information	Remarks and references to Appendices
HEUCHIN	8th October 1917	9.20 a.m.	H.Q. of 4th Cavalry Diff. Movement today. H.Q. A.S.C. Leaves 1st at 7am. Starting Point bank entrance of MINGEVAL. Route taken HEUCHIN LE-SEC., VAVRANS ANVIN HEUCHIN. Transport arrived 2.30 p.m. No motor office at MONCAY-CAYEUX. Roads & roads somewhat heavy. Horses in good condition. All horses & men under cover. Water from... men, most of horses soft muddy, weather fine. J.E.	
HEUCHIN	9th October 1917		All in same place. O.C. A.S.C. went to "Q" office. H.Q. R.H.A. & 3 Batteries approved. The Divisions today. A.O. 5th Cavalry Brigade called. Fine afternoon. Weather showery. J.E.	
HEUCHIN	10th October 1917		Still in same place. O.C. A.S.C. went to "Q" office. Amer. 4th Camp. Motor. Supply Column. Aux Park. Supply Column. A.O. 3rd Bde. came over in afternoon. A.D.O. & 6th Bde called this evening also A.D.V.S. called. No more water for men. Billets weather showery. J.E.	
HEUCHIN	11th October 1917		Still in same place. O.C. A.S.C. went to "Q" office. Water fine. J.E.	
HEUCHIN	12th October 1917		Still in same place. O.C. A.S.C. went to Railhead to see despatch of units. A.O. of S.& T. Can. Corps here as well. A.S.C. were all out night. Water Kent all day. J.E.	
HEUCHIN	13th October 1917		Still in same place. O.C. A.S.C. went to "Q" office. Orders came relative for return to a Supply Depot. Weather fine from morn. Rained most of the afternoon. J.E.	

HEADQUARTERS,
2nd CAVALRY DIV.
A.S.C. Army Form C. 2118.

WAR DIARY
or
INTELLIGENCE SUMMARY.
(Erase heading not required.)

Instructions regarding War Diaries and Intelligence Summaries are contained in F. S. Regs., Part II. and the Staff Manual respectively. Title pages will be prepared in manuscript.

Place	Date	Hour	Summary of Events and Information	Remarks and references to Appendices
HEUCHIN	14th October 1917		Still in same place. O.C. A.S.C. went to "Q" office. The fat ration to be reduced to CAESTRE as soon as arrangement can be made, ration from railhead to be received in bulk on morning of 15th Oktober. A.E. duty Officer dumps. Weather fine. P.S.	non-ration 4 days to WITTERNECK
HEUCHIN	15th October 1917		Still in same place. O.C. A.S.C. went to "Q" office. Supply Officers meeting held at H.Q. A.S.C. 3 p.m. to day. Supply Officers of three Brigades desired dumps. Weather fine & cold. P.S.	
HEUCHIN.	16th October 1917.		Still in same place. O.C. A.S.C. went to "Q" office. Received warning order from General Staff. Division to move on 18th, 19th & 20th Oct to S.W. of AMIENS. Weather fine. P.S.	to FREVENT area.
HEUCHIN.	17th October 1917.		Still in same place. O.C. A.S.C. went to "Q" office. Field Squadron R.E. moved to day to March Billets. Received. HQ Division march over Brigade a day. 5th Cavalry Brigade moves first starting on 18th with the Reserve Park. 50 too. Weather fine. P.S.	
HEUCHIN.	18th October 1917		Still in same place. O.C. A.S.C. went to "Q" office. 3rd Cavalry Brigade moved from Cart of Pol. Dro. to FREVENT area. Today orders came in the 4 Cavalry Brigade & Reserve line move to morrow to FREVENT area. 2nd Cavalry Brigade to CANAPLES area. Weather fine P.S.	
HOUVIGNEUL	19th October 1917.		H.Q. A.S.C. moved to day from HEUCHIN leaving billets at 9.a.m. route taken WAVRANS, ST POL, HOUVIGNEUL arriving at last place 2.30 a.m. 5 Cavalry Brigade moved today to CANAPLES area. Lightly from HEUCHIN to FREVENT. Remainder of Brigade not yet arrived. Bell 6.f.m. Weather fine. P.S.	

A/092 Wt. W2839/M1293. 750,000. 1/17. D. D & L., Ltd. Forms/C2118/14.

WAR DIARY or INTELLIGENCE SUMMARY

(Erase heading not required.)

Army Form C. 2118.

HEADQUARTERS,
2nd CAVALRY DIV.
A.S.

Instructions regarding War Diaries and Intelligence Summaries are contained in F. S. Regs., Part II. and the Staff Manual respectively. Title pages will be prepared in manuscript.

Place	Date	Hour	Summary of Events and Information	Remarks and references to Appendices
DOMART-EN-PONTHIEU	20th October 1917		H.Q. A.S.C. moved from HOUVIGNEUL this morning. Route taken PREVENT, FROHEN-LE-GRAND, BERNEVILLE, DOMART. Arrived at present place 4.20 p.m. Roads good. 5" Cavalry Brigade move from CANAPLE area to AMIENS and 2" Field Squadron Bray Dielin to 2" Cavalry Review Park marching with 5" Cavalry Brigade moved to GERBONNE area near the firing line. Remounts O.R.C. Cavalry Corps. 3" Cav. Brigade moved from BIZOL area to VIGNOY area near the firing line.	
ST SAULFLIEU	21st October 1917		H.Q. A.S.C. moved from DOMART at 8.30 a.m. this morning. Route taken ST VAAST, A VIENS, BURY, ST SAULFLIEU. At 5.15 p.m. Roads good. 3" Cavalry Brigade moved from PREVENT area to CANAPLE area today. Weather fine. My Pony lost in moving. Cloudy. Warmer. Fine rest day.	
ST SAULFLIEU	22nd October 1917		Still in same place. O.C. A.S.C. mounted "Q" office 3" Cavalry Brigade moved from CANAPLE area to the 5" & AMIENS area. He went to 2" Cavalry Division Hqrs billet in the AMIENS area. The 2" Field Squadron, His usual relation was lost in CRS Cavalry Corps. Weather fine. Little rain for some on in Paris this morning.	
ST SAULFLIEU	23rd October 1917		Still in same place. O.C. A.S.C. went to "Q" office. All supplies to be drawn by M.T. as much as possible. This has been arranged. Weather however now is of course fine and dry.	
ST SAULFLIEU	24th October 1917		Still in same place. O.C. A.S.C. went to "Q" office at Duffy. Column called this morning. Everything a bright weather rained most today.	
ST SAULFLIEU	25th October 1917		Still in same place. O.C. A.S.C. went to supply Duffy officers meeting. Held at H.Q. at 2 o'clock today. Weather fair.	

HEADQUARTERS,
2nd CAVALRY DIVL.
A.S.Army Form C. 2118.

No. ....

WAR DIARY

or

INTELLIGENCE SUMMARY.

(Erase heading not required.)

Instructions regarding War Diaries and Intelligence Summaries are contained in F. S. Regs., Part II. and the Staff Manual respectively. Title pages will be prepared in manuscript.

Place	Date	Hour	Summary of Events and Information	Remarks and references to Appendices
ST. SAULFLIEU.	26th October 1917.		Still in same place. O.C. A.S.C. went to "Q" office weather fine. FR.	
ST. SAULFLIEU	27th October 1917.		Still in same place. O.C. A.S.C. went to "Q" office. O.C. Supply Column called this morning; weather fine FR.	
ST. SAULFLIEU.	28th October 1917.		Still in same place. O.C. A.D.C. went to "Q" office weather fine. FR.	
ST. SAULFLIEU.	29th October 1917.		Still in same place. O.C. A.S.C. went to "Q" office also went to see S.O.H. # Div. of Brigade Dump.	
ST. SAULFLIEU	30th October 1917.		Still in same place O.C. A.S.C. went to "Q" office also went to Supply Column in afternoon. weather this morning; heavy shower in the afternoon a strong cold wind blowing FR.	
ST. SAULFLIEU.	31st October 1917.		Still in same place. O.C. A.S.C. went to "Q" office also went down in the afternoon with Supply officer of 3rd Cavalry Brigade Dump. weather fine FR.	

Hussey Capt A.S.C.
M.T. A.S.C.
2nd Cavalry Division.

HEADQUARTERS,
2nd CAVALRY DIVL.
A.S.C.

No.
Date

C O N F I D E N T I A L.

W A R   D I A R Y   O F

H E A D Q U A R T E R S 2nd C A V A L R Y   D I V I S I O N.

ARMY SERVICE CORPS.

FROM :-   1st NOVEMBER 1 9 1 7.

TO

30 th NOVEMBER 1 9 1 7.

VOLUME XXXIX.

Army Form C. 2118

HEADQUARTERS,
2nd CAVALRY DIVL
A.S.C.
Sheet No. 1

WAR DIARY
or
INTELLIGENCE SUMMARY.
(Erase heading not required)

VOLUME XXXIX

Instructions regarding War Diaries and Intelligence Summaries are contained in F.S. Regs., Part II. and the Staff Manual respectively. Title pages will be prepared in manuscript.

Place	Date	Hour	Summary of Events and Information	Remarks and references to Appendices
ST. GAUDELIEUR	1917 Novem. 14th		No detail. X.	
"	15th		Orders received to move tomorrow to MONCHY-LAGACHE in two days. X	
"	16 MERICOURT		H.Q. A.S.C. left Billets at 11.45 a.m. Route taken BOVES, VILLERS-BRETONNEUX, VILLERS-CARBONNEL, PROYART. 10.30 Employed. Billeted at 12 in rooms at ABANCOURT Barrack. X	
"	17 MONCHY-LAGACHE		H.Q. A.S.C. Left Billets at 10 a.m. Route taken FOUCAUCOURT, ESTRÉES-EN-CHAUSSÉE, MARICOURT, MONCHY LAGACHE. Movement arrived at 11.30 a.m. everybody billeted at 1.30 p.m. sniper proof X8.	
"	18th "		All empty teams called upon, with regard to hymn per fighting men. A "Eschelon a B" Eschelon X	
"	19 "		Orders came that Division move at 2.20 tomorrow morning all Gap rations were drawn & issued to every unit going forward. X	
"	20 VILLERS FAUCON E.16.c.3.7		H.Q. A.S.C. left MONCHY LAGACHE at 2.20.a.m. This morning arriving at E.16.c.3.7 at 8.30. approx found the whole Eschelon halted outside VILLERS FAUCON. after two hrs. turned off the road to roadside. The mobility part of the village. Owing to bad weather, the fighting troops moved off at 12.20 & the "A" Eschelon, "B" Eschelon assembly. Brgd. Sig. Column & Cash One Ren. & Car & half troops. the fighting troops moved & then at 3.30 pm. A. Sig. X.	
"	21st VILLERS FAUCON E.16.c.3.7		The 4 Cavalry Brigades returned about 4k; afternoon & the normal days Rations issued & were issued E.C. the rest of the Division returned at the evening. at 10.30.p.m. the normal days Ration arrived & were issued X.	
"	22nd "		H. remaining rations of the Division were delivered tonight, as the 3 & 4 Divisional Supply returned Last-night. The Brigadier gave notice on advance he lift rations. After which H.Q. fighting troops B. A. Eschelon & H.Q. had consumed their Another full days rations were issued in the afternoon B.Q. Rear park.	
"	23rd "		By Brigade waiting orders, ration come out again for the fighting troops of the Division to move forward to 7 ins. most of. the normal rations where issued. the rest of lots consumed by units were most out from Amo Park & the Rear Park made up again the normal days rations which were not issued. The Division will be ready at 5.30. a.m. & were all complete with & other rations & bulks of Amo. per base. X	

Army Form C. 2118

WAR DIARY
of
INTELLIGENCE SUMMARY.
(Erase heading not required.)

HEADQUARTERS,
2nd CAVALRY DIVN.

Sheet No II

Place	Date	Hour	Summary of Events and Information	Remarks and references to Appendices
VILLERS FALCON	24 November 1917	F.16.C.3.7	All Supply Officers ordered up with issues to take over dump at Carlope H.Q. Reserve, to all units in the FINS area. Stable	
23rd	"	F.6.26	Division still in FINS area. Rations issued to both days holding.	
24th	"	"	H.Q. A.D.S. move from VILLERS FALCON. to camp on FINS GOUZEAUCOURT ROAD. The Division taking at BOURLON WOOD. Full day ration issued. Lt. Supply Officers at Bourlon Road to-night to fetch troops.	
28th	"	"	No detail. H.R.	
29th	"	"	4th & 5th Car. Reg. returned to camp to-night. 3rd Car. Regt coming out of line, returning to-morrow. H.R.	
30th	"	"	About 11 a.m. this morning orders in packed trains ready to move at once. Germans had broken through and come round to our rear in the morning. Lot rations made at 6 a.m. The Supply Column ordered out to reserve in the anything. GOUZEAUCOURT. 4th & 5th Car. Regts went up mounted 3rd Car. Regt came up late & were in reserve. The Reserve Park moved to the Division on Fins area and to the Battle in GOUZEAUCOURT area. H.R.	

Henry Capt & Adjt.
H.Q. A.D.C.
2nd Cav Div.

C O N F I D E N T I A L.

W A R   D I A R Y

O F

HEADQUARTERS, 2nd CAVALRY DIVISIONAL A. S. C.

FROM:- 1st DECEMBER 1917.   TO:- 31st DECEMBER 1917.

(V O L U M E   40.)

Army Form C. 2118.

HEADQUARTERS
2nd CAVALRY DIVL.
A.S.C.

No. ....
Date ....

VOLUME 40

WAR DIARY
or
INTELLIGENCE SUMMARY
(Erase heading not required.)

Instructions regarding War Diaries and Intelligence Summaries are contained in F.S. Regs., Part II. and the Staff Manual respectively. Title pages will be prepared in manuscript.

Place	Date	Hour	Summary of Events and Information	Remarks and references to Appendices
	December 1st 1917.		H.Q. A.S.C. moved from camp. on GOUZEAUCOURT Road 2 cans. Wet Fins on METZ road. He Adv. up in GOUZEAUCOURT area.	
Camp Net 7/M5 on METZ road			Arrived, rations issued at 7pm. Supply column.	
	December 2nd 1917		No details.	
	3rd 1917		Colonel detailed to Division had been ordered out but stopped at NURLU. Arrived Coln. at 7.30 p.m.	
	4th "		Rations issued. y 12 noon. Division. 8 Bny 2/16 Hubs.	
	5th "		Orders Came on Re Division near Combles.	
CARNOY CARTIGNY	6th "		H.Q. A.S.C. moved today left camp at 11.a.m. arrived at CARTIGNY. 3.20. Route taken NURLU. BUSSU TINCOURT. Roads goods except the road from PERONNE to BUSSU. the road could have been improved in wet weather but been ballast in ground. made all passable but very rough.	
Bussy-les-Dours	7th "		H.Q. A.S.C. moved today left CARTIGNY at 9.45 a.m. Route taken. PERONNE. BIACHES. HERBECOURT. CAPPY. BRAY. CORBIE. AUBIGNY. arrived & piked at ODBY roads. Getting heavy owing to front going out of ground. arrived in at billets 9 h.m. very long march. Roads turnel in very bad, so two second very slippery. to the horses being sharped men BORDIE this day before 3 Roman no transport to arrive by. All harm is nearl pasted.	
	8th "		H.Q. A.S.C. Moved today left Bussy-les-Dours at 8.30 a.m. taken CAMON. SALOUEL. arrived & piked at QUEVAUVILLERS.	
QUEVAUVILLERS			Roads goods except for the road from BUSSY & CAMON but now actually motorised. Roads fairly except the 4th Cav. Bde. taken rations were changed outside this village owing to M.T. unable to get to mules. Horses having men drawn of the Mules in the morning.	
	9th "		Returned moved early to "Cav. Bde. ration tired: Rest Ride early on account of the days ration having time Ride in Yesterday afternoon & Mules been unable to draw upon bulk pasture.	
	10th "		Orders expected & all Supply Officers not Lemenials are before and only the Pot rations on H.A.A. to be lose over & period of 5 days. Canips Kant been 9 Rn 1001.	

D. D. & L., Ltd. Form/C2118/14.

Army Form C. 2118.

HEADQUARTERS
2nd CAVALRY DIV.
A.S.C.

VOLUME 40
Part II

WAR DIARY
or
INTELLIGENCE SUMMARY
(Erase heading not required.)

Instructions regarding War Diaries and Intelligence
Summaries are contained in F. S. Regs., Part II.
and the Staff Manual respectively. Title pages
will be prepared in manuscript.

Place	Date	Hour	Summary of Events and Information	Remarks and references to Appendices
December 11th/6/15 Quesnauvillers			No detail. YB.	
"	16th		Transport for the Divison moved off today with 3 days rations. Heavy fall of snow last night.	
"	17th/18		No detail. YB.	
"	19		O.E. Arrived from Transport, ground up, Chew & mc. Hays Action & proceed. Emerson & Dumbbell Brigade moved off Today.	
"	20.		4th Canadian Brigade moved today YB	
"	21st		3rd Canadian Brigade moved today YB	
"	22		All new Reserve ration for 2 days have been served to all S.D. YB	
"	22/23		No detail. YB	

Leon Capt & Adjt
H.G. A.S.C.
2nd Ca. Div.

CONFIDENTIAL.

WAR   DIARY

of

HEADQUARTERS, 2nd CAVALRY DIVISIONAL A.S.C.

JANUARY, 1918 - Volume XLI.

Army Form C. 2118.

WAR DIARY
INTELLIGENCE SUMMARY
(Erase heading not required.)

Sheet 1 Volume XLI

Place	Date	Hour	Summary of Events and Information	Remarks and references to Appendices
QUEVAUVILLERS	January 1st 1918.		2/Lt. R. Collis Lord Howes joined H.Q.O.S.C. on the 5th December. From the 8th Brady Division attached pending absorption. T/Major A.V. Craig A.S.C. Capt. A.Q.O.S.C. the 40th Divisional Train. T/Lieut. F.E. de la Barre A.S.C. S.O. 3rd Cavalry Brigade posted on 9.5.5. on the 23rd December. T. Lt. R.P.W. Paterson joined O.S. 3rd Cavalry Brigade on the 23rd December. T/Lt. V.B. Johnson A.S.C. joined H.Q.O.S.C. on the 26th December from A.G.C. Base Depot (M.T.R.S.) Paying & expenses who day & period of 12 days H.S. Pd.	
	January 2.6.12th		Mr. Colonel F. Major Shorter R.W.F. O.C. 2nd Cavalry Div Lark absorbed & expires who day & period of 12 days H.S. Pd.	
	January 13th		Lt. Colonel W. Scott Elliot proceeded this day on leave to Paris Major V.Y. Murray took over command. P.S.	
	January 13,14th		Q. Colonel P.S.	
	January 15th		Orders received. Horse Shows Come out force Manages 25th night 26th M.T. transport must be used on State & Corres Rs. Only to uced on State & Corres Rs.	
	January 16,17th		No detail P.S.	
	January 18th		Lt. Colonel W. Scott Elliot returned off leave today P.S.	
	January 19th		Horse detail order today. Report received at 6.1 am that horses below abnormal temperature for another 24 hours P.S.	
	January 20th		No detail O.S.	
	January 21st		Horse scheme ends. S.O. 6th Car. Bde returned from Divisional area P.Q. & New Dele reached up State over P.S.	
	January 22nd		Another Horse Scheme has been started 3 days to the Right on all S.D. always P.S.	
	January 23rd			
	January 25th		T/Major Edwin A.V. A.S.C. O.S. 46th Bde. Park. Iyould Rec & 9th. O.S. command of the 2nd Cavalry Division Rec Park was T/Major Iredale S.R. O.S.I examined to Coal M.	
	January 26,27,28th		No detail P.S.	
	January 29th		Orders received to Quevauv More from Quevauvillers T.Q.D.S. 3/2/18. To the forward area taking over billets H.Q. Cavalry Division. Horse shoes all made up & transferred before being transferred P.S.	

Army Form C. 2118.

WAR DIARY
or
INTELLIGENCE SUMMARY.

(Erase heading not required.)

Sheet II Volume XLI

Instructions regarding War Diaries and Intelligence Summaries are contained in F.S. Regs., Part II. and the Staff Manual respectively. Title pages will be prepared in manuscript.

Place	Date	Hour	Summary of Events and Information	Remarks and references to Appendices
OURVILLERS	January 30 & 31st 1918		In distt. 73	
	January 31st 1918		One Officer & other ranks app. H.Q. & C. 4th Coy by Division. 73. Balance on route to be forward area to take over division's duties.	

Roy Capt. & A.C.
H.Q. A.C.
2 Can. Div.

CONFIDENTIAL.

WAR DIARY.

OF

HEADQUARTERS 2nd CAVALRY DIVISIONAL A. S. C.

From 1st FEBRUARY 1918.

To 28th FEBRUARY 1918.

(VOLUME XLII)

* * *

WAR DIARY / INTELLIGENCE SUMMARY

Army Form C. 2118.

February 1918 Volume XLII

Place	Date	Hour	Summary of Events and Information	Remarks and references to Appendices
	February 1st/2nd 1918		No detail. PB	
QUEVAUVILLERS	February 3 1918		S.S.O. 4th Cavalry Division alongs & bill on a champ. etc all held such as know reserve. PB	
	February 4th "		No detail. PB	
" MARCELCAVE	5th "		H.Q. 2.A.C. moved today left QUEVAUVILLE at 9 a.m. with Divisional HQ details and 2nd Squad Squadron; arrived here TAISNIL, NEUVILLE, SANS LOUILLY, ST SAUFLIEU, REMIGNY, SAINS-EN-AMIÉNOIS, BOVES CACHY, VILLERS BRETONNEUX. MARCELCAVE waited & fed at SAINS-EN-AMIÉNOIS, moved at new miles 6-30 pm for CACHY & VILLERS BRETONNEUX Road, here bivouacked. The post was taken in place of the 3rd wagoned limber train wagon all roads were good except entering Marcelcave where was very what & as had caused half PB	
" MATHIES	February 6th 1918		H.Q. 2.A.C. & Signal Squadron Divisional H.Q. details left MARCELCAVE at 9 a.m. for MATHIES Road - Proud, PROUART - ARIEZ A 74/125 S. of PROYART where all the Divisional HQ after met, route taken Longueau, Road to ARIEZ, & from ARIEZ A 74/125 marched to just E. bank of the Somme, arrived at new place 3-45 p.m. to bivouac, one G.S. wagon arrived 7-0 pm to E.S. No detail. PB	
	February 7th 1918		No detail. PB	
	8th 1918		Routine & charge at from LA CHAPELETTE & ARIEZ 2nd Lt. T.L. HAMILTON A.S.C. M'road here presently taking over 2/32 at/sn. Lieut Cols. A E R.W. Baker I.F. 6th Cavalry Ambulance Post on 8.S.1119 & reported to O.C. 8 Squadron tank corps.	
	9th 13 "		No detail. PB	
	10th "		OX AT inspected Duff Officer attached 9 4th Cavalry Brigade	
	11th "		OX A.T. inspected 16 Am. A.T. Coml. PB	
	15th "		No detail. PB	
	16th "		Corps Commander distributed Medal ribbon today at DAVISE, Lt Col. M. Lacy DSO PB was awarded the D.S.O. & PGK Sergt R. Watchel P.S.M.	
	17th "		R.M.S.M. PB	

Army Form C. 2118

WAR DIARY
INTELLIGENCE SUMMARY

(Erase heading not required.)

Volume XLII

Sheet No. 2

Place	Date	Hour	Summary of Events and Information	Remarks and references to Appendices
February ATHIES	18th 1918		O.C. A.S.C. inspected Supply officer dump of 5th Cavalry Brigade. Enemy aeroplane over ATHIES his every between 6.30 & 7 a.m. Dropped some half dozen bombs, apparel of G.S. Anti-Aircraft gun opened off. Try returned by our later but this time did not drop any bombs P.E.	
February	19. 1915		S.O. 5th Cavalry Bde. sent to A.M. (S)A.S. to the schemes learnest exhausting, etc. for the Demonstration P.E.	
February	20 to 26. 1918		No detail P.E.	
February	27th 1918		S.O. 5th Cavalry Brigade returned from A.M.(S)A.S. having made arrangements to attend as an one received from Cavalry Corps regrey the Position. Bridges moved near its old positions P.E.	
February	28th 1918		2nd Cavalry Division have had 70 attached sents during this month.	

For Capt & Adjt
H.Q. 2. C. D. S. C.
2nd Cavalry Division

CONFIDENTIAL.

WAR DIARY

of

Headquarters, 2nd Cavalry Divisional
Army Service Corps.

FROM   1st. March

TO   31st March
1918.

VOLUME XLIII.

Army Form C. 2118

WAR DIARY
or
INTELLIGENCE SUMMARY.
(Erase heading not required.)

Sheet No. I.   Volume XLIII

Instructions regarding War Diaries and Intelligence Summaries are contained in F. S. Regs., Part II. and the Staff Manual respectively. Title pages will be prepared in manuscript.

Place	Date	Hour	Summary of Events and Information	Remarks and references to Appendices
ATHIES	March 1st 1918.		No detail. K.	
	March 2nd	14.16	A.D/S + T. Cavalry Corps. nve Bil. H.Q. A.S.C. Colony. K.	
	" 3rd	"	The Division started to go into Cantonments. 4th Cavalry Brigade today relieved 6th Cav. K.	
	" 4th	"	H.Q. 4 3rd Cavalry Brigade 9 the Assembled Parties moved to relieve 6 Cav. K.	
	" 5th	"	5th Cavalry Brigade & transport from the Reserve Park arrived today to relieve 6 Cav. K.	
	" 6,7th	"	No detail K.	
	" 8th	"	Warning order Armoured Division to be relieved by the 4th Division. Relief to be completed by 6 a.m. 14th March.	
	" 9th	"	Warning order received the Division will move about the 13th inst.	
	" 10th	"	Orders sent out to all staffs officers H.Q. Staff Commanded to Bedford on 12.13" or 15th so as to make the Division less the their	
	" 11-12	"	March up. K.	
QUESMY	" 13	"	No details	
			The Division moved from ATHIES today H.Q. A.S.C. left at 9.45am. Route taken MATIGNY, HAM. GUISCARD, ST MARTIN, Starting Point FOURQUES Cross roads arrived at Quesmy 3.40 p.m. Roads bad after arriving in Nelson Road the division lines own transport.	
	" 14	"	All groups of the Division drawn by their own House transport each Brigade getting supplies from own A.T. Coys. A.S.C. Divisional Troops all drawn by the Div. Park K.	
	" 15	"	No detail K.	
	" 16	"	Major H.V. Clark A.S.C. Commission H Cavalry Division as S.S.O. Capt. H.C. de la Run A.S.C. left the day for M.T. School of Instruction. STONER K.	

WAR DIARY

INTELLIGENCE SUMMARY

(Erase heading not required.)

Army Form C. 2118
Ahut II Volume XLIII

Place	Date	Hour	Summary of Events and Information	Remarks and references to Appendices
QUESMY.	March 17. 1919		"B" Battery mounted and divisional arms but also practised by the Batteries. Painting and transport cleaning from Railhead. Soft officers Camp. K.	
"	18"		No detail. K.	
"	19"		P.L. Cpt. W Scott Elliot proceeded on leave to England. Major Charles acting Adjt K.	
"	20"		H.Q. R.H.A. & D.T.L. Batteries march today. Rations drawn by own units transport; tomorrow M.T. will draw as above from Railhead at Ollezy. K	
"	21st		Heavy Bombardment started about 4 a.m. a belt of — E.W. taken at 7 a.m. 4th Cavalry Brigade Group moved off the morning to WREY-NOUREMIFONTAINES were out ate by Divisional S. from the Brigade. 3rd & 6th Cavalry Brigade Groups moved up in the afternoon to 3rd Line Brigade Front to BEAUMONT the Brigade Groups to BEAUMONT rations were drawn by the Lorries taking H.Q. 3rd Brigade R.H.A. rations still drawn by lorries. K.	
"	22"		Bombardment still continued from early morning till late in afternoon. Rations were delivered as above. 3rd Brigade R.H.A German aeroplane over at 9.20 a.m. flying very low, warning over to men received at 9 h.m. a counter at 9.20 h.m. K.	
PONTOISE	23"		Orders received that 3rd Brigade R.H.A. would be relieved by 1st Division this was carried out except Ammo transport. During morning more Rations were received that transport had been sent to draw Rations for them at NOYEN & Hot at 6 BABOEUF. Rations were drawn from APPILLY by M.T. for all as back area, & M.T. for the Divisions & Group. Rations were detailed. Lorries sent out to draw other orders came for the Division to move. AUXISTwh wagons were sent to Brigades. H.Q. A.Q.Q. march. 17" today at 3.15 pm QUESMY. 1st to MANCART GRANGES APPILLY, BREFIGNY, PLEGNY, PONTOISE arriving at Sept. march. 17" today at 10–30 pm. Rations were not sent where PARGNRY PONTOISE which was my nearest railhead. The H.Q. officers made for evening rations tomorrow by M.T. from APPILLY railhead, the Rations were ordered to be sent to Brigade & Septy to Officers when to take Rations to Railhead Divisional Sups. tomorrow.	

Army Form C. 2118.

WAR DIARY
~~INTELLIGENCE SUMMARY~~

(Erase heading not required.)

Sheet No III. V Volume XbIII

Instructions regarding War Diaries and Intelligence Summaries are contained in F. S. Regs., Part II. and the Staff Manual respectively. Title pages will be prepared in manuscript.

Place	Date	Hour	Summary of Events and Information	Remarks and references to Appendices
BAILLY	24-3-18		Orders received about 11 a.m. to be ready to move off at 2 hour notice after 1-30 p.m. all Details were drawn by H.T. as arranged. Moved from PONTOISE about 2-30 p.m. F CARLE PONT on arriving at the village there was found to be not enough accommodation we were all turned off into a small wood. Orders about further orders further orders received to proceed to BAILLY arriving there at 4-30 p.m. M.T.	
"	25-3-18		Orders received all transport & Pack horses to be ready to move by 7 a.m. Remained standing from Orders after further orders received later in the afternoon. ghostel. The Division be required to him out to-night the scored. "Saddle Up" will be sent out or if the order "turn out alarm posts" all troops billeted in BAILLY will proceed at once to the Church at ST. LEGER. Further orders received at 10-45 to move to CHOISY-LES-OISE above the bridge to cross further orders. Crossed the bridge at 4 a.m. (26th Tuesday) moved off at 10 a.m. to the other side of COMPEIGNE	
ROYALLIEU or ROYALLIEUS	26-3-18		arriving at Hotel's 12 noon. Rations were drawn for the whole Squadron on a scale normal. all units drew by their Own. H.T. Rations were sent out at Kells forward wards by lorries. Heavy bombing from German aeroplanes over the area took place between 9 p.m. and midnight. V.	
JONCQUIERES	27-3-18		Orders were received to march at 7 a.m. this orders were cancelled No transport movement during day until 6.2. noon. Lt. G.W. Scott Elliot Returned from leave. Further orders received to proceed to JONCQUIERES arriving 17 at 12 noon.	

Army Form C. 2118.

WAR DIARY
INTELLIGENCE SUMMARY.
(Erase heading not required.)

Sheet No IV Volume XVIII

Place	Date	Hour	Summary of Events and Information	Remarks and references to Appendices
JONCQUIERS.	27-3-18.		Arriving at billets 6 a.m. orders to the troops at LE MEUX not being considered safe. One squadron was sent after which took a very long time & also no definite orders received before the horses were done. Rallying the Radial Outside the village of JONCQUIERS for over an hour whereon orders arrived. The word came that German Cavalry were attacking.	
			The night in the village.	
MOYVILLERS.	28-3-18.	at 5 a.m.	Word came that the Germans had entered through the fighting troops moved off at 6 a.m. "B" Echelon had orders to remain in their billets & defend the villages later in the day. The Heavy Baton of the Res. Park moved up to be near the fighting troops also H.Q.A.S.C. moved to MOYVILLERS where our personnel remained in till 9 p.m. when we received orders together remain in the village. Word was sent back from O.C.A.S.C. to the personnel of "B" Echelon that they were sleeping the night in their present billets. Jt.	
ERQUINVILLERS.	29-3-18.	about 11.45	Orders received. "B" Echelon will move to new area. Personal kits over to go to ERQUINVILLERS arrival the village had been taken over by French troops all units sent into fields on the outskirts of village & cavalry bell for spartan orders. Orders came for Divisional troops to move to NOYONS-ST MARTIN. On the march. O.C.A.S.C. was taken away to Divisional H.Q. & the A.A.Q.M.G. On arriving at the village of ST REMY. A Staff officer of 3 Cavalry Division Rest gave orders for the Bn. Bak. to turn off the load remain in attachée village. This taking us out of the way. We lost quite 2 hours in getting four explanation arrived at NOYONS-ST MARTIN at 11 h.m. No rations had been delivered this day to "B" Echelon owing to another Army taking it. Jt.	

Army Form C. 2118.

WAR DIARY
INTELLIGENCE SUMMARY.
(Erase heading not required.)

War Diary Volume XLIII

Place	Date	Hour	Summary of Events and Information	Remarks and references to Appendices
PLACHY-BUYON	30-3-18		Orders received about 1 a.m. to branch rations from the Res. Park as no rations could be obtained from Echelon by lorries, this was not done owing to arriving too late & the Echelon being too far apart but arrangements were made that the Res. Park to make a dump on the S. side of road at TILLOY. This was done. As the divisible forward sup. received Dets. & P.M. & knowing won't to PLACHY-BUYON b.m. transf. Rations dump at BACOUEL. Details of "B" Echelon were bivouacked along the road from PLACHY-BUYON to VERS. W. side of main rd.	
PLACHY-BUYON	31-3-18		All "B" Echelon still in same place awaiting further orders. Rations were delivered by lorries direct to Brigades of 1st Corps. dump as yesterday.	

Percy. Capt. A.V.C.
H.Q. A.D.C.
2nd Cavalry Division.

CONFIDENTIAL.

WAR DIARY.

of Headquarters, 2nd Cavalry Divisional
Army Service Corps.

FROM. 1st APRIL.

To. 30th APRIL.

1918.

VOLUME XLIV.

Army Form C. 2118.

WAR DIARY
INTELLIGENCE SUMMARY.
(Erase heading not required.)

Instructions regarding War Diaries and Intelligence Summaries are contained in F. S. Regs., Part II. and the Staff Manual respectively. Title pages will be prepared in manuscript.

H.Q. 2ND CAVALRY DIV. A.S.C.
No. Sheet 1 Volume XLIV
Date.

Place	Date	Hour	Summary of Events and Information	Remarks and references to Appendices
PLACHY-BUYON.	1-4-18.		All "B" Echelons still in same place except the two tanks who moved to SALOUEL this morning. German aeroplane flew over the valley this morning when heavy fire was opened on passing over AMIENS. Orders received at 5.30 p.m. to move to SALOUEL. Left PLACHY at 5 p.m. arrived at ALLONVILLE 8 p.m. taking billets of Lorries. J.E.	
SALOUEL	2-4-18		As usual P.C.	
"	3-4-18		Orders received at 8 a.m. all units in SALOUEL & "B" Echelons will move today to RIVERY leaving at 9 a.m. via POIX-AMIENS road, arriving at 11.30 a.m. where the whole Divisional troops will billet. "B" Echelons went to their respective Brigades. Rations delivered by Lorries to R.Q. Dupus. J.E.	
RIVERY.	4-4-18		As usual P.C.	
"	5-4-18.	8.30pm	Warning orders received	
		9.0	Reserve Park and Div H.T. Coy moved and marched via ST. SAUVEUR and FLIXECOURT to AILLY-LE-HAUT-CLOCHER . LONG area.	
		9.30	5th Cav Bde "B" Echelons left CAMON.	
		10.0	4th Cav Bde "B" Echelons left LAMOTTE. Both then marched to AILLY-LE-HAUT-CLOCHER by the route above mentioned.	
		11.0	March table was received for now however unnecessary orders issued	

Army Form C.2118.

WAR DIARY

INTELLIGENCE SUMMARY.
(Erase heading not required.)

Instructions regarding War Diaries and Intelligence Summaries are contained in F.S. Regs., Part II. and the Staff Manual respectively. Title pages will be prepared in manuscript.

Sheet II Volume XLIV

Place	Date	Hour	Summary of Events and Information	Remarks and references to Appendices
AILLY LE HAUT CLOCHER.	6.4.18	AM 8.30. 9.30.	Reserve Park, Aux A.T. Coy and "B" Echelons arrived at destination. Div: H.Q. details under orders of Camp Commandant moved today from RIVERY, following the ST. SAUVEUR. FLIXECOURT route. Watered and fed on the road between Reformer place and LA CHAUSEE (TIRANCOURT) arriving at 5.45 p.m. and were billeted. Rations delivered by lorries to S.O. Dumps.	
"	7.4.18		Railhead HANGEST.	
"	8.4.18		T/Capt F. EVERY Adjt HQ A.S.C. admitted 12 C.C.S (sick) T/Capt. S. E. SKEEN reported for duty on transfer from 4th Cav: Div.	
"	9.4.18		T/Capt S.L.E. SKEEN assumed duties of S.O.D.T. vice T/LIEUT R.F.R.F. SHEPPEY GREEN	
"	10.4.18	12 Noon	Warning orders received. March orders received.	
AUXI LE CHATEAU.	10.4.18	3.30pm	Div. H.Q. details moved today at 3.30 pm Route taken ERGNIES, GORENFLOS, DOMQUEUR, LONGVILLERS, DOMLEGER, MAIZICOURT, AUXI LE CHATEAU arriving at the last named place at 8 pm. The Light Section Reserve Park moved at 4 pm. Taking same route. Billeted in the Town. "B" Echelon moved at 5 pm to	

Army Form C. 2118.

WAR DIARY
INTELLIGENCE SUMMARY.
(Erase heading not required.)

Instructions regarding War Diaries and Intelligence Summaries are contained in F. S. Regs., Part II. and the Staff Manual respectively. Title pages will be prepared in manuscript.

Sheet III Volume XLIV

Place	Date	Hour	Summary of Events and Information	Remarks and references to Appendices
AUXI.LE.CHATEAU.	10.4.18.		EAUCOURT. Rations moved by lorry to "A" Echelon at AUXI.LE.CHATEAU at 10 p.m. and to "B" Echelon at EAUCOURT.	
"	11.4.18	11 pm	Warning orders received.	
"	"	8.30 pm	Railhead "A" Echelon as in margin. Warning orders received.	
"	12.4.18.		Division moved at 12.45 pm. H.Q. A.S.C. and high Echelon Reserve Park left at 2 pm. H.Q. A.S.C. took route QUOEUX - GALAMETZ - WAIL - BLANGY-SUR-TERNOISE. AMBRICOURT. VERCHIN. to FRUGES where information received that the Division had moved to BOMY so	
BOMY.			Travelled via LUGY - BEAUMETZ.LEZ.AIRE. GREUPPE. BOMY arriving there at 11-55 pm. Watered and fed at BLANGY.SUR.TERNOISE. A long march starting at in the day. Reserve Park also went to FRUGES and then on to BEAUMETZ arriving there at 12 midnight. Rations were issued to all units by lorry.	
"	13.4.18	1 am.	Warning orders received.	
BLARINGHEM	13.4.18.	12 noon	Orders received. Division moved this day. H.Q. A.S.C. marched at 1-30 p.m. via ENGUINGATTE - MARTHES - MAMETZ - REQUETOIRE. LE MONTDUPIL. BLARINGHEM. arriving at destination 7. p.m. Reserve Park marched by same	

Army Form C. 2118.

WAR DIARY
or
INTELLIGENCE SUMMARY.
(Erase heading not required.)

Sheet IX Volume XLIV

Place	Date	Hour	Summary of Events and Information	Remarks and references to Appendices
BLARINGHEM	13.4.18.		Route and bivouacked about 2 miles N.W. of BLARINGHEM on BLARINGHEM - RENESCURE road. Roads good. "HQ A.S.C. weekend autled at MARTHES. No casualties. Railhead today PERNES. Rations drawn to accounts by lorry. Railhead WARDRECQUE.	
"	14.4.18		"	
"	15.4.18		"	
"	16.4.18		all night. Rations received from 75% fresh 15 between 40% to 50% fresh. Heavy bombardment started at 6 p.m. and continued at intervals	
"	17.4.18 9 a.m.		Very heavy bombardment all the morning. Lieut E. Bolton proceeded to report to O.C. 1st Cav: Div: A.S.C. for duty.	
"	18.4.18. 9.30 a.m.		Orders received - 3rd Cavalry Bde= move to FLETRE area. Quiet day. "B" Echelon moved to day to RECLINGHEM	
"	19.4.18		Orders received "B" Echelon marched at 10 a.m. via PETIGNY ENGUINGATTE MARTHES MAMETZ ROQUETOIRE BLARINGHEM arrived BLARINGHEM at 5.30 p.m.	
"	20.4.18		Transport rejoined units. No details.	
"	21.4.18		A quiet day. Church Parade in the girls School this morning. During the evening starting till April 6 a.m. (22.4.18) a fairly heavy bombardment heard. E.A. row in the morning	

Army Form C. 2118.

WAR DIARY
or
INTELLIGENCE SUMMARY.
(Erase heading not required.)

Instructions regarding War Diaries and Intelligence Summaries are contained in F. S. Regs., Part II. and the Staff Manual respectively. Title pages will be prepared in manuscript.

Reed T. Volume X L II

Place	Date	Hour	Summary of Events and Information	Remarks and references to Appendices
BLARINGHEM	22.4.18.		No detail	
"	23.4.18		No detail	
"	24.4.18		Intermittent bombardment by enemy during evening up to 24.25 h.	
"	25.4.18		No detail	
"	26.4.18		No detail	
"	27.4.18		No detail	
"	28.4.18		Warning order received at 4.45 p.m. March order received 9.15 p.m. and acknowledged	
COYECQUE	29.4.18	10 a.m.	H.Q. A.S.C. moved following 2nd Field Squadron, the letter being already on the road to WARDRECQUES STA: Halted some time on this road. Watered at THEROUANNE which would be. Moved and pulled off road at S.W. end of village with permission of A.P.M. and there fed. Proceeded at 3 p.m. arriving destination at 4.15. Arrived reported at Headquarters. Route taken from WARDRECQUES STA — THEROUANNE — COYECQUE. 3rd Bde WANDANE. 4th Bde DOHEM. 5th Bde RADINGHEM. Reserve Park ENGUINGATTE. Roads good throughout, being fine. Supply & ordnance lorries found according to address and delivered H.S.O. dumps in new area. SGJ	
"	30.4.18		T/Lieut R.F. SHEPPEY-GREENE A.S.C. rejoined this day from Cav. Corps Reinforcement Camp ABBEVILLE where he had been since the 14th April. SGJ	

Army Form C. 2118.

WAR DIARY
or
INTELLIGENCE SUMMARY.
(Erase heading not required.)

Chap. VI Volume XLIV

Place	Date	Hour	Summary of Events and Information	Remarks and references to Appendices
COYECQUE	30.4.18	—	The Division was put on divisional scheme as from thingf. April 30th	

Prob. Division. 2nd Lum
apart HQ. A.D.C.
2nd Cavalry Division

Vol 23

H.Q.
2ND CAVALRY DIVL.
A.S.C.

WAR DIARY

Headquarters
OF 2ND CAVALRY DIVISIONAL, ARMY SERVICE CORPS.

From : 1st May, 1918.
To : 31st May, 1918.

VOLUME XLV.

Army Form C. 2118.

Remarks and references to Appendices

Sheet I. Volume XLV.

WAR DIARY
or
INTELLIGENCE SUMMARY
(Erase heading not required.)

Instructions regarding War Diaries and Intelligence Summaries are contained in F. S. Regs., Part II. and the Staff Manual respectively. Title pages will be prepared in manuscript.

H.Q. 2ND CAVALRY DIVL A.S.C.

Place	Date	Hour	Summary of Events and Information
COYECQUE	1.5.18.		1/Lieut. R.F. SHEPPEY GREENE A.S.C. proceeded to join 3rd Divisional Train.
"	2.5.18.		2nd Cavalry M.T. Company moved from present Licencing at GONDARDENNE to ENGUINGATTE Railhead QUALWARDRECQUES.
"	3.5.18.		The Reserve Park Light Section was inspected at 10.30am by the Divisional Commander at ENGUINGATTE.
"	4.5.18	12.30	Warning Orders received.
		9 pm	March orders received.
"	5.5.18		Railhead to MARESQUEL. The Division moved to LONGVILLERS - BEAURAINVILLE Headquarters closed at COYECQUE and opened at MONTCAVREL & environs. Headquarters A.S.C. moved in accordance with March table. Route taken WANDONNE - HENOVILLE - MANINGHEM - CLENLEU. To destination reached at 2.15 PM Very heavy going after MANINGHEM. Rain very heavy during the early part of the march. Watered and fed at HENOVILLE. Supplies to S.Os. dumps in new area by M.T.
ALETTE	6.5.18		Heavy Section Reserve Park reported arrival at VIEIL HESDIN.
"	7.5.18		Heavy Section Report Park reported arrival at ESTREE when consider'd. MARESQUEL.

Army Form C. 2118.

WAR DIARY
INTELLIGENCE SUMMARY
(Erase heading not required.)

Sheet II Volume XLVI

Instructions regarding War Diaries and Intelligence Summaries are contained in F. S. Regs., Part II. and the Staff Manual respectively. Title pages will be prepared in manuscript.

Place	Date	Hour	Summary of Events and Information	Remarks and references to Appendices
ALETTE	8.5.18		No detail	
"	9.5.18		No detail	
"	10.5.18			
"	11.5.18		No detail	
"	12.5.18			
"	13.5.18			
"	14.5.18		No detail	
"	15.5.18			
"	16.5.18		The M.T. Company was inspected at 11-30 a.m. by the Divisional Commander.	
"	17.5.18		The A.D.V.S. inspected horses and mules of the Reserve Park at 10.30 a.m.	
"	18.5.18		No detail	
"	19.5.18		E.A. over and dropped bombs in the neighbourhood 11 p.m. Church Parade with the this morning.	
"	20.5.18		No detail	
"	21.5.18		E.A. over. 11 p.m.	
"	22.5.18		No detail	

Army Form C. 2118.

WAR DIARY
or
INTELLIGENCE SUMMARY.
(Erase heading not required.)

Volume XLV

Instructions regarding War Diaries and Intelligence Summaries are contained in F. S. Regs., Part II. and the Staff Manual respectively. Title pages will be prepared in manuscript.

Place	Date	Hour	Summary of Events and Information	Remarks and references to Appendices
ALETTE	23/5/18		No details	
"	24/5/18		Following warrant officers in detachment (see papers of 25/5/18) T./Maj H.J.CLARK, A.S.C. T./Capt. H.C. dela Bère (S.S.O.) - 16 hours 1918) T./Capt. J.EVERY Act'g H.Q., A.S.C. T/23363 San. Corp'l (A/Qm S/Sgt R.ELLIS) Reserve Park, and S.S./1122 Sgt. R.W. HAIGH S/S 2nd Army Div. l. Troops.	
"	25/5/18		Voluntary Service held in the school ALETTE at 6.30 p.m.	
"	26/5/18		No details	
"	27/5/18		No details	
"	28/5/18		O.C., A.S.C., inspected heavy section RESERVE PARK this afternoon also McCaulff No details	
"	29/5/18		No details	
"	30/5/18			
"	31/5/18		No. of vehicles repaired in Divisional Workshop at ALETTE 6 daly 33.	

Lus Swanson ? Lieut
9/Adjt, H.Q., A.S.C.
2nd Cavalry Division

CONFIDENTIAL.

WAR   DIARY

OF

HEADQUARTERS, 2ND CAVALRY DIVISIONAL A.S.C.

From   1st JUNE, 1918.
TO   30th JUNE, 1918.

VOLUME. XLVI.

Army Form C. 2118.

XLVI
Chief I Volume X-VII

H.Q.
2ND CAVALRY DIV.
A.S.C.
No ....
Date ....

WAR DIARY
or
INTELLIGENCE SUMMARY.
(Erase heading not required.)

Instructions regarding War Diaries and Intelligence Summaries are contained in F. S. Regs., Part II. and the Staff Manual respectively. Title pages will be prepared in manuscript.

Place	Date	Hour	Summary of Events and Information	Remarks and references to Appendices
ALETTE	1.6.18		Montreuil.	
"	2.6.18		Voluntary Service at 7 pm in Cudehire ALETTE.	
"	3.6.18		Railhead to-day AUBIN ST VAAST.	
"	4.6.18		Railhead MARESQUEL	
"	5.6.18		Reserve Park moved this day from ESTREES to SEMPY.	
"	6.6.18		Montreuil	
"	7.6.18		Montreuil	
"	8.6.18		Montreuil	
"	9.6.18		Montreuil.	
"	10.6.18		T/Capt J. Every Capt H.Q. A.S.C. rejoined from Rouflict HQ	
"	11th,12th 13.6.18		Montreuil	
"	14,15,16.6.18		Dismounted Coyte	
"	17-6-18		A.D.S. & T.N 2nd Cavalry Divn Park. 2nd Cavalry Divn Transport Coys were all good.	
"	18th,19th,20.6.18		Montreuil	
"	21.6.18		O.C.H.Q. 2nd Cavalry Division presented Complementary Cards today to N.C.O's & men of H.Q. Coy, M.T. Coy & Res. Park.	
"	22.6-18		O.C.H.Q. 2nd Cavalry Division presented Complimentary Cards today to N.C.O's & Men of H.Q. A.S.C. M/73727 Cpl. Ott H.Q. A.S.C. S/8696 A Cpl. Mankelow S.J. H.Q. A.S.C. T4/059207 Pr. Lloyd W.H. H.Q. A.S.C. "Wells R.S. 2nd Cav. M.T. Coy Pte. Kelly J.F. H.Q. A.S.C. T.S/7574 Sherring Smith, Netherway VH.D. H.Q. A.S.C. S/33923 A/Cpl.	

Army Form C. 2118.

H.Q.
2ND CAVALRY DIV.
A.S.C.

WAR DIARY
or
INTELLIGENCE SUMMARY

(Erase heading not required.)

Instructions regarding War Diaries and Intelligence Summaries are contained in F.S. Regs., Part II. and the Staff Manual respectively. Title pages will be prepared in manuscript.

[Sheet 1] Volume XVI

Place	Date	Hour	Summary of Events and Information	Remarks and references to Appendices
ALETTE	29-6-19		No details yet	
	30.6.19.		"B" Bde Reserve "S" Brigade R.H.A. moved forward towards Lille went regard to the Brigade since today	D + E R.H.A.
			Moved to MARESQUEL AREA. H.Q. & E Bait Reserve in present site & rations lorries & lorries yet	

Henry, Capt & Adjt
H.Q. A.S.C.
2nd Cavalry Division.

"ease"
Jy 25

WAR DIARY

CONFIDENTIAL

Vol. XLVII   of

H.Q
2nd Cav. Divn. A.S.C.
from
1st to 31st July 18.

Army Form C. 2118.

H.Q. A.S.C.
Volume
XLVII
Sheet I.

WAR DIARY
INTELLIGENCE SUMMARY.
(Erase heading not required.)

Instructions regarding War Diaries and Intelligence Summaries are contained in F. S. Regs., Part II. and the Staff Manual respectively. Title pages will be prepared in manuscript.

Place	Date	Hour	Summary of Events and Information	Remarks and references to Appendices.
	July 1918			
ALETTE	1 to 12		No detail. K.	
ALETTE	13		Received warning order. Division might move tomorrow or the morning. 13th July. To Lurigean.	
			Move to WAIL area. K.	
WAIL	14		H.Q. A.S.C. moved this morning along to ALETTE at 9 a.m. Route taken BEAUMERIE - ST MARTIN. BEAURAIN, CHATEAU d'valuin to ford on the road arrived in time to water at 3.30 p.m. Orders received the Division will move tomorrow to LA CAUROY, and take the 3rd Cavalry Bgde. H.	
LA CAUROY	15		H.Q. A.S.C. left WAIL at 6 a.m. Route taken FREVENT ETREE — arriving in billet at 8 a.m. watered before coming into billets. Word received the 3rd Cavalry Brigade move on the 16th inst. K.	
LA CAUROY	16		3rd Cavalry Brigade moved to ANVIN. K. Supply officer reported everything alright. K.	
LA CAUROY	17th to 19th		No detail. K.	
" "	20th		3rd Brigade R.H.A. rejoin the Division from the 1st Corps. K.	
" "	21st		Warning orders received. The Division will move tomorrow to WAIL area. March table received at 12 midnight to move K.	
WAIL	22nd		H.Q. A.S.C. moved off at 9.30 a.m. Arriving at WAIL at 2.30 p.m. Route taken HESDIN, WAIL. March table issued at 8 p.m. Division move to MONTCAVREL area. K.	
ALETTE	23rd		H.Q. A.S.C. moved off at 11 a.m. Arriving at ALETTE 6.30 a.m. Route taken BOUIN, BRIMEUX, ALETTE. Supply of day march table issued. All well. F. March. K.	

2353 Wt W2544/1454 700,000 5/15 D. D. & L.   A.D.S.S./Forms/C. 2118.

Army Form C. 2118.

WAR DIARY
of
INTELLIGENCE SUMMARY.

(Erase heading not required.)

Instructions regarding War Diaries and Intelligence Summaries are contained in F.S. Regs., Part II. and the Staff Manual respectively. Title pages will be prepared in manuscript.

Volume _____
Sheet II
XLVII

Place	Date	Hour	Summary of Events and Information	Remarks and references to Appendices
ALETTE	July 1916 24th	4.30ᵃ	As detail 72.	
"	30th		O.C. asc. inspected the transport of 3rd Cavalry Brigade. Horses in very good ft.	
"	31st		Orders received that 4th Cavalry Brigade & 2nd Cavalry Reserve Park moved tomorrow to new billets 72.	

J. Furry. Capt-asc.
H.Q. A.S.C.
2nd Cavalry Division.

CONFIDENTIAL.

WAR DIARY.

of

Headquarters, 2nd CAVALRY DIVISIONAL, A.S.C.

FROM. 1st AUGUST, 1918
TO. 31st AUGUST, 1918.

VOLUME XLVIII.

Army Form C. 2118.

WAR DIARY

INTELLIGENCE SUMMARY.

(Erase heading not required.)

Instructions regarding War Diaries and Intelligence
Summaries are contained in F.S. Regs., Part II.
and the Staff Manual respectively. Title pages
will be prepared in manuscript.

August 1918   Volume XLVX

Place	Date	Hour	Summary of Events and Information	Remarks and references to Appendices
1st & 2nd August 1918.	ALETTE		No detail. JR.	
3rd	"		Orders received at 6 p.m. The Division will move tomorrow night from "B" Echelon. JR	
4th	MOULNEL		March table received. H.Q. etc. move off at 9 p.m. route taken, MONTREUIL STATION. BRIMEUX, STREMY AUX BOIS, TORTE FONTAINE. Transport arrived in 5-30 a.m. JR.	
5th	COAURS		March table received. H.Q. etc. move off at 9-9-15, route taken DOMVAST, MILLECOURT arrived in billets at 4-16 a.m. Very bad night. Rained most of night and going through one village the road horses packed on the road. Given transport very little room. JR.	
6th	BREILLY		March table received. H.Q. etc. moved off at 9 p.m. route taken. LA FOLIE FLIXECOURT LA CHAUSSEE PICQUIGNY, arriving in billets at 4 a.m. JR	
7th	"		Rations were delivered to a dump near PICQUIGNY. and the M.T. of the Division drew rations were delivered by 7 a.m. The Division drew Rations for 8th. Two men rations per man & rations for horse order were received The Division move off at 12-15 midnight. from Rear Q. Jr.	
8th	LONGUEAU		The Division moved off at 12-1K a.m. Rations were received that H.Q. A.S.C. move to LONGUEAU move completed by 10 p.m. Supplies were sent out to a dump at POMART, were all the S.O. were able to take over the rations & issue. Later orders received. The Oats & men rations were to be dumped & they left on the lorries JR	

2353 Wt. W2544/1454 700,000 5/15 D. D. & L. A.D.S.S./Forms/C. 2118.

Army Form C. 2118.

WAR DIARY

~~INTELLIGENCE SUMMARY~~

(Erase heading not required.)

Sheet I Volume XLIX

Instructions regarding War Diaries and Intelligence Summaries are contained in F. S. Regs., Part II. and the Staff Manual respectively. Title pages will be prepared in manuscript.

H.Q.
2ND CAVALRY DIV.
A.S.C.

Place	Date	Hour	Summary of Events and Information	Remarks and references to Appendices
LONGUEAU	9th August 1918		M.T. train up today. Rations were delivered to all fighting troops. Rations dump moved to MAISON BLANCHE. Lorry remain at the new dump for the night. Returned with the morning. Railhead LONGUEAU. Y.F.	MAISON BLANCHE
"	10th "		Horse Park moved Rations today & were loaded up again from dump at MAISON BLANCHE. Ration lorries dead out again today. Railhead LONGUEAU. Y.F.	
"	11th "		Ration lorries went out this morning & returned at 8.30 p.m. Railhead LONGUEAU. Y.F.	
Proof Ref. Sheet 66E 1/40000 E.13.b.6.3.	12th "		H.Q. A.S.C. moved from LONGUEAU at 9 a.m. & marched to IGNACOURT. En route orders were received for transport to move to E.4.b.6.3. Sheet 66E. Also S.O. Division troops dumps moved from Place. Railhead LONGUEAU. Y.F.	
"	13th "		Orders received late the ready force brew camp tomorrow. The Division took & all above together. Railhead LONGUEAU. Y.F.	
"	14th "		New Camp found good but on return to camp the orders had been cancelled. Further orders received to move tomorrow to ST SAUVEUR area. Railhead LONGUEAU. Y.F.	
BELLOY-SUR-SOMME	15th "		H.Q. A.S.C. moved from camp at 9 a.m. and taken DEMUIN-GLISY LONGUEAU-LONGPRÉ arrived at Billets 6.30 p.m. Railhead AMEINS MAIN. Y.F.	
CANAPLES	16th "		H.Q. A.S.C. moved at 9.30 a.m. route VIGNACOURT arrived at 11 a.m. H.	
FONTAINE L'ETALON	17th "		H.Q. A.S.C. moved 7/8 at 9 a.m. route taken BERNAVILLE AUX-LE-CHATEAU arrived in billets at 3 a.m. Railhead Yr. 16+17. AMEINS MAIN. N.O. PACK horse left today. Y.S.	

(A8041) Wt. W1771/M031 750,000 5/17 Sch. 52 Forms/C2-18/14
D. D. & L., London, E.C.

Army Form C. 2118.

Sheet III. Volume XLIX

WAR DIARY
INTELLIGENCE SUMMARY
(Erase heading not required.)

Instructions regarding War Diaries and Intelligence Summaries are contained in F. S. Regs., Part II. and the Staff Manual respectively. Title pages will be prepared in manuscript.

H.Q.
2ND CAVALRY DIVL.
A.S.C.

Place	Date	Hour	Summary of Events and Information	Remarks and references to Appendices
FONTAINE L, ETALON	18th August 1918		"B" Echelon of the Division joined up today R.Q. are B" Echelon arrived into billets at 8 p.m. Orders received at 6 p.m. 3rd Brigade R.H.Q. move this evening to come under Command 5th Cav. and to be relieved by 5th Cavalry Division. Railhead AUX-LE-CHATEAU. K.	
"	19th "	"	Ammn Squadron of "B" Cavalry Brigade went up today. Relieved by G.O. 3rd Cavalry Brigade. Railhead AUX-LE-CHATEAU. K.	
"	20th "	"	One Squadron of 3rd Cavalry Brigade's remainder of bty, a late in the day orders received 1 & 3rd Cavalry Brigades Moved forward this evening. Railhead AUX-LE-CHATEAU. K.	
GRENAS	21st "	"	Orders received. The Division moved today. Ammn [Echelon] "B" Echelon & GRENAS area H.Q. Q.C. moved off at 9 p.m. Route taken AUX-LE-CHATEAU FROHEN-LE-GRAND, REMAISNIL GRENAS, arrived in billets at 6 a.m. Railhead AUX-LE-CHATEAU. K.	
"	22 "	"	No detail given.	
"	23rd "	"	Orders received at 3 p.m. Division to move forward immediately. H.Q. O/c moved off at 6 p.m. via Mondicourt - Lahertoire to Camp S of Doullens-Arras Road by the Bavincourt-Bailleulmont Rd arrived 9 p.m. Railhead WARINCOURT. ARCH.	
Camp Bavincourt - Bailleulmont Road	24 "	"	No detail given.	

Army Form C. 2118.

H.Q.
2ND CAVALRY DIVL.
A.S.C.

WAR DIARY
or
INTELLIGENCE SUMMARY.
(Erase heading not required.)

Volume XIX

Instructions regarding War Diaries and Intelligence Summaries are contained in F. S. Regs., Part II. and the Staff Manual respectively. Title pages will be prepared in manuscript.

Place	Date	Hour	Summary of Events and Information	Remarks and references to Appendices
Beauval Amiens Railway Road	25 August		Received orders from N° D/G was moving back to Frevas area. H.Q Q/i HSC to move off anytime after 9A.M. Moved off at 9AM via Lahereleuse - Hondicourt arrived Frevas 11 x 30 A.M. dtd	
	26 "		No Details. N/L.	
	27 "		"B" Echelon joined up. Watching from Gerye - Ivergny at 9AM via Le Ponchel - Quivy Chateau Doullens - Pommera - Frevas dtd.	
	28 "		Raithea Saulty dtd.	
	29 "		No Details dtd.	
	30 "		No Details dtd.	
	31 "			

Stephens Capt.
H.Q Q/i KRC
2nd Cav Div.

War Diary

of

Headquarters, 2nd Canadian Divisional A.S.C.

From 1st September
To 30th September
1918

Volume XIX

Army Form C. 2118.

Instructions regarding War Diaries and Intelligence
Summaries are contained in F. S. Regs., Part II.
and the Staff Manual respectively. Title pages
will be prepared in manuscript.

WAR DIARY
or
INTELLIGENCE SUMMARY.

(Erase heading not required.)

Sheet I Volume XLIX

Place	Date 1918	Hour	Summary of Events and Information	Remarks and references to Appendices
FRENAS	1-10 September		No Detail.	
MONDICOURT	11 Sept		A.S.C. N⁰ 95 moved to Billets in MONDICOURT.	
"	12 Sept		CAPT (T/Mjr.) J.C. SPENCER-PHILLIPS D30 A.S.C. (T.F.) posted from 19th Divisional Train to take command of 2nd Cavalry Divnl. Train. T/Major a/j. EDEN A.S.C. from 07 Res. Park to 19th Divnl. Train.	
"	13 Sept		T/Lieut. H. GOODALL A.S.C. from H.Q. 2nd Cavalry Res. Park to transfer appt H.Q. 3rd Cavalry Brigade vice 2 Lt D.A. RAWLENCE from transfer appt. 3rd Cavalry Brigade to Reserve Park.	
"	14.30 Oct		No detail.	

Henry G. H. Capt
A.Q. etc.
2nd Cavalry Division

(6339) Wt. W150/M3016 1,500,000 10/17 McA & W Ltd (E 1898) Forms W3091. Army Form W.3091.

Cover for Documents.

CONFIDENTIAL.

Nature of Enclosures.

WAR   DIARY

of

Headquarters 2nd Cavalry DivnL. A.S.C.

From 1st to 31st October, 1918.

VOLUME L.

Vol 29

Notes, or Letters written.

Army Form C. 2118.

H.Q.
2ND CAVALRY DIVL.
A.S.C.

WAR DIARY
of
INTELLIGENCE SUMMARY

Sheet 1 Volume

(Erase heading not required.)

Instructions regarding War Diaries and Intelligence Summaries are contained in F. S. Regs., Part II. and the Staff Manual respectively. Title pages will be prepared in manuscript.

Place	Date 1918	Hour	Summary of Events and Information	Remarks and references to Appendices
MONDICOURT	1st-31st		Battalion for billets. Nothing to disengage the 3 Brigades being away from the Division HQ.	
			Percy Cyril & Cpt	
			H.Q. A.S.C.	
			2nd Cavalry Division	

Confidential.

WD 30

War Diary

of

H.Q. 2nd Cavalry Divl. A.S.C.

November, 1918.

Volume LI.

Army Form C. 2118.

2ND CAVALRY DIVL.
H.Q.
A C.

WAR DIARY
or
INTELLIGENCE SUMMARY.
(Erase heading not required.)

Army Form C. 2118.

Shed. T. Volume XXVII

Instructions regarding War Diaries and Intelligence
Summaries are contained in F. S. Regs., Part II.
and the Staff Manual respectively. Title pages
will be prepared in manuscript.

Place	Date November 1918	Hour	Summary of Events and Information	Remarks and references to Appendices
MONPICOURT	1st, 2, 3		No detail. YE.	
"	4th		Warning Order received. Divisional H.Q. and Divisional troops will move two motor cars on 5th to BAPAUME away H CAMBRAI ans.	
"	5th		Moved late received at 6.17.YR.	
BIHUCOURT	6th		H.Q. and moved off (two motor) at 08.15. Road good, heavy rainfall & feel on the road. Arrived at billets in BIHUCOURT at 15.30. YR.	
CAMBRAI	7th		H.Q. and moved off (two motor) at 08.00. Roads not so good, rainfall & feel on the road. Arrived at billets in CAMBRAI at 15.30. YR	
CAMBRAI	8th, 9, 10th		no detail. YE	
"	11th		Warning order received that the Division will move to an area S. of MAUBEUGE. March table 3 stages YR.	
"	12th November		March received for 13th-14th YR.	
BOUSSIES	13th		H.Q. 2 A.C. moved off (two motor) from CAMBRAI at 10-00. Rainfall & feel arriving in billets at BOUSSIES at 18-00. YR	
TAISNIERES	14th		H.Q. 2 A.C. moved off (two motor) at 08-00 [illegible] arriving at billets 13-00. YR	
South side of road MAUBEUGE - BOUX LES MAUBEUGE	15th		H.Q. 2 A.C. moved off (two motor) at 09-00, rainfall and feel before entering villages of DOUX LES, arriving at billets 15-00 roads very bad. Motor left CAMBRAI at 09-30 arriving at billets 17-00. YR	

Army Form C. 2118.

2ND CAVALRY BDE.
A.S.C.

WAR DIARY

INTELLIGENCE SUMMARY.

(Erase heading not required.)

Volume XLVII April 18

Instructions regarding War Diaries and Intelligence Summaries are contained in F. S. Regs., Part II. and the Staff Manual respectively. Title pages will be prepared in manuscript.

Place	Date	Hour	Summary of Events and Information	Remarks and references to Appendices
	November 1918			
	16th	South side of road between DOUZIES and MAUBEUGE	Modinit. 78	
	17th		H.Q. A.S.C. left HILLIS at 06·00. arriving at TAININ 13·00. roads fairly good. owing to bad s'post. March Order received for tomorrows march to MORIALME via the Divisor Polit for 2 Augs 78	
TAININ				
	18th		H.Q. A.S.C. left billets at 09·13. arriving at MORIALME. 13·30. roads still good but v. angl. Had before coming into village. 78	
MORIALME				
	19th		No details 78	
	20th		March Order received for 21st to 22nd. 78	
	21st		H.Q. A.S.C. left MORIALME 09·00. arriving in billets at BOUVIGNES at 14·45. 78	
BOUVIGNES				
	22nd		H.Q. A.S.C. left BOUVIGNES. 09·00. arriving in billets at LEIGNON at 13·00. 78	
LEIGNON				
	23rd		H.Q. A.S.C. left LEIGNON 09·15. arriving in billets at MARCHE at 9·30. 78	
MARCHE				
	24th to 30th		No details. 78	

Percy. Capt. A.S.C.
H.Q. A.S.C.
2nd Cavalry Division

(6339) Wt. W160/M3016 1,500,000 10/17 McA & W Ltd (E 1898) Forms W3091. Army Form W.3091.

Cover for Documents.

H.Q.
2ND CAV DIV.
A & Q

Nature of Enclosures.

CONFIDENTIAL.

WAR DIARY

of

Headquarters, Royal Army Service Corps, 2nd Cavalry Division.

FROM :— 1st December, 1918.

TO :— 31st December, 1918.

VOLUME LII.

Notes, or Letters written.

Army Form C. 2118.

WAR DIARY
OF
INTELLIGENCE SUMMARY.
(Erase heading not required.)

Place	Date December 1918	Hour	Summary of Events and Information	Remarks and references to Appendices
MARCHE	1st		Arrived MARCHE the first Supply arrived MARCHE 26th of November. As train arrived yesterday & today. This delay of Supply trains was owing to congestion of traffic further down the line. Ninth A.S.C. train had to be diverted by the Constitutions of the A.S.C. Brigadier to the Constitutions of the Economisers of the Economisers.	
	2nd		The first S Train arrived on this day at 11-50. The Suffices on this train was normally for consumption this day. The Suffices for the 5 Canadian Brigade which had crossed the frontier to relieve our troops at GIVET for the 30th November so were this day had been left on rail up of rations and Supply collected in various ways, day ration however could not be made up of Supply Officers' requisitions. On arrival of brown rations & proper Supply Officers on units were instantly to make up deficiencies, & make recommendations which were available out of this & following days Supplies. Owing to decision of the 5th Brigade to move by road by bounding to reach destination after having reviewed of the decision of the 3rd Echelon of Lorries were provided each solution, it was impossible to move it around the following day it was the night these and required to transport to units were for conveyance of the mobile transport this and day 26th Echelon Broadcast 3 arriving troops the 2nd August 3rd for conveyance to 5 Canadian Brigade it was arranged that 3 Coach & Signals had to depart with one & two cars and 5 Canadian Brigade were fast on Revisional stages one main day deter than that frontier. The Overpaid Venture arrived at NOCHAMPS had to have Supplies delivered by Lorries, Y2.	
	3rd		From time of the 3rd Brigade were going to Rauheabout & were able to drawn by Horse transport from Supply Officers' Dumps, the Remainder had to have there Supplies delivered by Lorries Y2.	
	4th		Owing to there being no A.S.O. at MARCHE the Division Post orders to yard have been A.S.O. McCahoney. was able to take over the A.S.O. duties. Y2.	
5#6/13	5th		The above arrangements were carried out for the period. Y2.	

Army Form C. 2118.

WAR DIARY
INTELLIGENCE SUMMARY

(Erase heading not required.)

Instructions regarding War Diaries and Intelligence Summaries are contained in F. S. Regs., Part II. and the Staff Manual respectively. Title pages will be prepared in manuscript.

Place	Date 1918	Hour	Summary of Events and Information	Remarks and references to Appendices
MARCHE	December 14th		Two days rations were drawn from Railhead & delivered to the 4th Cavalry Brigade. This was floated to helping the day in hand held by the 5th Cavalry Brigade and so broad arrangement for Railhead. Marche table was accessible, and the necessary arrangement made. YE	
	15th			
THEUX	16th		The motor lorries portion of D.A.Q. R.A.S.C. moved from MARCHE to THEUX, the Rail Transport arrived at Marche Point 08:15 Orders stating the close of HOTTON & 12:00 Again taking HOTTON, BOMAL xxxx SOMA 13:30 Reserve Park & Divc H.T. Comp. B.H. this lukat of MARCHE & WAHA, moved from route as above & went Jostled MY and VIEUXVILLE. The Rations began to arrive in R.S.O. Dump Railhead BOMAL, the Rations above, relief arrangement was made & Divisional troops	
	17th		The motor transport D.A.Q. moved from BOMAL to THEUX according with motor lorries arriving details 13:30 H.Q. Reserve Park KOEIGNES Assoc H.T.Comp. & MONT-THEUX. Railhead BOMAL Rations were delivered to Divisional Troops & 3rd Brigade. Self H.Comp & R.H.A.S.C Brigades arrived, and two days rations may sent to 4th Brigade. YE	
	18th		Railhead BOMAL Rations issued. Personal truck 9 3+5 Brigade dump, no issue to 4 th Brigade. YE	
	19th		Railhead PEPINSTER. The Division Helpforuund their own R.S.O. Rations were delivered to Sb. Divisional dumps for Ammunition Column & Reserve Park but route without Rations for 3rd Brigade Dump. 3 H.Comp at Celled. YE	
20.4.22.4 H.123			Reserve Park moved this day from, DEIGNE to WEGNEZ YE. Reserve Park truck this day from WEGNEZ to LAMBERMONT. Two lorries of Rations made to the Division as on Set an issue on their Depot	

Army Form C. 2118.

WAR DIARY
or
INTELLIGENCE SUMMARY.
(Erase heading not required.)

Sheet III Volume [?]

Instructions regarding War Diaries and Intelligence Summaries are contained in F. S. Regs., Part II. and the Staff Manual respectively. Title pages will be prepared in manuscript.

Place	Date	Hour	Summary of Events and Information	Remarks and references to Appendices
December	1918			
	24th		Rations drawn & issued 4F	
	25"		Xmas cleaned no issues. F2	
	26"		R.Q.O. reported & took over the duties relieving Lt. 2.D.Q.3" Can M.T. Coy - 19	
	27-6 31		Issues - 5 days Rlts M.T. Coy - none delivery. A snow reserve of 4 supply officers depots the snow reserve consists of 9 + 4 days rations for men & horses 75.	

Hrews Cpt + Qgt
H.Q. R.O.L.C.
2nd Cavalry Division

Appendix 1 to Dec 1918 war diary.

The general system adopted by regulations for the supply of a Cavalry Division in the Field allowed of two echelons of lorries, each capable of carrying one days supply for the Division. Originally this did not allow for carrying hay or fuel. After the commencement of hostilities additional lorries were allotted for hay.

No horse transport was allotted for Supplies.

The difference between Infantry and Cavalry is, that Cavalry has two echelons of lorries while Infantry have one echelon and the Divisional Train Supply Section.

It was thought before the war that the maximum distance of 40 miles from Railhead to UNITS would be the limit. This was worked out on the supposition of good roads and a free run for lorries during the hours of darkness.

No provision was made for transport from the lorries to Units or Squadrons, no vehicles thus being available unless unloaded. It became obvious from the beginning that supplies could not be drawn by the Division in bulk from Railhead as many miles frequently seperated Brigades. The same for drawing by Brigades as the Units were frequently far apart and this necessitated additional work for Horse transport who had already done their allotted work. The first system was to draw in bulk and split up on M.T. Park. This system included a proportion of the Supply Officers personnel being permanently with the M.T. Coy. It also necessitated the Supply Officers being continually at Supply Column to superintend the splitting up and resulted in their being too much away from the formation area. Further, if they did not attend the splitting up, questions were settled by the Column Supply Officer which should have been settled by the Supply Officer., the general result being that supply officers had not sufficient control of the allocation of supplies to various units. Responsibility for losses and errors could not be fixed.

On the instructions of the then A.D.S. & T. this system was changed when the A.F.B55 was brought into use, the Supply Officer sending in a form shewing what each unit was to get. The Supply personnel were returned to Supply Officer and the lorries were loaded in detail at Railhead. This may be called the 1915 system. At that time the control of Supplies was loose, the ration was big and accounting was simple. Units, as long as there was sufficient, were not exacting as to the last lb of flesh. As the system of accounting economy etc. became more strict and the ration was reduced this system was found to have many disadvantages:

(1) Formation Supply Officers had practically nothing to do with the supplies, till they were delivered to Units.
(2) The A.F. B55 being also a receipt resulted in Units naturally expecting to get everything demanded.
(3) There was a suspicion that other Units were done better than they were.
(4) Continual mistakes were made in loading at Railhead and issues were made short to units which it was impossible to rectify or

trace responsibility in spite of the trial of many forms of waybill.

(5) Drawing in detail takes longer at Railhead and is objected to by Transportation and Railhead Authorities for that reason. Trains have to be cleared quickly and at all times of the day or night if other Divisions are drawing from the same Railhead.

(6) Supplies remaining all night split up on the lorries was simply asking for peculation of odd tins and small items.

In the winter of 1915-1916 as far as possible in the large area occupied, Supply Officers commenced the dump system; supplies for the formation being dumped in bulk in a central place and split up by Supply Officers. Units drew from the dump by their own transport, assisted by A.H.T. Coy. wagons.

When the Division is stationary this has been found the only satisfactory system. A fair division of the Supplies can be made, units see what they are getting and what others are getting. Shortages and complaints can be made and frequently settled on the spot. The Supply Officer has full control of the issue and give and take has a chance.

Railhead has usually been a long way from the troops, but on a few occasions, as at ROISEL, ATHIES etc, Railhead was within H.T. distance of troops. Supplies could be drawn by Horse transport from Railhead. In these places the most satisfactory system was found to be for units to draw their forage in detail and A.S.C. transport to draw the men's rations from Railhead to a dump for issue the next day. To equalize the days the Supply Officer held one days forage on his dump.

With Supply Officers dumps it has been possible to work with one echelon of lorries. The lorries draw in bulk from Railhead and deliver to Supply Officers dump for issue the next day. One echelon of lorries was therefore available for extraneous duties or for overhaul. This system could be varied by the lorries standing loaded at night issuing early and loading up again at Railhead, which was the most convenient, depending on the time of the arrival of the train. This system was possible during stationary periods and during trench warfare. A convenient Railhead was necessary.

The dump system is now the normal system when the Division is stationary, but in the large area necessary for a Cavalry Division it is usually necessary for lorries to deliver from the dump to outlying units.

The dump system does not work satisfactory on the move and a detail issue by lorry system is necessary. The normal system is for lorries to draw in bulk at Railhead.

Between the time of drawing and the Brigade or Division rendezvous, the next days supplies are split up in detail by units on the lorries. This splitting up is done by the Supply Officers personnel who remain with the M.T. Coy. during the move. It is left to Supply Officers to say when and where the supplies are split up, but the lorries should arrive at the rendezvous ready to proceed to issue. The Divisional rendezvous is fixed by "Q" with due regard to the March Table and positions of Brigades.

Before the rendezvous the Supply Officers find out the billets of their units and report to the rendezvous. Instructions are issued by "Q" as to when issue can be made. The Supply Officers then conduct or give direction to Section Officers for the issue.

In the winter of 1917-18 it was decided to reduce the M.T. Coy. to sufficient lorries to provide only one echelon for Supplies.

The second echelon was withdrawn on 19th March 1918, two days before the enemy offensive.

During the move from NOYON to AMIENS and the operations round Amiens it was conclusively proved that two echelons were necessary. Additional lorries to make up the number required were attached to the M.T. Coy.

One echelon only might be sufficient during trench warfare and with convenient Railheads when stationary, but there are certain extraneous duties for which lorries are necessary. These lorries with two echelons are available, leaving one echelon for Supplies.

There are thus two systems of issue :-
(1) Dump system.
(2) Detail issue system.

During the recent advance owing to long distances and various other handicaps it was necessary to reduce the time spent by lorries in Brigade areas about 4 to 7 hours.

A.S.C., Horse Transport was allotted to Brigades and was used as a train. The lorries delivered in bulk to a dump and the A.S.C. transport conveyed rations to units.

This entailed very long hours for the A.S.C. Horse Transport but enabled the lorries to get back to the staging point in time for the next load.

The billeting areas made it difficult to fix a dump, and billets for Horse Transport at a reasonable mileage from all Units.

It is not a system to be recommended, unless, absolutely necessary.

Appendix 2 to Dec 1918 War diary.

2nd CAVALRY DIVISION.
Supply arrangements THEUX Area. Railhead, PEPINSTER.

DIVISIONAL TROOPS.

Supplies loaded at Railhead by lorry and issued to Supply Officers dump THEUX same day. Units draw by Horse Transport from Supply Officers dump.

3rd CAVALRY BRIGADE.

Supplies loaded at Railhead by lorry and issue direct same day to Supply Officers dump, AYWAILLE, except forage for 5th Lancers which goes direct by TROOZ and THIER des FORGES to SPRIMONT.
Units draw by Horse Transport from Supply Officers dump, except 16th Lancers, at MY, to whom lorries deliver from Supply Officers dump.

4th CAVALRY BRIGADE.

Supplies loaded at Railhead by lorry and issued direct same day to Supply Officers dump at CHAUDFONTEIN Station. Units draw by Horse Transport from dump, except Brigade H.Q. MERY, 3rd Hussars, 9th M.V.S. at ESNEUV and 2nd Field Squadron at TILFF to whom lorries deliver from dump.

5th CAVALRY BRIGADE.

Supplies loaded at Railhead by lorry and issued direct same day to Supply Officers dump at PEPINSTER.
Supplies for 12th Lancers sent on returning lorries to ENSEVAL.
Supplies for 20th Hussars, SART, Brigade H.Q., Signal Troop and M.V.S. FAYS, and 5th M.G.S. POLLEUL, delivered by lorry.
There will therefore be in Brigade areas at midnight 2 days Rations and forage.
All formations work with single echelon of lorries.

In addition, a reserve of 4 days supplies is held by the Division, in case snow or frost causes the roads to be impassable.

Forage is held by units, except units in neighbourhood of dumps.
Mens rations at Supply Officers dumps.

December, 1918.

Copy :- War Diary.
"Q" for information.
A.D.S. & T., Cav. Corps. for information.

WAR DIARY

OF

HEADQUARTERS, 2nd CAVALRY DIVISIONAL R.A.S.C.

FROM 1st to 31st January 1919.

Army Form C. 2118.

H.Q. 2CASC

Sheet 1 Volume XXXIV

WAR DIARY

(Erase heading not required.)

January 1919.

Place	Date	Hour	Summary of Events and Information	Remarks and references to Appendices
In the Field	1st to 12th 1919		No Detail. WEL	
	13th		Major Clark took over Command from Lt Col Scott-Elliot DSO who was proceeding to England on leave. WEL	
	14th to 17th		No Detail. WEL	
	18th		Instructions received from A.D.S.&T. Cavalry Corps. that all R.A.S.C. personnel of the Division would be administered by this Office for demobilization. WEL	
	19th to 30th		No Detail. WEL	
	31st		Veterinary Board of Animals of H.Q. Qrs. R.A.S.C. 1st Cav. Scott-Elliot returned Command on returning from leave. WEL	

W Kleen Capt & QMr
HQ Qrs R.A.S.C.
2nd Cavalry Divn

CONFIDENTIAL.

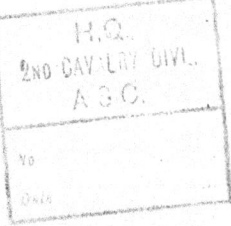

WAR   DIARY

of

Headquarters, 2nd Cavalry Divisional R.A.S.C.

From:- 1st February, 1919

To:- 28th February, 1919.

VOLUME LIV.

Army Form C. 2118.

WAR DIARY
or
INTELLIGENCE SUMMARY
(Erase heading not required.)

HQ RAMC
Chat I Volume XLV

Feb 19

Place	Date	Hour	Summary of Events and Information	Remarks and references to Appendices
	February, 1919			
	1st	T4ELX	No detail. FS.	
	6-11 "	"		
	12 "	"	Two Y.L.D. proceeded this day to England — Demobilisé FS	
	13 "	"	No detail FS	
	14 "	"	2nd Y.M. Severn, R.A.M.C. proceeded this day to England. Demobilisé FS	
	15 "	"	4 + L.D. proceeded to Ste H Cerisy (Bicycle) this day. a 4 Z L.D. brought back than demobilised. FS	
	16 "	"	Capt/Lt-Col Bhan, R.A.M.C. left until 9 went pile hospital. FS	
	17 "	"	4 Z LD went to ENSIVAL & one L.D. ditto. to Belgian Frontier FS	
	19 "	"	No detail FS	
	25 "	"	3 Rodin Z. went to SERAING Foster, FS	
	26 "	"	No detail. FS	
	27 "	"		
	28 "	"	1 Chargen Y. went to ENG'S this day, 1 man demobilised FS	

Piercy Coffro acct.
A. D. Rose
2nd Count Reinforce

Confidential
War Diary
of
Hq. 2" Cav. Div. R.a.S.C

1/3/19 — 31/3/19

(VOLUME LV)

Army Form C. 2118.

WAR DIARY
INTELLIGENCE SUMMARY.
(Erase heading not required.)

Instructions regarding War Diaries and Intelligence Summaries are contained in F. S. Regs., Part II. and the Staff Manual respectively. Title pages will be prepared in manuscript.

Sheet I Volume XIV

Place	Date	Hour	Summary of Events and Information	Remarks and references to Appendices
	March 1919.			
THEUX	1st to 9th		holiday, H.	
HEUSY.	10th		H.Q.R.A.C. moved from THEUX to HEUSY move completed by 12 noon. H	
"	11th to 31st		to alint. H.	

Huey Capt.
H.Q. R.A.C.
2nd Cavalry Division.

www.ingramcontent.com/pod-product-compliance
Lightning Source LLC
Chambersburg PA
CBHW080918230426

43668CB00014B/2156